Electronic
Music Synthesis

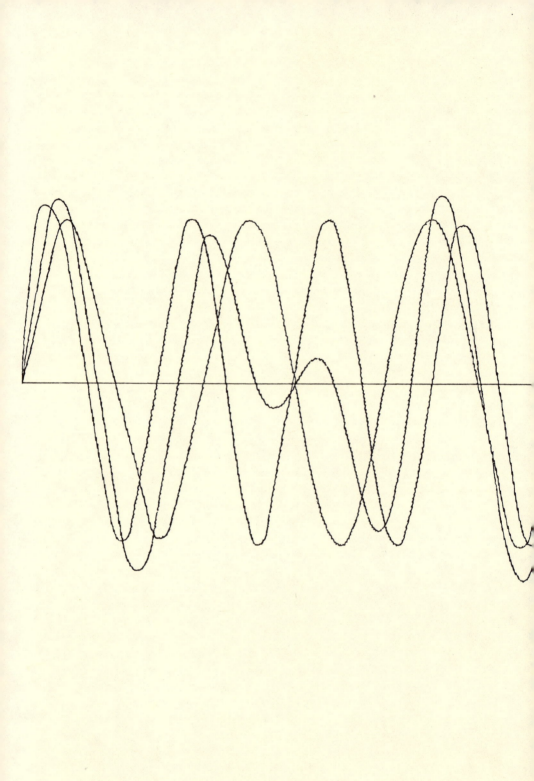

Electronic Music Synthesis

Concepts, Facilities, Techniques

HUBERT S. HOWE, Jr.

ASSOCIATE PROFESSOR OF MUSIC
QUEENS COLLEGE OF THE CITY UNIVERSITY OF NEW YORK

W · W · NORTON & COMPANY · INC ·
NEW YORK

To Susan

Copyright © 1975 by W. W. Norton & Company, Inc.
FIRST EDITION
Library of Congress Cataloging in Publication Data
Howe, Hubert S
   Electronic music synthesis.
   Bibliography: p.
   1. Composition (Music)—Mechanical aids.
2. Music—Acoustics and Physics. 3. Musical
instruments, Electronic. 4. Computer composition.
I. Title.
MT41.H735E4   789.9   74–10722
ISBN 0–393–09257–3
Published simultaneously in Canada
by George J. McLeod Limited, Toronto
This book was designed by Robert Freese.
Typefaces used are Times Roman and New York.
Manufacturing was done by The Haddon Craftsmen.
PRINTED IN THE UNITED STATES OF AMERICA

1 2 3 4 5 6 7 8 9 0

Contents

Illustrations

Preface

This book has been developed over a period of several years, during which time I have taught courses in electronic music at Queens College of the City University of New York and at several summer institutes devoted to electronic music at Southern Illinois University and at Dartmouth College and the University of New Hampshire. There were never any adequate teaching materials for these courses, and I hope that the present book will help fill that gap for others who will be trying to teach or to learn electronic music in the future.

Electronic music is a young field. Its history is traced back to the end of World War II, but, of course, it really goes back to long before then. At the present time, while it might be fair to say that electronic music has passed the period of its "youth," it has certainly not outgrown its "adolescence," and there seems to be a "generation gap" between many of those involved in electronic music and those involved in other facets of contemporary music, of which electronic music represents, after all, only a small portion. This dichotomy is actively encouraged and sustained by the traditional musical educational establishment, which has admitted electronic music into its curriculum, but which is otherwise so narrow and fearful of any field requiring technical "scientific" or "mathematical" training that it cannot distinguish between serious and pseudoserious work.

In order for electronic music to grow and to flourish, there must be greater communication between the two sides of this dichotomy, and, of course, there must be a more solid educational structure for electronic music. I have been appalled to discover the educational content of many courses supposedly concerned with the subject. It is no wonder that so few students or even serious composers have produced respectable work in this field.

Crucial to the presentation of technical courses in electronic music, for

which this book is intended, is the use of the word *composition.* Usually this
term is reserved for courses in which the student is concerned with writing
music and with the reasons why he would decide to do one thing or another.
While many courses in electronic music are actually called *composition,*
they do not really deserve this name, for they do not deal with such considerations in any serious or competent manner. Instead, they talk about
synthesis, which concerns the technical problems encountered in creating
the sounds that represent a piece of music by electronic means. Synthesis
is more analogous to orchestration or to performance than to composition
in the sense described above; and yet, perhaps even more than in traditional
instrumental music, it is impossible to separate composition from synthesis
in electronic music. The limitations of the means of synthesis available to
a composer have a great effect upon the music that he may create; and,
unlike the traditional orchestrational classification of the instruments, nobody has been able to map out the sound structures that may be produced
by electronic means in any simple manner.

This book is called *Electronic Music Synthesis* because it concerns the
concepts, facilities, and procedures necessary for creating sounds that represent music in the sense described above. It is only when people are competent at synthesis that they can begin to consider the problems of the music
itself. These have unhappily been neglected all too often in the training of
electronic music composers. It is partly a consequence of this fact that
electronic music has attracted a number of people because they think they
can avoid this kind of study. I sincerely hope that this book will help
composers become competent at electronic music synthesis so that they can
begin to confront the many important compositional issues that have been
raised by early electronic music.

I am also hopeful that this book will help to uncover some of the problems
in the current methods of electronic music synthesis and thus lead to
improved facilities as well as to better understanding of old facilities. Recent
developments in technology offer truly great potential to electronic music,
but any research requires financial support beyond the means of almost all
those people who are in a position to know what to do. Here, too, we must
hope for improvement in the future.

Introduction

This is a technical book about electronic music. It is intended for readers who are interested in gaining first-hand knowledge of how electronic music is created. All of the major methods of producing electronic music are discussed in detail: tape-splicing and editing techniques, electronic music synthesizing equipment, and computers.

The book is divided into three major sections in order that it may be used in a variety of ways and in a number of different college-level courses. The material in Part I, which concerns acoustics and psychoacoustics, will probably be of interest to anyone involved with electronic music, although it may also be used in courses on these subjects alone. Part II may be used in a semester or year course that involves working in an electronic music studio or with electronic music equipment. Part III may be used in a semester or year course in computer music, although this section assumes a knowledge of the technical terms and concepts explained in the preceding sections. In both Parts II and III it is assumed that the material in the book will be supplemented by regular sessions in which the reader will have direct, "hands on" experience with the facilities discussed, although not necessarily with all of them.

The order in which the materials are presented in the book—acoustics and psychoacoustics, analog systems, and computer systems—does not necessarily mean that these materials must be studied in this order. For courses in analog synthesis or computer music, it is usually best to begin by getting the students to work with the equipment immediately and then returning to the subject matter of Part I after they are familiar with the facilities. Not starting in this way only has the effect of reinforcing the students' fears about the equipment. Nevertheless, in planning an entire sequence of courses in an electronic music program, it would be best to have the first course involve the students in much listening and familiarization with the concepts in Part I, for these materials are really basic to all the rest.

In Part II, the book describes tape-recording and synthesizing equipment from a generalized viewpoint, without reference to specific systems and devices. The reader must realize what features his equipment possesses and lacks. For a person beginning work with this equipment, the emphasis of his study should be on discovery of the kinds of sounds he can make and how they can be controlled and modified.

The discussion of computer music in Part III consists of a chapter on basic concepts, which is introductory in nature, and a large chapter that should be read more as a reference manual than as a description of the program. When working with computer music, the emphasis of study should be on composition itself and on how the characteristics of a piece of music can be generated accurately and efficiently. This process assumes some of the semantic familiarity that can be gained by working with a synthesizer.

While the book will be of primary concern to composers, it will also be of interest to anyone who wants to gain insight into the technical processes involved in electronic music synthesis. No assumptions have been made about the compositional orientation of the reader; rather, it is intended that readers of any stylistic viewpoint be able to use this book to help them understand how to create their music with greater skill and facility. It is assumed, however, that the reader has *some* viewpoint, since prescriptions for the kind of music he should write will not be found in the book.

The book covers technical procedures but not the history of electronic music, except with regard to what people may be associated with the invention or popularization of various techniques discussed. The reader will have to consult other books, recordings, and information to find out what composers have used what procedures, etc. Nevertheless, it would be better for the reader to have some knowledge of the history of electronic music, and he or she is encouraged to pursue this study while reading this book.

The book presents what could fairly be described as the "state of the art" circa 1973. In a field such as electronic music, which has undergone such rapid growth and development in a short period of time, it is possible that some of this information may become obsolete in a few years. If this occurs, new editions of the book will be prepared to bring it up to date. Readers are encouraged to communicate with the author through the publisher regarding their reactions to the material, in order that the book may be revised to accommodate viewpoints that may not have been foreseen by the author at this time.

Instructors who use the book will have to devise their own exercises and problems to test their students. This kind of information has not been included in the book, except for the four examples at the end of Chapter 8, which may be regarded as illustrative "solved problems." It has been the author's experience that class exercises and such material must continually be revised and adapted to suit the needs of the individual students taking the course at a given time and the equipment available. It is often better to encourage each student to pursue his own interests at his own speed than to create artificially competitive situations through group tests.

The bibliography lists several books and articles that may be consulted for further information about any of the topics covered in the book. The material in this book, however, is probably a sufficient description of the technical and "mathematical" knowledge that is required for someone to be able to create electronic music competently. Many people have shied away from studying electronic music because they were apprehensive about the amount of technical knowledge required before they could work with it. It is hoped that the information in this book will be a sufficient remedy for this situation, although in stating this it is also necessary to issue the warning that no one should expect to develop a proficiency in this field any faster than he would expect to develop a proficiency in instrumental music.

ACKNOWLEDGMENTS

Many people have been of great help to me in preparing this book. I owe my greatest debt of gratitude to John Rogers, who read the manuscript as I wrote it and helped me to achieve a more complete and comprehensible presentation. Others who have made many valuable suggestions to me include Robert A. Moog, Richard Cann, Godfrey Winham, A. James Gabura, and Diane Thome. Last, but not least, I would like to thank all of my students on whom I forced much of this material, often before it was as well organized or presented as it appears here. Their success or failure was a convenient way of measuring the success of the text, although I regret that I have sometimes created misunderstandings that caused them difficulty in their work.

Hubert S. Howe, Jr.
September 2, 1973

PART 1

Acoustics and Psychoacoustics

Sound, and hence music, can be analyzed in two ways: *physically,* by using instruments such as meters or other devices that display or record measurements of the properties of the sound; and *psychologically,* by listening to the sound and attempting to ascertain its properties on the basis of our immediate experience. Since this is a book about music, we are ultimately more interested in the latter process than in the former, although we are interested in the former as a way of getting at the latter. We are also concerned with training a listener to become aware of things in music that he or she may not hear at the present time, and that require some directed experience and skill to be able to hear.

The important thing we must understand at the beginning of this presentation is that there is no one-to-one correlation between the physical and the psychological attributes of sound. The two chapters that constitute Part I of this book present both sides of this issue. Only those aspects of acoustics and psychoacoustics relevant to electronic music are included in these chapters. The material in Chapter 1 is just a brief review of the physical properties of sound; more detailed explanations may be found in other books.

In both of these chapters, since we are more interested in a qualitative than in a quantitative understanding of the issues, we present a minimum of mathematics and technical data. One thing that must be borne in mind throughout Chapter 1 is that the physical properties discussed are not things that are heard as such; rather, what we hear are the psychological properties, which are discussed in Chapter 2. They are the correlates of these properties, and are usually described as functions of more than one physical property. For example, we do not perceive the intensity of a sound, but rather its loudness, which is a function of both frequency and intensity.

CHAPTER ONE

Physical Attributes of Sound

1. SOUND

Sound is *vibration in air.* While this is a fact that is easily conveyed to us by our everyday experience with sounds, understanding the precise nature of this phenomenon requires some study. Three elements are necessary for sound to be created and received: a *vibrating source,* which generates the sound: the *medium,* which is the air; and the *listener.*

The vibrating source comes in direct contact with the air, which consists of billions of tiny particles packed under pressure into a space. When the vibrating source moves forward, some particles are pushed into others, causing *condensations* in the air; and when the source moves back, particles are pulled apart, causing *rarefactions.* The particles that move forward bump into others, which both push the first particles back and which, in turn, are pushed into others, continuing the process. Thus, although the particles move only a short distance back and forth, the wave motion started by the vibrating source continues to expand outward through the air, and the sound is dispersed through the space.

If we plot the path in which an individual air particle moves during the course of a sound, the resulting graph is called a *displacement waveform.* A displacement waveform is graphed in Figure 1–1.1. In this graph, time moves from left to right, and the motion of the particle back and forth is shown in the vertical dimension (positive is up and negative is down).

Sound travels through the air at a constant speed (approximately 1,100 feet per second, the exact figure depending on the temperature of the air). As the sound travels through space, it may be reflected off objects in the environment, and thus what reaches the listener is a combination of both direct and reflected sound. (This situation is elaborated on in our discussion

3

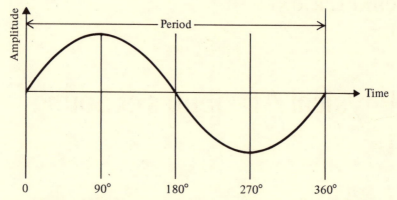

Figure 1–1.1: Displacement waveform of a sample sound. The vertical axis represents amplitude and the horizontal axis time. The period of the waveform is the duration of one cycle. The phase is the instantaneous amplitude of the waveform. A single cycle of a periodic wave is divided into 360 degrees as shown.

of reverberation, below). The sound energy decreases as the sound travels farther from the source, until it finally dissipates into the background motion of the air particles.

2. PROPERTIES OF SOUND WAVES

Let us assume that the sound represented in Figure 1–1.1 repeats indefinitely the motion shown. The displacement waveform itself has only two dimensions: amplitude and time. It is important to note at this point that all other properties of sound must be defined in terms of these characteristics, or in terms of regularities in the variations of amplitude with respect to time. The displacement waveform is identical in shape to a graph of the variations in air pressure above and below the ambient pressure, which is called a sound-pressure waveform. (Many books describe the following properties in relation to the sound-pressure waveform instead of the displacement waveform.)

The *period* of a sound wave is the duration of one cycle of the motion. Period is measured in seconds. The *frequency* of the sound is the number of cycles completed in one second. Frequency is measured in *cycles per second* (abbreviated cps) or *Hertz* (abbreviated Hz), which is another name for the same thing.[1] The period and frequency of a sound are related by the important formula

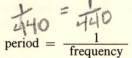

$$\text{period} = \frac{1}{\text{frequency}}$$

Thus, one cycle of a sound with a frequency of 440 cps has a period of 1/440 of a second.

The *phase* of a sound is the instantaneous amplitude at a given point in time. This definition of phase allows for both periodic and nonperiodic waveforms. When considering a periodic wave such as that illustrated in Figure 1–1.1, the term *phase* is employed to denote the portion of the cycle that has been completed at a given time. The entire cycle, beginning usually at the point where the amplitude crosses from negative to positive,[2] is divided into 360 equal parts called *degrees*. Phase is thus a measure of time with respect to frequency or period.

(We will avoid discussing most of the other complex properties about sound, which are adequately covered in books on acoustics written from a physics viewpoint.)

3. SOUND INTENSITY

Sound intensity is a measurement of the amount of power in a sound at a given location. To envision this concept precisely, we must imagine a sphere surrounding the sound source; the intensity is the amount of power passing through a unit area of the sphere at any point.

Intensity is usually measured in *decibels* (abbreviated dB), which is a measurement of the ratio between the power of a given sound and a reference sound, usually a standard reference sound. The formula for calculating the intensity level of a sound I_1 is

$$dB = 10 \log \left(\frac{I_1}{I_0}\right),$$

[1] In this book the term *cycles per second* (or *cps*) is used exclusively for frequency measurement instead of *Hertz*, since this term is more descriptive of the concept of frequency. Most scientific work today uses the term *Hertz*, however.

[2] This does not necessarily denote the beginning of a cycle, for there are many periodic waveforms that make several zero crossings in one cycle.

where I_0 is the intensity of the reference sound, which is often taken as the threshold of hearing. The ratio of the threshold to itself is 1, and the intensity level of that sound is therefore 0 dB. Above this level, human beings can hear sounds up to a level of approximately 120 dB before the sound becomes physically painful. Various other intensity levels are often described in terms relating these levels to everyday sounds, such as 30 dB for the level of background noise, 80 dB for heavy traffic on a city street, etc. (In these terms, note that most sounds that we hear in music would have intensities between 30 and 80 dB.) For practical purposes, we must realize that dB is not an absolute measurement and also that it is not a measurement of loudness but rather of intensity. Another confusing fact about decibels is that an increase of approximately 6 dB at any point corresponds roughly to a doubling of the power of the sound.

4. NOISE

Noise is supposedly a simple kind of sound that we are all familiar with but that resists any attempt at simple definition. Perhaps the best description of noise is that it is the sound, produced by random motion of the air particles, which exists in the background of any acoustical environment. This noise can be heard when the volume is turned up on a sound-reproduction system with no input. Noise is a category for sounds that are *nonperiodic* and that contain unrelated frequency components. *White noise,* so named by analogy with white light, is a mixture of all frequencies in equal proportions. When the frequencies are weighted in some unequal manner, noise is sometimes called a different color—e.g., "pink noise" for noise that contains a constant power per octave, or "blue noise" for noise that has more power at high frequencies.

Noise is sometimes defined as "unwanted" sound, or in other informal ways. Such definitions are rejected here, for if taken seriously they usually cause various kinds of confusion.

5. COMPLEX SOUNDS

Most sounds we hear, even those that have only a single pitch, actually consist of several separate frequency components whose amplitudes vary constantly over the course of the duration of the sound. These frequency components may be divided into two general categories: *harmonic* and *nonharmonic partials.* All frequency components of a sound constitute its *spectrum.*

Harmonic partials are tones whose frequencies are integral multiples of a fundamental frequency. Tones above the fundamental are called *overtones.* The number of an overtone is always one less than the number of a harmonic partial—e.g., the first overtone is the second partial, etc. A fundamental frequency and its harmonic partials constitute a *harmonic series* or an *overtone series.* Although the frequency between each successive pair of overtones is always the same, the musical interval or distance in pitch between the overtones gets smaller as the series goes higher. The intervals at the lower end of the overtone spectrum are very close to equal-tempered intervals, and played an important role in the evolution of early Western music.

A tone consisting of a single frequency with no overtones is called a *sine wave,* which is the acoustical manifestation of simple harmonic motion. Each harmonic partial of a complex tone is a sine wave.

Nonharmonic partials are any components of a single tone that are not harmonic partials of the fundamental frequency. This term is simply a convenience for referring to these elements under a single category; they do not necessarily have other common features.

6. RESONANCE

Whenever a vibrating body is placed in contact with another object also capable of vibrating, vibrations are induced in the second object so that the resulting sound is determined by both objects acting as a single system. The vibrations in the second object are produced by *resonance.*

Most musical instruments use a system of this kind in the production of their tones. A vibrating body such as a string, a reed, or a mouthpiece is adjoined to a tube or box or other object which resonates the original tone into the characteristic sound of the instrument.

The frequencies of the original tone and those of the resonators are usually different. Many types of resonators, such as cylindrical tubes open at one or both ends, will provide maximum response at frequencies that constitute a harmonic series of some kind; other resonators may have irregular responses. A graph showing the amount of amplification of a resonator along the frequency continuum is called a *response curve*. Response curves are illustrated in our discussion of filters in Chapter 4. (See Figure 4–8.1.) For a given tone, the response is determined both by the frequency content of the tone and by the frequency response of the resonator.

7. ENVELOPE

Envelope refers to the growth and decay characteristics of some property of a sound. It is thus a "catchall" category describing the way in which one property varies in relation to another. When the term is used in most situations in electronic music and not qualified by an adjective, it means *"temporal* envelope," which describes the way in which some property varies with respect to time. A *"spectral* envelope" describes the way in which the amplitude of a sound varies with respect to frequency, or, in other words, a frequency-response curve. This term is encountered more in the literature of acoustics than in that of electronic music.

The temporal envelope of a sound describes the manner in which its amplitude varies with respect to time. Envelope generators are devices that have been constructed to control these variations. Specific shapes and other aspects of envelopes are discussed in Chapter 4 under "Envelope Generators." The important point about envelopes and envelope generators is that they may apply to any characteristic of a sound—not just to amplitude. Most of the characteristics of sounds in live music undergo some kind of change during the course of their durations. Sounds are not attacked instantaneously; they grow gradually from zero up to some peak and back. The term *envelope* denotes a concept that is useful for describing changes in these characteristics, and the complexity of the envelopes as they apply to each property of the sound is a measure of the complexity of the sound.

8. SOUND ABSORPTION AND REVERBERATION

When a sound wave strikes a surface, a certain amount of the energy of the sound is *reflected* off the surface and a certain amount is *absorbed*. Different materials have different reflective and absorptive properties. These properties are of particular relevance for the science of room acoustics.

One important fact about concert halls is that the sound absorption will be greater if an audience is seated in the hall. Thus, when electronic music is played in concerts, it is not possible to set the volume level of tapes played back before the audience arrives. For this reason, it is a good practice to set up the tape recorder so that the levels may be adjusted from the audience during playback.

The reflective properties of the walls, floor, and ceiling of a room have a very important effect on the quality of sounds that are played within them. As we noted above, when a sound strikes the wall, a certain amount of its energy is reflected off the wall. Some of the sound will be reflected from the wall directly to the listener, just as some of the sound reaches the listener directly from the vibrating source. However, most of the reflected sound is sent in other directions, where it bumps endlessly into the other walls and ceiling. Thus, the sounds that reach the listener actually come from all directions, since the sound bounces off all the walls of the room; and some of the sound arrives directly, some after reflecting off just one wall, some after reflecting off two walls, etc.

The cumulative effect of the sound reflecting off all of the walls in this manner is called *reverberation,* and it is clear that this is a property that depends on the shape and construction of the room. Let us note that the difference between the direct and reflected sound is simply the duration that it takes the sound to reach the listener's ear, and, of course, the amplitude of each successive reflection is smaller. The important variable in this situation, therefore, is the size of the room; and the larger the room the longer it takes the sound to travel from one wall to the next.

When a sound is produced in an actual room, the most noticeable effect of the reverberation is the length of time it takes the sound to die away after it is cut off at the source. This duration is referred to as the *reverberation time* of the room. There is much material in the literature of room acoustics

describing such qualities as "optimum reverberation time" and other characteristics. These qualities depend on subjective factors about which there
is much disagreement.

It must also be noted that the reverberant qualities of a room affect
sounds of different frequencies in different ways, in such a manner that the
reflections of the sound act as a kind of filter. The manner in which this
occurs is described in detail in our discussion of reverberators in Chapter
4, below.

9. BEATS AND COMBINATION TONES

When two tones are played simultaneously, the resulting sound wave is
the sum of the sound waves of each individual tone. When the two waves
are both positive or negative in amplitude, they reinforce one another,
producing a greater amplitude in the result; this process is called *construc-
tive interference*. When one wave is positive and the other negative they
cancel one another out; this process is called *destructive interference*. In the
unusual case that one wave is exactly the reverse of the other, the result is
a total cancellation of the sound—silence.

When two waves of slightly different frequencies are sounded together,
the result is a periodic amplitude modulation of the sound called *beating*.
The frequency of the beating is equivalent to the difference in frequency of
the two sounds. The production of beats is illustrated in Figure 1–9.1, *which
displays* separate frequencies of 3 and 4 cps and the resulting wave.

When the beat frequency approaches the lower limit of pitch discrimination (approximately 20 cps—see our discussion of pitch in Chapter 2), it
becomes audible as a separate pitch component of the sound, and it is called
a *combination tone* or *difference tone*, since its frequency is equal to the
difference between the two input tones. The amplitude of this tone is not
as great as either of the original components. Nevertheless, since this happens whenever any two or more tones are combined, combination tones are
present in almost all sounds that we hear, and certainly in all music.

This discussion shows that combination tones are physically present in
the signal, and they must, therefore, be distinguished from subjective tones,
which are produced in the ear by its nonlinearity of response; but see our
discussion of subjective factors in Chapter 2. Furthermore, combination
tones produced by the interference between the tones of a harmonic series

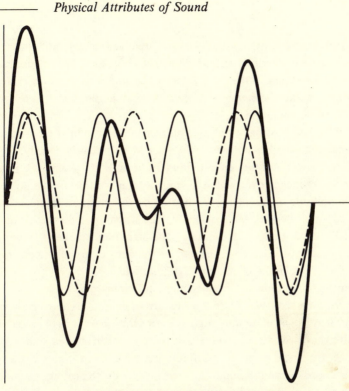

Figure 1–9.1: Beating between tones of 3 and 4 cps.

will only serve to reinforce the fundamental frequency, since the difference between each successive pair of partials is the same frequency as the fundamental. This does not mean, however, that the perception of the fundamental is explained on the basis of difference tones. (This can easily be demonstrated by experimenting with a frequency shifter—see Chapter 4.)

10. MODULATION

Modulation refers to the _periodic change_ in any characteristic of a sound. The term _modulation_ must, therefore, be qualified by a term denoting the characteristic that is varied. The most common types of modulation are _amplitude modulation, frequency modulation, location modulation,_ and _timbre modulation_ (or _filter modulation_).

Two signals are involved in modulation: the _carrier_ signal, or the "original" signal before modulation, and the _modulating_ signal, or modulator, or program signal, which produces the periodic change in the carrier signal.

There are always three characteristics involved in any modulation: the *speed* or *rate* of modulation, which is the frequency of the modulating signal; the *amplitude* of the modulator or *amount* of the characteristic that is modulated; and the *shape* or *pattern* of modulation, which is the wave-shape of the modulating signal.

In radio broadcasting, amplitude and frequency modulation are used in the transmission and reception of AM and FM respectively. Briefly, the way in which this works is that an individual radio station is assigned a particular carrier frequency over which it sends a signal of that frequency that is either amplitude or frequency modulated by the program signal, which is the "program" or message received by the listening audience. A radio is essentially a device to "demodulate" the signal and makes it intelligible again. In radio broadcasting, the carrier frequencies are all supersonic, or above the upper limits of pitch discrimination.

In music, amplitude and frequency modulation are described as *tremolo* and *vibrato* respectively. (These terms are often confused, even by musicians.) There are no common-language terms for other kinds of modulation.

In live music, whatever modulation there is occurs at frequencies below the lower threshold of pitch discrimination. In electronic music, there are no restrictions on modulation frequencies, and, as with beating, a significant change occurs as the modulating signal approaches and exceeds the lower limit of pitch discrimination. When the modulating frequency is below this limit, it is possible to hear each individual variation in the carrier frequency resulting from the modulation; but when the modulating frequency is above this limit, the ear perceives instead a complex spectrum. The frequencies in this complex spectrum are called *sidebands*. The band of frequencies above the carrier frequency is called the upper sideband, and the band below, the lower sideband. In order to know what frequency components are present in this spectrum, one must know the specific details of the modulation involved and the theory of that type of modulation.

Most of the characteristics that we have covered in this chapter are known by most people relatively familiar with live music. Modulation at frequencies above the lower limit of pitch discrimination, however, is an unknown experience, and yet it is very important in electronic music. When the sidebands that result from a complex modulation are known, it is possible to predict the results of a modulation very precisely. This knowledge can be used to produce complex spectra without a corresponding complexity in the signal generation. Therefore, we include a detailed discussion below of amplitude modulation, ring modulation, and frequency modulation in which both the carrier and modulating signals are sine waves. This information is of primary interest to people working in computer synthesis and to people working with analog oscillators capable of modulating themselves or with harmonic generators.

Amplitude modulation produces the *sum* and *difference* of the carrier and modulating frequencies. The original carrier frequency is also present in the result, and it has a greater amplitude than the sidebands. For example, suppose that a carrier signal consisting of frequencies of 100, 200, 300, 400, and 500 cps (the first five harmonic partials of a fundamental of 100 cps) is modulated by a sine wave of 27 cps. The output would consist of frequencies of 73, 100, 127, 173, 200, 227, 273, 300, 327, 373, 400, 427, 473, 500, and 527 cps; this is obviously an inharmonic spectrum. If the modulating frequency were changed to 25 cps, however, the output would consist of frequencies of 75, 100, 125, 175, 200, 225, 275, 300, 325, 375, 400, 425, 475, 500, and 525 cps, or partials number 3, 4, 5, 7, 8, 9, 11, 13, 15, 16, 17, 19, 20, and 21 of a fundamental frequency of 25 cps. In general, if there is a simple ratio between the carrier and modulating frequencies (4:1 in our example), the result is a harmonic spectrum.

Ring modulation is a special case of amplitude modulation that produces only the sum and difference of the carrier and modulating frequencies. For our first example above (carrier frequencies of 100, 200, 300, 400, and 500 cps and a modulating frequency of 27 cps), ring modulation would produce frequencies of 73, 127, 173, 227, 273, 327, 373, 427, 473, and 527 cps. For our second example above (modulator changed to 25 cps), the output would contain 75, 125, 175, 225, 275, 325, 375, 425, 475, and 525 cps, or partials 3, 5, 7, 9, 11, 13, 15, 17, 19, and 21 of a fundamental of 25 cps. Ring modulation is produced by multiplying the two input signals.

When a sine wave is frequency modulated by another sine wave, sidebands are produced above and below the carrier frequency at intervals of the modulating frequency. Although a theoretically infinite number of sidebands is produced, only a few of them have a significant enough amplitude to be heard. The amplitudes of these resulting frequencies are determined by Bessel functions of the first kind and *n*th order,[3] the argument to which is the *modulation index,* which is the ratio of the frequency deviation (or amplitude of frequency modulation) to the modulating frequency:

[3]Tables of Bessel functions are found in standard books of mathematical functions.

$$\text{modulation index} = \frac{\text{frequency deviation}}{\text{modulating frequency}},$$

$$I = \frac{d}{m}.$$

In general, there are frequencies of significant amplitude on both sides of the carrier frequency within a band which is slightly larger than the frequency deviation.[4] Figure 1–10.1 illustrates the frequencies and amplitudes of components in the upper and lower sidebands of a frequency-modulated signal.

When m in Figure 1–10.1 is large enough for the expression $(c - nm)$ to yield a negative frequency, it must be remembered that negative frequencies are simply positive frequencies reversed in phase and are perfectly audible components.

Using the information in Figure 1–10.1, it is possible to determine the spectrum for any given carrier and modulating frequency. In general, spectra containing various harmonic partials can be produced by employing carrier and modulating frequencies that exist in a simple ratio to one another. The fundamental frequency of the spectrum produced is the largest common factor of c and m. For example, if $c = 100$ and $m = 300$, the carrier and the first three order sidebands contain partials 1, 2, 4, 5, 7, 8,

Frequencies		
Upper side band	Lower side band	Amplitudes
c		$J_0(I)$
$+(c+m)$	$+(c-m)$	$J_1(I)$
$+(c+2m)$	$+(c-2m)$	$J_2(I)$
$+(c+3m)$	$+(c-3m)$	$J_3(I)$
.	.	.
.	.	.
.	.	.
$+(c+nm)$	$+(c-nm)$	$J_n(I)$

Figure 1–10.1: Frequencies and amplitudes present in a sine wave of carrier frequency c frequency modulated by a sine wave of frequency m with modulation index I. $J_n(I)$ indicates the Bessel function of the nth order.

[4]For this knowledge, the author is indebted to John Chowning, who originally developed all of the information presented here. This work is described in his paper "The Synthesis of Complex Audio Spectra by Means of Frequency Modulation," *Journal of the Audio Engineering Society,* XXI/7 (Sept., 1973), 426.

and 10 of the fundamental frequency 100 cps. If $c = 500$ and $m = 200$, the carrier and the first three order sidebands contain the partials 1, 3, 5, 7, 9, and 11 of the fundamental 100 cps. Figure 1–10.2 illustrates the partials obtained through the first four orders of the sidebands for various simple ratios of $c{:}m$.

	1/1		1/2		1/3		2/3		3/4		2/1		5/1		4/3		5/4	
0	1		1		1		2		3		2		5		4		5	
1	2	0	3	1	4	2	5	1	7	1	3	1	6	4	7	1	9	1
2	3	1	5	3	7	5	8	4	11	5	4	0	7	3	10	2	13	3
3	4	2	7	5	10	8	11	7	15	9	5	1	8	2	13	5	17	7
4	5	3	9	7	13	11	14	10	19	13	6	2	9	1	16	8	21	11

Figure 1–10.2: Partials obtained from sine-wave frequency modulation for various simple ratios of c to m. The ratio $c{:}m$ is shown in the top row, and the nth order side frequency is shown opposite the number n in the extreme left column. Within each group, the left column shows the partials in the upper sideband, and the right the lower sideband. In the middle is the carrier. A 0 indicates a frequency of 0 cps.

Inharmonic spectra can be produced by employing complicated ratios of $c{:}m$. Although some of these spectra are technically harmonic, the only significant elements are distributed in such a way that the series is heard as inharmonic. For example, if $c = 100$ and $m = 210$, the carrier and the first three order sidebands contain the frequencies 100, 110, 310, 320, 520, 530, and 730 cps. These are technically a subset of a fundamental of 10 cps, which is below the lower threshold of pitch discrimination. Figure 1–10.3 illustrates the spectra obtained for various ratios of $c{:}m$.

	2/11		11/2		9/11		11/9		1/1.4		1/.7		1/2.1	
0	2		11		9		11		1		1		1	
1	13	9	13	9	20	2	20	2	2.4	.4	1.7	.3	3.1	1.1
2	24	20	15	7	31	13	29	7	3.8	1.8	2.4	.4	5.2	3.2
3	35	31	17	5	42	24	38	16	5.2	3.2	3.1	1.1	7.3	5.3
4	46	42	19	3	53	35	47	25	6.6	4.6	3.8	1.8	9.4	7.4

Figure 1–10.3: Partials obtained from sine-wave frequency modulation for various complicated ratios of c to m.

Perhaps the most significant aspect of sine-wave frequency modulation is that spectra with dynamically changing amplitudes can be produced by varying the modulation index, which is easily controlled by placing an envelope on the frequency deviation. This method of producing dynamically varying spectra is illustrated in detail in Chapter 8, Example 4, pages 242–248. It is of great interest, not only because the method is so inherently simple, but also because almost any sounds can be produced by employing proper amounts and manners of deviation. Further research is necessary to establish data for specific sounds. This method is most significant to computer sound-generating systems, since most present analog equipment cannot be controlled precisely enough to produce these results.

CHAPTER TWO

Psychological Attributes of Sound

Psychological attributes of sound are properties identified by listeners who are describing their own immediate experience with music. To a certain extent these can be correlated with physical attributes of sound, but in doing so the response of the ear must also be taken into account. It has been discovered through much research in the field of psychoacoustics that the ear is not linear in its response to sounds, a fact that introduces many complexities into the situation. Unfortunately, since much psychoacoustical research has focused primarily on such problems as deafness, its results are frequently not relevant to music.[1]

In the following summary of psychological attributes of sound, only those aspects deemed relevant to music have been included. Much of this material, while speculative and controversial, is presented in the hope of stimulating the reader to think about these issues and to reflect upon his own experience, and also to encourage the further research that is necessary to solve some of these problems.

[1] J. K. Randall, in his article "Theories of Musical Structure as a Source for Problems in Psycho-acoustical Research" (the first lecture in "Three Lectures to Scientists," *Perspectives of New Music*, V/2 [spring–summer, 1967], 124–140), not only makes this point, but also finds some serious flaws in the methods by which psychoacoustical tests have traditionally been carried out.

1. PITCH

For many reasons, pitch is one of the most important dimensions of music. First, pitch can be broken down into several separate component properties. Second, listeners are quite sensitive to very small changes in pitch, and are able to hear extremely fine differentiations in this property —much finer than with any other attribute of sound. Finally, pitch helps to explain characteristics of musical styles to a much greater degree than any other properties of sound; indeed, most musical theory deals primarily with pitch organization.

There are at least three separate component properties of pitch that can be identified by listeners and that are basic to practically all music. The most basic is the "higher than" relationship, by which any tone can be recognized as either higher, lower, or the same in pitch as another tone. The second property is the octave relationship. Tones one or more octaves apart possess a similarity that can be described as "identity" or "duplication" of pitch at a higher or lower level. The third property is somewhat more difficult to describe, since it is a property of pairs, or groups, of pitches. Two pitches sounding together form an "interval," and it is possible to compare intervals on the basis of the distance between the component pitches. In particular, it is possible to hear whether two intervals are equal or unequal. This property is called the "equal interval" property, and it is basic to the notion of an "equal-tempered" scale.

Pitch is the psychological attribute that corresponds to frequency in the physical domain in a sense explained further below. A low frequency seems to begin to be heard as a pitch somewhere between 20 and 30 cps. Below this frequency, we hear each cycle of the vibration as a separate pulse. Frequencies below the lower threshold of pitch discrimination are called *subsonic* or *subaudio,* and they do occur in music as beating and modulation frequencies.

The upper threshold of pitch discrimination varies greatly with individual listeners. Most people cannot hear frequencies above approximately 16,000 cps. This limit recedes with age, and older listeners may be unable to hear frequencies above 12,000 cps. Frequencies above the upper threshold of pitch discrimination are called *supersonic* or *ultrasonic,* and they are also present in music. When such tones produce beats or combination tones with other frequencies in the signal, their effects are audible; unfortunately, we do not now know how often these occur and how important they are.

Most pitches in (older) music tend to occur within the range of human voices, which extends approximately four octaves, from 125 to 1,000 cps. (In view of the upper limit for this range, it appears strange that many psychoacoustical tests have been conducted using a 1,000-cps sine tone as a standard of reference.) Below this level, pitch discrimination becomes even more difficult, and above that range most frequencies that are present are overtones of lower fundamentals. This fact is in no way meant as a prescription for what may be written, but only as an observation that is a relevant concern when the means of exceeding these limitations are provided by electronic devices.

Much psychoacoustical research concerning pitch measurement has been of little benefit to music. One of the reasons for this problem is that the differences have been measured in terms appropriate to frequency rather than to pitch. This difference must be explained carefully.

The basic difference between frequency and pitch is that one is a physical attribute of sound and the other a psychological attribute. As noted above, the octave relationship has special significance in identifying a perceptual similarity between sounds of different frequency. The physical relationship between octaves is that there is a 2:1 ratio between their frequencies. A series of octaves from a low to a high pitch produces frequencies that are related according to powers of 2, and the twelfth root of 2 is also the basis of the equal-tempered chromatic scale.

According to the experience of almost all listeners, and disregarding some inconsistencies that occur under laboratory conditions but not in actual music, it does seem to be the case that frequency corresponds absolutely to pitch according to this exponential relationship, without any other physical properties affecting the perception of the pitch. In asserting this as a fact, we must note the following circumstances as well. First, intonation deviations in almost all live music are so great that it is irrelevant to use laboratory measurements made in nonmusical contexts as a basis of pitch measurement that would have meaningful application to music. Second, the musical concept of "single pitch" customarily denotes the fundamental of a harmonic series rather than the pure tones used in psychoacoustical experiments, and each element of the series may vary in both frequency and amplitude during the course of a tone; yet the perception of the pitch is rarely in doubt because of these variations.

In this book we will use the terms *frequency* and *pitch* interchangeably, depending on whether we intend to suggest a physical or psychological point of view. More subtle, perhaps, is the use of terms for the measurement of these properties. Frequency is measured in cycles per second. Pitch is measured in terms denoting musical intervals, such as octaves or semitones, or in absolute terms by the identification of a particular pitch. The most convenient notation for pitch outside of musical notation itself is the octave-point pitch-class form or 8VE.PC form, introduced in Chapter 8.

Returning to our original point about measurements in terms of frequency rather than in terms of pitch, we can see from our discussion above that the concept of an interval of x cps has no absolute meaning, but would denote one quantity at a low frequency and a smaller quantity at a higher frequency. The most useful form of measurement for small quantities of pitch is the *cent*, which is $\frac{1}{100}$ of a semitone or $\frac{1}{1200}$ of an octave.

One concept that has been explored extensively in psychoacoustical research provides a good illustration of the kind of confusion that abounds in this field, and helps reveal why the results are of such little value to music. This is the issue of *consonance* and *dissonance*. These terms are used in music-theoretical work as a classification of intervals; the concept of some intervals being "more consonant" than others does not occur.

In psychoacoustical research these terms have been confused with their common-language use in other situations, and the result has been a hopeless mix-up of objective and subjective factors. "Consonant" is confused with "pleasing," and both the experimenters and their subjects have lost track of whether they were trying to recognize a property of the sound or to make a value judgment about it.

Even more ridiculous is the psychoacoustical concept of the *mel scale*, which was constructed by asking listeners to find the pitch that was "one half as high" as another pitch. This concept simply has no meaning for music, and it has not been taken seriously by musicians. Examples of such fruitless ideas are abundant in the psychoacoustical literature, and have detracted from the more serious research that may have practical value for musicians.

2. LOUDNESS

As pitch corresponds to frequency, loudness is the psychological attribute most closely related to the physical attribute of intensity. In this regard psychoacoustical research has provided the valuable insight that loudness is not determined by intensity alone, but rather as a function of both frequency and intensity. This concept also requires careful explanation, since it was not discovered by research pertaining to music.

In 1933, Fletcher and Munson published an important paper[2] in which they explained the dependence of loudness upon both frequency and intensity. What they showed in particular was that in order to make a pure tone appear to have the same loudness as a 1,000 cps reference tone, it was necessary to increase the amplitude considerably as the frequency became lower and lower. They plotted a number of curves called "equal-loudness contours" that indicated what intensities were necessary to produce equal loudnesses at different levels. Equal-loudness contours are indicated in Figure 2–2.1.

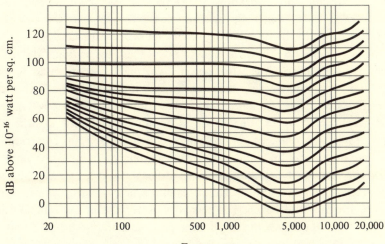

Frequency

Figure 2–2.1: Equal-loudness contours. (From Harvey Fletcher and W. A. Munson, "Loudness, Its Definition, Measurement and Calculation," *Journal of the Acoustical Society of America,* V (Oct., 1933), 83–103.)

Later research has hypothesized that the basis of these contours is the frequency response of the first mode of the outer ear's canal, which

[2]Harvey Fletcher and W. A. Munson, "Loudness, Its Definition, Measurement and Calculation," *Journal of the Acoustical Society of America,* V (Oct., 1933), 82–103.

is about 10 dB up at approximately 3,000 cps.[3]

To avoid confusion, it must be remembered that this is a measurement of sine tones only, and that it does not describe the terms in which different loudness levels may be measured or related to one another. For the latter question, unlike pitch, for which we were able to identify three separate perceptible characteristics, there seems to be only one property for loudness —the "louder than" relationship. Furthermore, in musical notation as well as common language, it appears that there is only an *ordinal scale* for loudness—that we are able to rank tones with regard to their loudness, but that we do not measure the difference between levels of loudness nor do we assign any absolute meaning to a particular level. In musical notation, loudness is denoted by dynamic markings such as *p* (piano, soft), *f* (forte, loud), *ff* (fortissimo, very loud), etc.

Nevertheless, these intuitive factors have not deterred psychoacoustical researchers from attempting to devise a *ratio scale* for loudness by asking subjects to find a tone that was "twice as loud" or "half as loud" as a reference tone. The *sone* scale for loudness was developed in this way,[4] but it is not regarded today as having much significance for music.

We can apply the knowledge about equal-loudness contours discussed above to a practical musical situation involving the comparison of two complex tones containing a harmonic series. If the partials of two complex tones of different pitch and overtone content are adjusted by a factor proportional to an equal-loudness contour, they seem to have the same subjective loudness.[5] While this problem requires further research so that its extents and limits may be ascertained, it is an example of how the results of previous psychoacoustical research can be used for practical benefit in music. Another example of employing previous research for practical benefit has been the use of the power function obtained from the development of the sone scale to produce a "linear" crescendo.[6]

[3]J. L. Flanagan, *Speech Analysis, Synthesis and Perception,* 2nd ed. (Berlin and New York, 1972), p. 88.

[4]S. S. Stevens, "The Measurement of Loudness," *Journal of the Acoustical Society of America,* XXVII/5 (Sept., 1955), 815–829.

[5]This adjustment is an optional feature of the MUSIC4BF unit generator FORMNT.

[6]Marks and Slawson, "Direct Test of the Power Function for Loudness," *Science,* CLIV (1966), 1036–37.

3. TIMBRE

The timbre of a sound is less easily grasped than the qualities of pitch or loudness. The reason for this has more to do with the way in which this term has been used in application to live or instrumental sounds than to electronic music. After reviewing some of the history of this subject, we will suggest that the use of this term be restricted in the future.

The timbre or "tone quality" of a musical instrument has been used to denote that property which enables a listener to identify the instrument. It is thus a "bushel basket" or "catchall" concept that has caused many difficulties because not all listeners are equally successful in identifying certain instruments, nor are they at all sure about just what qualities enable them to make the identification. It is clear, though, that there are many distinct qualities subsumed under the term *timbre*.

It has always been assumed, or at least suggested, that the most important element in the timbre of a sound was its overtone structure. What was uncertain about this explanation is what it was about the overtone structure that constituted the timbre. Many books contain graphs of the spectrum of a sound that show a number of vertical bars of different heights, representing the amplitudes of the partials of the tone. These graphs are labeled with descriptions such as "French horn, middle c," or worse, simply "French horn." What is often missing in these descriptions is the disclaimer that these amplitudes represent the *average* taken over a particular time. Tones electronically synthesized on the basis of these descriptions usually don't sound anything like the instruments from which the information is supposedly derived. At best, they may resemble organ stops that are also made in imitation of the instruments.

Recent studies of musical instruments have achieved more satisfactory results by obtaining graphs describing the envelope of each partial over the duration of the tone. From these we learn that for some tones certain partials are present only during certain portions of the duration, and the amplitudes may be affected by complex factors. Also, not all components of the tones are harmonic partials. Elements present only for a very short portion of the duration, often only during the attack of the sound, are called *transients*. Sometimes these are nonharmonic partials, but not all transients are of this nature. (Sometimes this fact is confused in the literature, where writers assume that transient elements are always nonharmonic.)

It is indeed difficult to form generalizations about musical instruments and how they are identified from data so complex in nature. Even studies that have been successful in suggesting important qualities that aid in the identification of certain classes of instruments[7] leave the impression that something has been lost in the whole process. The listener, in learning how to identify instruments, has learned to disregard some musically significant distinctions and to summarize others under a single category called "timbre." This situation is part of the whole package that a listener inherits from his experience with live music; but it should not hinder his experience with electronic music.

It is suggested here that the term *timbre* be retained to describe the overtone structure of sounds, including whatever variations in amplitude may occur over the course of their durations, but that the connotation that this has to do with identifying instruments be dropped. Thus, any factors other than the overtone spectrum that are involved in identifying sounds may be disregarded as far as the timbre is concerned and subsumed under other dimensions, such as "articulation." Furthermore, this redefinition still allows for higher-order generalizations about similarities and differences in overtone structure.

At least two simple kinds of similarities may be used to form generalizations about tones on the basis of their overtone structure.[8] The most direct is similarity of *waveshape,* or of the specific partials present and their amplitudes. According to this theory, two tones that have the same waveshape would have the same timbre. This idea is used intuitively when people refer to two sawtooth or two square waves as having the same timbre.

More important, however, is the similarity between two tones on the basis of *formants.* A formant is a fixed frequency area in which the loudest partials of a tone occur. A formant actually defines a relationship between frequency and amplitude for the entire frequency continuum, and it is the exact analogue of a filter network. Formant similarities differ from waveshape similarities in that the area of maximum response is associated with

---

[7]Risset, for example, suggests that one of the important clues in recognizing brass sounds is that increases in the overall amplitude of the sound are correlated to increases in the amplitudes of higher partials. (Jean-Claude Risset, *Computer Study of Trumpet Tones* [Murray Hill, N.J., 1968].)

[8]In "Operations on Waveforms" (the third lecture in "Three Lectures to Scientists," *Perspectives of New Music,* V/2 [spring–summer, 1967], 124–140), J. K. Randall suggests several other ways in which the partials of tones can be related.

fixed frequencies, which affect different partials of different pitches. For example, if a strong formant occurs at 1,000 cps, this would resonate the tenth partial of a frequency of 100 cps, but the fourth partial of a frequency of 250 cps.

It is on the basis of formant similarities, rather than wave-shape similarities, that speakers of a language recognize the same vowels, even when these are spoken by people with different voice qualities, on different pitches, or with other differences due to age or sex. Hence, vowels already constitute a kind of intuitive theory of timbre, although one obviously too crude to account for most sounds occuring in electronic music.

While much discussion in the literature of timbre assumes that the object of attention is a "single tone," which could mean "single pitch," nothing about the considerations we have mentioned implies any such restriction. It would thus be completely correct to speak of the timbre of a chord or of a collection of unrelated frequencies. Obviously, such tones are distinguished by the fact that different pitches can be perceived in the collection.

When we think about differentiations in the overtone structure of a sound, the fact that a series of harmonic partials is heard as a single pitch becomes all the more remarkable. Changes in frequency and amplitude which may occur throughout the range of the frequency continuum are heard as changes in the quality of a single tone.

4. MODULATION

Since modulation occuring at a frequency above the audio range causes a complex spectrum to be perceived, because the sidebands result in audible frequencies, the properties of these sounds must be considered in the same way as any complex tone that is produced in any manner. It is possible to consider that modulation below the audio range actually introduces a new property into the sound; but for this property it is more useful to employ terms like _vibrato_ and _tremolo_ rather than _modulation,_ since the latter involves using one term to describe both a psychological and a physical property. No corresponding musical terms are available to describe timbre modulation, location modulation, or any other complex kind of modulation, however.

The physical properties of modulation have been explained as the rate, amplitude, and shape of modulation, and in the absence of any extensive or conclusive research in these areas, it seems unwise to try to summarize these differentiations under a single concept like Stevens's and Davis' "richness."[9]

What more complex kinds of modulation are there? Since modulation has been defined in such completely general terms—a periodic change in any characteristic of a sound—it seems logical that the process will eventually be applied to still further new properties.

5. *SOUND LOCATION*

The location from which a sound emanates is an important characteristic, and it is a property always present in any sound. Not until recently, however, has it been possible for composers to structure sound locations in their music in any sophisticated manner, and thus this property has often been overlooked.

There are, of course, numerous exceptions to the above statement. There are works from many historical periods in which different instrumental ensembles are directed to be situated in different locations. It may be asserted that many composers intended that their orchestral music be played with the different instrumental groups in certain locations, and there are many works that specify the locations of their instruments or voices. Since the advent of stereophonic recording, these properties have been preserved in recordings of live music—or at least they can be preserved. (They are often destroyed in the recording process.)

Moving sounds, on the other hand, cannot be specified in any convenient manner in instrumental music. One fact that must be noted about moving sounds when they occur in nature is that they always produce the Doppler effect—a change in the pitch of the moving sound, depending upon its velocity and direction relative to the listener—and this phenomenon might conceivably affect some of the pitch relationships in the music. Using electronic means, it is possible to produce moving sounds without the Doppler effect.[10]

How is it that listeners are able to perceive sound locations? The customary explanation for this phenomenon is that the sound reaching one ear is

[9]S. S. Stevens and Halowell Davis, *Hearing, Its Psychology and Physiology* (New York, 1938), pp. 236–239.
[10]The Doppler effect is a physical and not a psychological property of sound.

at a slightly different *phase* from the otherwise identical sound reaching the other ear. While this suggests that phase is responsible for producing the sense of the location of the sound, one should not conclude from this that phase in itself is a perceptible characteristic of the sound. Furthermore, informal experimental results have concluded that the phases of the partials of a complex sound make no difference to the perception of the timbre. Other remarks about the effects of the phase of sounds are included in our discussion of phase shifters in Chapter 4.

6. SUBJECTIVE FACTORS

In addition to the "objective" properties of sound perceived by a listener, there are several other characteristics produced by the ear itself as a result of its *nonlinearity* of sound transmission through the middle ear. These properties are called "subjective" because they are not actually present in the stimulus, but are created by the manner in which the ear responds to the stimulus. It is not within the scope of this book to discuss the physiology of the ear or to survey the current state of knowledge about these subjective factors; but since we are interested in the effects of music on human observers, we present the following summary of the more important nonlinearities of the ear.

Aural harmonics is a term used to describe subjective tones produced when the stimulus to the ear is a pure sine tone; the ear perceives a complex sound because of these additional tones. When the stimulus consists of a mixture of two or more frequencies, the tones that are produced are called *combination tones,* and they happen to have the same frequencies as the identically named tones discussed in Chapter 1. These tones can beat with one another or with the other tones in the stimulus. When the stimulus is at a low amplitude level, these subjective tones may not even be perceptible, but their effect becomes more and more pronounced as the amplitude increases. The change in tone quality that we hear when a single tone increases in intensity is due to the increasing amplitude of the subjective tones.[11]

Masking is the technical term describing the capacity of one tone to

---

[11]Paul Hindemith's *The Craft of Musical Composition* [originally *Unterweisung im Tonsatz*], trans. Arthur Mendel (New York, 1942), asserts a "theory" of composition based upon "roots" derived from combination tones produced in collections of tones used as "chords."

"drown out" another. High-frequency sounds are more easily masked by low-frequency sounds than the reverse. High frequencies are usually overtones of low frequencies, so that the masking affects the tone quality of the sounds. When the frequencies of the sounds are moved apart, the masking effects are decreased but not eliminated.

Masking is well known to orchestral musicians. Frequently they are asked to play along in passages when they cannot even hear themselves. More important nuances of masking arise when instruments attempt to balance one another in amplitude. In electronic music, the only practical suggestion that can be made is that problems involving masking will inevitably arise, and they can be solved only by trial-and-error methods.

7. RHYTHM

It would be foolish to omit the concept of rhythm from an enumeration of the psychological properties of sounds, but this is often what is done in books and articles on psychoacoustics. This is especially true of psychoacoustical tests that attempt to test sounds in isolation from other sounds and with no control of their rhythmic characteristics. The results of these tests do not reveal properties relevant to musical situations in which the sounds might appear and, therefore, ought to be relegated to a category called "nonmusic."

Rhythm is a very difficult term to define, and even harder to explicate out of its usage in common language. Fundamentally, it is the concept that includes time relationships in music, in particular the starting points and durations of individual sounds (which are two separate characteristics), and higher-order similarities arising out of patterns among these properties of sounds in musical contexts. *Meter,* for example, is a higher-order similarity arising out of patterns in the starting points and durations (and sometimes harmonic characteristics) of sounds in a musical context.

One useful way of thinking about the rhythm of a musical passage is to consider it the manner in which two sounds *not* associated on the basis of any other characteristic may be related to one another. The sweeping nature of the importance of rhythm to music is succinctly expressed by the statement that music is a function of time. So regarded, it is clear that rhythm is a conceptual property that is of most value to the analysis of individual works or groups of works, and would not be a fruitful subject to explore for universal truths by traditional psychoacoustical testing methods.

An understanding of the conceptual nature of rhythm is of great importance to composers, and also to anyone who is really interested in that subset of our overall auditory experience that constitutes music. It is also clear that much more research could be done on the investigation of higher-order rhythmic characteristics of music.

8. OTHER PROPERTIES

There are many other properties that are present in sounds and in music. It must be recognized that the nature of music is such that the discovery and recognition of any property of sound is a conceptual process that can never be concluded, but must be renewed continually as new observers and new music come to the fore. Some ideas may be of importance only to certain musical works and not to others. In fact, if the focus of attention could be directed more toward individual works rather than toward sounds in the abstract, the conclusions reached would be of much more importance to distinctly _musical_ experience.

The musical properties that fall into the general area of _articulation_ have not been studied extensively as to their physical correlates. These include such characteristics as phrasing and the manner in which individual notes may be performed, such as legato, staccato, pizzicato, sforzando, etc. Certainly the most important relevant physical property is the envelope of the tone, but the reader is cautioned against forming generalizations from the overall envelope of a tone and not the constituent envelopes of each partial.[12]

One of the more important properties that we have not yet mentioned is that of _chorus effect._ This is a quality that applies to instrumental music, and that includes whatever aspects are present when two or more instruments of the same type are playing the same music at the same time. When instruments are doubled the effect is quite different from a single instrument, even if the amplitude of the single instrument matches that of the group of instruments. Chorus effect, like timbre, is a "bushel basket" quality that includes a great number of separate properties under a single heading. Studies have been made attempting to find generalizations about these

---

[12]A rather farfetched scheme for classifying these characteristics in instrumental music is described in Donald Martino, "Notation in General—Articulation in Particular," _Perspectives of New Music,_ IV/2 (spring-summer, 1966), 47–58.

characteristics, but no really satisfactory conclusions have been reached. The reason for this lies partly in the nature of the problem. The whole concept of chorus effect is an attempt to summarize the many deviations in all tonal characteristics of a musical passage under a single heading, and such an attempt seems destined to lead to confusion.

Certainly, however, tonal deviations are an important aspect of music. Precisely because these deviations have not been adequately understood, methods of electronic music synthesis have often failed to take them into account. Experienced practitioners of electronic music have sometimes overreacted to this problem once they have become aware of it, by introducing all kinds of random elements and deviations into practically every aspect of their music. More research is obviously needed before we can understand what deviations are actually present in what kind of music. One possibility that ought not to be overlooked in electronic music is the opportunity to structure tonal deviations in such a way that they relate to the structure of the music.

The literature of psychoacoustics is replete with other qualities that seem to have little or no relevance to music. Examples of these are *volume* (size, extensity), *brightness*, and *density* (compactness). These attributes are explained as follows:

> The tones of a tuba sound bigger than those of a piccolo, and a bugle blast appears to be hard and compact and to have a luster that is lacking in the more diffuse sound of an organ.[13]

It seems obvious in these cases that such qualities are the product of the listener's imagination, especially when grounded in some physical characteristic of the instrument that the listener already knows, such as the shininess of the bugle or the size of the tuba. It is not our intention, however, to disparage the search for new dimensions of musical experience, or the explication of old ones. Because this is a conceptual process involving the development of listening skills, it is hard to draw the line between reality and fantasy. A listener's attention must first be directed to the qualities he is seeking in the music, and then he may discover new aspects of music he was already familiar with.

It is the author's belief that most musical research, including particularly analysis, could profit by being conducted from the viewpoint of the listening

[13]J. C. R. Licklider, "Basic Correlates of the Auditory Stimulus," in S. S. Stevens, ed., *Handbook of Experimental Psychology* (New York, 1951), p. 1004.

experience rather than from the score, except when the score is used as a guide to the listening experience. There seems to be no reason why such traditional concepts as *tonality* could not be explained as an attribute of sound—namely, as a quality possessed by musical compositions judged to be tonal. People who approach music in this inquisitive manner will certainly be well prepared for the many varieties of experience that are to be found in electronic music.

PART 2

Electronic Music Equipment

CHAPTER THREE

Recording and Playback Equipment

1. BASIC COMPONENTS OF SOUND-REPRODUCTION SYSTEMS

The invention of electronic sound-reproduction systems preceded the invention of electronic sound-generation systems, at least as far as general consumer products are concerned. By now most people are familiar with the kinds of devices that are available for these purposes. In this section we will review these systems in general, and in separate sections below we will cover individual devices in detail.

There are four basic components of a sound-reproduction system, illustrated in Figure 3–1.1. All such systems employ two kinds of *transducers,* which are devices that convert one kind of energy into another. An input transducer converts acoustical energy into mechanical or electrical energy, and an output transducer performs the reverse conversion. The most common input transducers are microphones, phonographs, radio receivers, and magnetic tape recorders. Following the input transducer, the energy is transmitted to a *preamplifier,* which amplifies the signal without distortion. Preamplifiers generally incorporate *equalization,* which is essentially a filter that boosts frequencies in certain areas. Following the preamplifier comes the *power amplifier,* which transforms the signal so that it will be capable

Figure 3–1.1: Basic components of a sound-reproduction system.

of driving a loudspeaker. Finally comes the output transducer, which is either a loudspeaker or a pair of headphones.

Microphones

Microphones are one of the most common kinds of input transducers. The microphone is activated by the acoustical energy it senses in the air, and it delivers this energy in electrical form to the preamplifier. The accuracy of the microphone's conversion is expressed by its sensitivity and frequency response. The sensitivity indicates approximately the range of amplitude to which the microphone can react, and the frequency response indicates the range of frequencies. No microphone is uniformly sensitive to the entire range of frequencies audible to the human ear. The frequency response of a particular microphone is given by a curve showing how the response varies over the frequency continuum. These curves are similar to equalization curves for tape recorders and are exactly analogous to the frequency-response curves for loudspeakers. As we pointed out in Chapter 2, even the human ear has a frequency-response curve.

Since the microphone is the mechanism that defines the character of live sounds when a recording is made, it is extremely important that the user know the qualities of his equipment. This information is available in many books,[1] and only the most essential points will be repeated here.

There are two basic types of microphones: low impedance and high impedance. Most microphones used for musical recordings are low impedance. Contact microphones and the microphones found on electric instruments such as guitars are high impedance. Contact microphones sense the mechanical vibrations in a body instead of the acoustical energy in the air. High-impedance microphones cannot be located more than a few feet from the preamplifier, and special devices called "bridges" are available that convert high-impedance lines into low-impedance lines.

Different microphones have different directional characteristics—which is to say that some microphones are more sensitive to sounds emanating from certain directions. A nondirectional microphone picks up sounds coming from all directions with equal efficiency. Pressure microphones, such as carbon, crystal, magnetic, condenser, and dynamic microphones,

---

[1]See, in particular, the discussions by Allen Strange, *Electronic Music: Systems, Techniques, and Controls* (Dubuque, 1972), pp. 108–110, and Harry F. Olson, *Music, Physics, and Engineering* (New York, 1967), pp. 325–336.

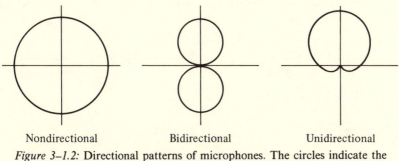

Nondirectional   Bidirectional   Unidirectional

Figure 3–1.2: Directional patterns of microphones. The circles indicate the area in which the microphone picks up sounds. The intersection of the two lines shows where the microphone should be located for maximum efficiency.

are nondirectional. A bidirectional microphone responds well to sounds in front and in back of the microphone but not on the sides. The most common bidirectional microphone is the ribbon microphone, which is very useful for recording dialogues. A cardioid or unidirectional microphone responds well only to sounds in front of it, thus blocking out sounds in the rear. Unidirectional microphones are constructed by combining a nondirectional and a bidirectional microphone or by other special designs that inhibit or reinforce sounds from one direction. Unidirectional microphones are used in motion pictures, television, and for similar stage applications. Microphone directional patterns are shown in Figure 3–1.2.

When a microphone is situated near a loudspeaker to which it is connected, care must be taken to avoid acoustic feedback from the loudspeaker to the microphone. Anyone who has used a public-address system is familiar with the "microphone howl" that results in this situation. It is eliminated by reducing the gain of the microphone, which limits the area of the field to which it reacts, or by moving the microphone away from the loudspeaker.

Many different materials are used in the construction of the various microphones that are available today. The least expensive and most common type of microphone is the carbon microphone. Unfortunately, carbon microphones also have a very limited frequency response, usually from about 80 to 7,500 cps.[2] Carbon microphones are normally regarded as suitable only for speech and not for music, and are used almost exclusively in telephones.

[2] Quoted by Strange, *op. cit.*, p. 109.

The best microphones, which are used for most professional sound recordings, are condenser or electrostatic microphones. These microphones
are naturally more expensive than most other varieties, and they require a
separate amplifier and power supply as part of the operating components.
If professional sound quality is desired, these microphones are essential
components of an electronic music studio.

Phonographs

Most people today are familiar with phonographs since, indeed, most
people have one in their home. The phonograph has several distinct components, which are illustrated in Figure 3–1.3. These include the motor,
turntable, stylus (or needle), pickup, and tone arm. The output of the
phonograph is transmitted to a preamplifier and to the remaining components of the sound-reproduction system. The basic reason why phonographs
have acquired their status as the most popular sound-reproduction device
is cost. Once a master disc has been cut, individual pressings can be stamped
out for only a few cents each. Inexpensive phonographs are also much
cheaper to manufacture than tape recorders. Unfortunately, there are also
many problems with phonographs that make these systems generally of
poorer quality than tape recorders.

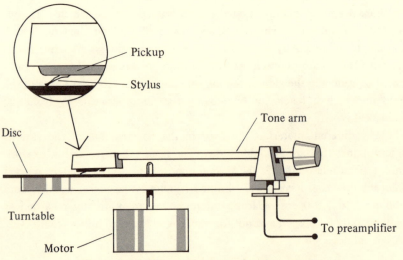

Figure 3–1.3: The components of a phonograph.

The most common problem with phonograph recordings are "scratches" or "jumps" in the music. These are invariably produced by imperfections on the surface of the disc. Often these imperfections are caused by a faulty stylus or poor balance of the tone arm. Once they are present on a disc, however, there is no way of removing the distortions they produce during playback. In order to lessen their effect, many preamplifiers include a "scratch filter." Such a device is simply a low-pass filter and reduces the amount of high frequencies uniformly, thus removing part of the music as well. More serious disc imperfections occur when the disc is warped or cracked. There is no way of salvaging discs with these problems, and they often cannot be played back at all.

Another common problem with phonographs is called "rumble." Rumble is characterized by low-frequency sounds present in the background when the turntable is moving. This problem is usually caused by improper isolation of the turntable or its motor from the pickup, so that the mechanical vibrations of the turntable are sensed as part of the playback signal. Only the most expensive turntables eliminate rumble completely. As with scratches, many preamplifiers include a "rumble filter," which is simply a high-pass filter that reduces low frequencies uniformly, thus eliminating part of the music as well.

A phonograph that is to be used as a high-quality sound-reproduction device must be carefully installed and maintained. Instructions for these purposes are usually provided when the unit is purchased, but we will mention the most important points here. The tone arm must be carefully mounted so that the needle will "overhang" the turntable spindle if it were swept past the center of the disc.[3] The arm must be balanced so that the center of gravity passes through the pivot.[4] The stylus should be checked periodically and replaced when worn. While diamond needles cost much more than other needles, they provide significantly longer wear and better reproduction quality.

Preamplifiers

Preamplifiers are standard components of "hi-fi" systems, and nowadays are often combined with power amplifiers into "integrated" amplifiers. Preamplifiers in hi-fi systems contain inputs for any of the devices that may

[3] Edgar Villchur, *Reproduction of Sound* (Cambridge, Mass.: 1962), pp. 40–41.
[4] *Ibid.*, pp. 41–43.

be patched into them, and they also provide gain controls and "treble" and "bass" filters for each output channel. Treble and bass filters are simply high-pass and low-pass filters respectively, with a mild slope, that boost frequencies in each of these regions uniformly. (Actually, they attenuate frequencies in the opposite region.) Sometimes even an AM/FM radio tuner will be combined with a preamplifier and amplifier in a single device, known as a *receiver*. Preamplifiers are usually built into tape recorders, and the line-level output of the tape recorder may be connected directly to a power amplifier.

Power Amplifiers

Power amplifiers usually have no controls at all except a "mono-stereo" switch, which combines both inputs into a single output. The power-level outputs of power amplifiers are rated in watts. Different loudspeakers require different amounts of power to be driven efficiently. Most can be satisfactorily driven by 40 to 60 watts; more watts are required in order to make the output level louder. It should be pointed out that many amplifiers rated at nominal power levels of 200 to 400 watts in fact produce only half this amount in each channel. Further-more, hardly any commercial loudspeakers require constant power levels on the order of 100 or 200 watts, and if driven at this level, they produce very loud but greatly distorted sounds.

Loudspeakers

Loudspeakers are the weakest components of sound-reproduction systems. Whereas a typical amplifier may be close to 100-per-cent efficient in reproducing its input signal, a typical loudspeaker may be only 5-per-cent efficient; the loss is both in power and in linearity of response. Loudspeakers come in a variety of sizes and price ranges. Many "speaker systems" mounted in attractive wooden cabinets actually contain several individual speakers, each with a different range of response. The largest speaker is called the *woofer* and responds well to low frequencies; the smallest is called the *tweeter* and responds well to high frequencies. Intermediate speakers are called *midrange*.

The subject of loudspeakers and which ones are appropriate for electronic music is beyond the scope of this book. Much information about loudspeaker construction and use is available in books[5] and in literature provided by manufacturers. Users must select loudspeakers that are appropriate for their own requirements of power, quality, and cost, and there are a great number of products on the market from which to choose.

Nevertheless, one comment about loudspeakers is included that reflects practical experience. Some of the best loudspeakers available from the point of view of reproduction quality, physical size (i.e., smallness), and cost are *acoustic suspension* systems. These speaker systems must be used with extreme caution when they are in an electronic music studio. They can be severely damaged if sine tones are played through them for long periods of time or if they are driven with too much power. For this reason, we recommend that any studio with acoustic-suspension loudspeakers have another pair or group of other speakers available for monitoring sounds during everyday work, and that the acoustic suspension speakers be reserved for playback of tapes and discs only when reproduction quality, particularly in the bass register, is essential for the listening experience.

2. MAGNETIC TAPE

The invention of magnetic tape recording was the most important historical event in the evolution of electronic music. Many early attempts at electronic music had been made before tape recorders appeared on the general consumer market, but nothing on the scale that followed. Magnetic tape provided a convenient means for *storing* and *editing* sounds. Sounds could be experimented with in a manner previously impossible. Other systems such as disc and wire recordings had provided methods of storing sounds, but these could not be manipulated with the ease of magnetic tape. Even today, the tape recorder remains one of the most central devices in the production of electronic music, and anyone who is seriously interested in composing or understanding the production of electronic music must be familiar with the characteristics of magnetic tape and tape recorders.

---

[5]See, for example, Edgar Villchur, *op. cit.,* chs. 11 and 12, or Harry F. Olson, *op. cit.,* ch. 9.

Characteristics of Magnetic Tape

Magnetic tape consists of a thin ribbon of plastic, referred to as the *backing* or *base,* that is coated with a layer of extremely fine magnetic particles, referred to as the *oxide* or *coating.* Each of these particles acts as a tiny "bar magnet." When a signal is recorded on magnetic tape, the particles are magnetized in such a way that the characteristics of the signal are reflected in their alignment, and these characteristics can then be sensed as the tape is played back. The coating is applied on the side of the tape that is wound facing the *inside* of the reel. The outside of the tape is the only side that should be used for marking. On older brands of tape, the outside of the tape was always shiny and the inside dull in appearance. On some newer brands, the coated side is shinier than the outside, so this general principle can no longer be relied upon.

The most common backing materials used for magnetic tape are *acetate* and *polyester* or *mylar.* (*Mylar* and *polyester* are different names for the same material.) According to extensive tests made by the 3M company,[6] polyester tape has greater strength and stability, although acetate tape may be preferable for editing purposes. The most significant characteristic of these tape backings, in the context of electronic music, is that polyester tape has a tendency to stretch when force is exerted on it, but it does not break easily. Acetate tape, on the other hand, will break under less force than will cause polyester tape to stretch. Nevertheless, this comparison is misleading, because once a tape is stretched even slightly the signal recorded on the tape will be distorted on playback.

When polyester tape is spliced, there may be a sudden "pop" or "click" at the point where the two edges are joined. This happens also with acetate tape, but usually the pop is much less noticeable. For this reason, acetate tape may be preferable for electronic music. Nevertheless, polyester backing is now used almost exclusively for magnetic tape. Anyone seriously interested in all of the differences between these two tape backings should consult the results of the 3M company's tests.

Tape *thickness* is measured in *mils,* the most common thicknesses being 0.5, 1.0, and 1.5 mils. The advantage of thin tape is that more of it can be stored on a reel; furthermore, it is cheaper for equivalent lengths. The fact that the cost of high-quality magnetic tape is so high, along with the cost

[6]"Polyester and Acetate for Magnetic Recording Tape Backings," *Sound Talk,* II/1 (1969).

of duplication, explains why tape cannot compete with disc recordings on the consumer market. Nevertheless, there are serious disadvantages with thin tape: it is more difficult to handle than thicker tape; it is less resistant to print-through (see below); and it stretches or breaks much more easily than thicker tape. Since the disadvantages far outweigh the advantages, 1.5-mil tape is used for most professional recording purposes.

Magnetic tape may be purchased on reels of different sizes, and sometimes, when it is bought in large quantities, "on the hub." The standard diameters of reels are 5 inches, 7 inches, and 10½ inches. A 5-inch reel can contain 600 feet of 1.5-mil tape; a 7-inch reel, 1,200 feet of 1.5-mil tape; and a 10½-inch reel, 2,500 feet of 1.5-mil tape. These lengths correspond respectively to slightly more than fifteen minutes, thirty minutes, and one hour of recording time at a speed of 7½ inches, recording in only one direction. Professional tape recorders usually can accommodate reels up to 10½ inches in diameter.

An important property of a magnetic tape reel is the diameter of the *hub,* the central portion that mounts on the tape recorder. The standard hub sizes of 5-inch, 7-inch, and 10½-inch reels are 1¾ inches, 2¼ inches, and 4 inches, respectively. The smaller the hub, the greater the tension on the tape when it is wound to the end of the reel. Since tape tension can cause the tape to break or stretch, it is a good idea to use reels with hubs as wide as possible. Reels of 7 inches are also made with 4-inch hubs, although tape is not sold commercially on reels of this size. The resultant loss of capacity on the reel amounts to only a few minutes of running time. When practical, the use of 7-inch reels with the wider hub, and complete avoidance of 5-inch or smaller reels, is strongly recommended.

The standard *width* of magnetic tape used on most musical tape recorders is ¼ inch. Multitrack tape recorders employ tape of the same thickness, backing, and length as two-channel tape recorders, but with a greater width; the standard is ⅛ inch for each track. Therefore, four-track, eight-track, and sixteen-track tape recorders employ tape that is ½ inch, 1 inch, and 2 inches wide, respectively.

The reader must be warned, however, that not all ¼-inch tapes are compatible with one another. The significant property is the *head format* of the tape recorder—whether it is quarter-track, which is standard for nonprofessional tape recorders, or half-track, which is standard for professional tape recorders. (These factors are explained in detail under "Tape Recorders" below.)

When magnetic tape is tightly packed onto a reel, the magnetization of one layer of tape can be impressed on an adjacent layer. This process is known as *print-through*. Print-through can never be completely eliminated, although audio noise-reduction systems may reduce it markedly. Its effect on the playback of a recording can be minimized by storing the tape *"tails out,"* or with the beginning of the recording on the innermost portion of the reel. (The tape must then be rewound *before* playing, rather than after.) In this manner, the print-through of loud passages preceded by silence or by soft passages follows rather than precedes the entrance of the loud sounds. The most noticeable effect of print-through when tapes are stored "heads out" is that loud entrances are preceded by the printed-through entrance, which ruins any sudden changes in dynamics. Most professional tapes are stored "tails out."

Other problems encountered with magnetic tape recordings are *crosstalk* and *tape hiss*. Crosstalk occurs when a portion of a recorded signal on a given track of a multitrack tape recorder "leaks over" to an adjacent track. This problem may be caused by faulty alignment of the heads of the tape recorder. Tape hiss is a low-amplitude background noise that can interfere with the reproduction of weakly recorded signals. In fact, the dynamic range of a tape recorder must be measured with respect to the level of background noise upward, rather than with respect to any absolute dynamic level. The problem of tape hiss can be greatly reduced by an audio noise-reduction system.

Magnetic tapes can be purchased in a variety of qualities that are supposedly geared to these sundry problems: "low noise" has a lower level of tape hiss; "low print-through" minimizes print-through; "standard" has neither of these properties. While most professional recording outfits use "low noise" tape, these differences are not nearly as important as the thickness and backing of the tape. Even more important is that tape recorders must be individually adjusted for the type of tape used. Once you decide on the type, it is difficult to change, unless you want to readjust all your machines, which will then not be exactly right for all your previous tapes.

Tape Splicing and Editing

At one time, tape splicing was the only way in which electronic music compositions could be assembled, and it still remains one of the most basic procedures in an electronic music studio. Anyone who works in a studio must be familiar with proper splicing procedures.[7]

Splicing requires a *splicing block, marking pencil, razor blade,* and *splicing tape.* The splicing block is sometimes fastened to the top of the head assembly of the tape recorder, conveniently close to the tape travel path. Standard blocks have two cutting grooves, and should be mounted with the diagonal cut to the left and the 90-degree cut to the right. A professional splicing block is always made of metal—not plastic—and is a machine-tooled, precision instrument. The groove in the block grips the tape firmly while it is being spliced. The tape should be placed in the groove with the *uncoated* side facing up, and pressed squarely down in the groove. Tape should *never* be removed from the groove by peeling. The best way to remove the tape is to grasp it by both hands at the ends of the block, pull it taut and snap it out of the groove. If only one end of the tape is to be removed from the block, it can be pulled out slowly from the end of the block. Peeling the tape out of the groove wrinkles the edges, causing permanent damage.

Sound recorded on magnetic tape is reproduced from the playback head (see "Tape Recorders" below), and sounds must be located on the tape in relation to this head. On most professional tape recorders the distance between the playback head and the nearest edge of the head-assembly shield is exactly 1½ inches, and this is also the distance between the center of the diagonal cut and the perpendicular cut on professional splicing blocks. Therefore, the tape can safely be marked at the edge of the head-assembly shield when the desired sound is exactly at the playback head. Tape can be marked with a grease pencil, but it is best not to let the marking material accumulate on the back of the tape lest it rub off onto the coated side when the tape is wound. If this occurs, the material can be removed with head cleaner or lubricant.

Splicing is most easily accomplished when the tape deck is mounted horizontally rather than vertically. In this position, tape does not fall to the floor when wound off the reel, and markings are more easily spotted as the tape moves past the heads. Some people prefer to have the deck mounted at a slight angle.

Locating a specific sound in the middle of a musical context, in order to make a splice at exactly that point, can be very difficult. Probably the best

[7]A more detailed explanation of these procedures is contained in the "Instructions for Mounting and Use of Editall Blocks" by the Tall Co., 158 South Terrace Avenue, Mount Vernon, N.Y. 10550. This pamphlet comes free with Editall splicing kits.

method is to play the tape repeatedly at the slowest speed at which the sound remains recognizable until you are thoroughly familiar with the musical context, and then to hit the stop button at exactly the right moment. This spot can then be marked on the tape, and as the tape is played back again the user can watch for the mark to see when it passes the marking point in relation to the specific sound. After a few tries, one can come fairly close by this method.

The procedure for locating the beginning of a sound following a silence is much easier: turn the playback volume up very high and, placing one hand on each reel, move the tape manually past the head until the sound is heard. With the volume so high, even the softest sound can be located in this manner.

Tape is normally spliced *diagonally* in order to avoid "clicks" if the splice occurs between two sounds. The diagonal merely causes the sounds on each end of the splice to fade in and out gradually. However, if a multichannel tape is spliced this way, there will be a very slight time lag between the entrances of the channels, which might be noticeable if sounds occur in more than one channel at that time. If this is not acceptable, then the tape must be spliced vertically, and there is no way to avoid the "pop" that occurs at the splice.

The splicing tape should also be cut at an angle, to prevent a sudden change in the thickness of the tape as it moves past the playback head, possibly causing a slight change in pitch when the tape is played back. Only the best-quality thin polyester splicing tape should be used. The adhesive of cheap splicing tape tends to ooze or "bleed" out of the splice in warm temperatures or when the tape is stored tightly packed on the reel. This causes adjacent layers of the tape to stick together, and the stray adhesive will peel the oxide coating off the tape, ruining the recording. A length of approximately 1 inch of splicing tape is satisfactory for a single splice.

Splicing tape should be slightly narrower than the width of the tape being joined. When the splicing tape is the same width as the recording tape, the splicing tape must be exactly aligned or it will hang over the edges slightly. The overhanging portion may then adhere to an adjacent layer of tape on the reel.[8]

It is best to use a single-edge razor blade for splicing. Before cutting the tape, make certain that the blade is not magnetized. A magnetized blade will

[8]More complete information about splicing tapes and their use is provided in "Splicing Tapes and their Proper Application," *Sound Talk*, II/2 (1969).

cause a "click" on the tape at the splice. When the tape is solidly in place in the groove of the block, hold the razor with its forward point in the cutting slot, and cut the tape by pulling the blade toward you.

It is essential that the two edges joined in a splice be placed exactly adjacent to one another, with no overlap or gap between them. If this is not accomplished on the first attempt, the splicing tape should be peeled off and the tape respliced.

Splicing should be done with clean hands. A fingerprint, especially an oily or greasy one, on the oxide coating of the tape can cause the output level of the signal to drop appreciably. Even fingerprints on the back of the tape are a problem, because dirt will be transferred to the oxide side of the tape which wraps in front of the back on the next revolution of the reel. The sticky surface of the splicing tape should not be touched with the fingers. To avoid this, lay down a stretch of masking tape in a convenient place, and put a long piece of splicing tape on top of it; 1-inch pieces of splicing tape can then be cut, and picked up with the edge of the razor blade. Alternatively, a splicing-tape dispenser can be used.

It is customary to splice leader tape at the beginning and end of a composition recorded on tape. The leader tape should always be spliced on the tape *after* it has been recorded, so that the "pop" caused by starting the tape and hitting the record button can be removed. Since there should be no change in the level of background noise before the recording begins, it is a good idea to have leader tape all the way up to the first sound attacked in the music. When splicing silences into the middle of a composition, one could use leader tape or, even easier, timing tape (which is marked every 7½ inches for measurement of duration). However, this tape would have a lower level of background noise than the recording, and would not be perceived as a "silence" but as an indication of the ending of the piece. It is best to use blank tape for silence within a piece. These considerations may not apply if a good audio noise-reduction system is used.

Leader tape is made from either plastic or paper. Plastic leader is stronger and thinner than paper, but it can accumulate static electricity, causing "pops" as it goes past the playback head. Layers of plastic leader may also stick together and be difficult to remove from the inside of a reel when one is mounting a tape on a tape recorder. Paper leader does not have these drawbacks, but it is rather easily torn by a careless operator or even broken by a tape recorder with improperly adjusted tension. Leader attached to the beginning of a tape should be several feet long to allow for threading and for the tape recorder to attain a constant speed before the music begins. A similar length at the end also prevents the tape from coming off the machine the second after the music stops.

Tape Storage and Handling

Electronic music compositions are created and preserved on magnetic tape. The tape represents the only real form in which the piece exists. While a given realization of a composition might be regarded as a "performance" of the composition and not as the composition itself—a philosophical view to which not all people active in the field may subscribe—the only way in which the composition may be heard is by playing the tape. If the tape is damaged in any way, the piece is damaged and may even be lost. Electronic music composers have a vital stake in learning and observing proper tape handling and storage procedures.[9]

In the first place, the environment in which tape is handled should be kept clean and especially free of air-borne dust and dirt. Smoking should not be allowed in the area where the tape recorders are kept; although smoke itself is not harmful, cigarettes ashes and especially matches and burning tobacco can be very hazardous. Eating and drinking should also be prohibited: a spilled drink may ruin not only the tape but the tape deck as well; food particles not only contaminate tape, but may also leave a residue of grease and oil on the fingers. In general it is always a good idea to wash your hands before beginning work with tape, especially if you are going to be splicing.

Dust creates a special problem. When dust or excess oxide that has rubbed off the tape onto heads or other surfaces over which the tape passes accumulates on the surface of the tape, it interferes with the correct play-back or recording. Dust covers should be placed over tape decks when they are not in use, and the entire studio should be cleaned regularly.

Temperature and humidity conditions in the recording area must be carefully controlled. Ideally, the temperature should be kept in the 70s, with a variation of ± 5 degrees, and the relative humidity at about 40 per cent, with a variation of 10 per cent. Tape should be allowed to adjust to these conditions before it is used. These conditions of environmental control and cleanliness will have an important psychological effect on the users of the equipment, who will be encouraged to maintain good operating habits.

---

[9]These procedures are summarized in "The Handling and Storage of Magnetic Recording Tape," *Sound Talk,* III/1 (1970). This article has served as the basis for many of the points covered here, and is the source of all quantitative data.

When a tape reel is handled, it should always be grasped by the hub and not by the flanges. Applying pressure to the flanges in handling or in storage may warp the reel and damage the tape. Take-up reels should be inspected for warping, cracks, chips, and for cleanliness before they are used. Reels with the smallest holes in the flanges provide the best protection from dust and other air-borne contamination.

Before a recording session begins, it is always good practice to clean the heads and all portions of the tape path with head cleaner. At the same time, the heads should be demagnetized, and any other dirt should be cleaned off of the tape deck. Finally, the tape can be mounted on the deck.

When operating certain tape recorders, particularly older or badly adjusted machines, one must hit the button for the reverse direction of the tape when it is traveling at high speed before stopping; otherwise, a sudden stop may exert great tension on the tape, causing it to stretch or break. Before a tape is started, the slack between the feed and take-up reels should be eliminated by manual rotation of the reels.

There are several ways in which magnetic tape may be damaged, just as there are specific causes that may be associated with each type of damage. One of the most common is known as "edge damage," which consists of wrinkles along the edge of the tape. Edge damage can cause the track that runs along the edge to be lost or distorted, but it can also cause debris to be deposited along the entire width of the tape. Edge damage can be caused by a warped or broken reel, or by the misalignment of the components of the deck along the tape path.

Tape "cinching" occurs when adjacent layers of tape wound on a reel become loose and slip. Cinching creates wrinkles along the length of the tape, which cause the tape to be lifted back and forth as it passes across the heads, producing fluctuations in the signal. If the cinching is observed immediately, a proper rewind may save the tape. Cinching is caused when the wind tension on the take-up reel is too weak.

When the wind tension is too great, other problems may occur. Extreme tension may stretch or even break the tape, while a very tight wind may result in backing distortion if the temperature rises while the tape is in storage.

"Scattered wind" occurs when individual strands of tape on a reel protrude above the others. The exposed strands are subject to damage since they are not protected by the body of the tape. A properly adjusted tape recorder should pack the successive layers of tape onto the reel so that they create a smooth edge, and if the wind tension is properly adjusted, the flanges of the reel can even be removed for storage without harm.

None of these forms of damage is necessarily disastrous, and damaged tape can frequently be salvaged.

Magnetic tape should be stored under atmospheric conditions resembling those of the recording area itself: temperature between 60 and 80 degrees Farenheit, humidity between 40 and 60 per cent.

Tapes should always be stored in their containers or boxes, and these should be placed upright, on edge propped up by a bookend. The tape should not be placed at an angle, which exerts uneven pressure on the reel and may cause warping. Stacking them on top of one another may crush reels at the bottom of the stack. Of course, the tape should be wound on the reel with proper pressure and wind quality.

Surprisingly, there is little possibility of accidental erasure of magnetic tape during storage or shipment. Magnetic fields strong enough to cause erasure of magnetic tape are simply not found in a home or office environment. A distance of as little as 3 inches from a strong magnetic field is enough to prevent erasure.

This last fact is relevant to packaging tapes for shipment—packing material can be placed around the tape to insulate it from the possibility of accidental erasure. Shipping containers should, of course, be strong enough to resist crushing in transit, and should also be water resistant. It is also a good idea to fasten the outer end of the tape to the reel, to prevent slippage and maintain pressure. The one thing that cannot be controlled in transit is the temperature, which may vary from −40 to +120 degrees Farenheit. Tapes received in the mail should be allowed to reach the environmental conditions of the recording area before being played.

3. TAPE RECORDERS

The essential components of a tape recorder are illustrated in Figure 3–3.1. The machine consists of two main portions: the *deck,* which contains the mechanical features concerned with handling the tape, and the *electronics,* which contain the circuitry for processing the signals. These portions may be physically separated. For ease in editing tape, the deck is often mounted horizontally and the electronics vertically above the deck.

The deck contains two hubs on which the *feed reel* and *take-up reel* are mounted. On some decks the reels must be held in place by *reel locks.* When

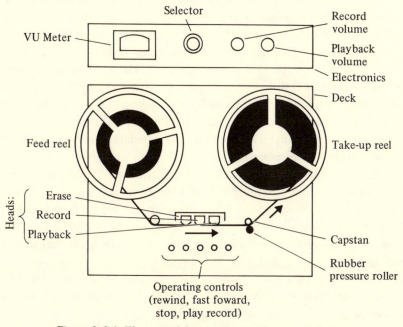

Figure 3–3.1: The essential components of a tape recorder.

the tape is threaded, there may be *guides* that help keep the tape in alignment along the tape path. The tape itself moves past an array of *heads* that produce or detect magnetic fields on the oxide. First it passes the *erase head,* which erases any signals previously recorded on the tape. Next is the *record head,* which records signals on the tape. The erase head and record head are used simultaneously, so that tape is erased only when it is to be recorded. Last is the *playback head,* which detects the signals on the tape. The tape path is usually from left to right past the heads. Sometimes a machine will have only a playback head, or it may have more than one of these functions combined in one head. Some machines have even additional heads. *Tape lifters* lift the tape off the surface of the heads during high-speed winding, in order to reduce wear on the heads.

The tape is made to move past the heads by the *capstan,* a rotating shaft driven by a motor with a very carefully controlled speed. The tape is held against the capstan by a rubber *pressure roller,* which is locked into place when the play button is hit. The capstan motor often is capable of operating at two or more speeds. Professional tape recorders generally employ speeds of 7½ and 15 inches per second (abbreviated ips). Nonprofessional machines may employ speeds of 7½, 3¾, 1⅞, and even $\frac{15}{16}$ ips.

The heads of most tape recorders are divided into a number of parallel *tracks* or *channels*. Each track has separate heads and electronics, and an entirely separate signal is recorded on each track. The width of tape covered by each channel is called the *track width*. Professional tape recorders employ a track width of ⅛ inch (actually 0.082 inches)[10] and, therefore, can record two parallel tracks on ¼-inch tape. Professional tape recorders are also made with four, eight, and sixteen tracks, requiring tape widths of ½, 1, and 2 inches wide respectively.

Nonprofessional tape recorders employ tracks half as wide as professional tape recorders, $\frac{1}{16}$ inch (actually 0.043 inches),[10] and, therefore, fit four parallel tracks on ¼-inch tape. These tracks are not always used together, however. On *quarter-track stereophonic* machines, tracks 1 and 3 are combined into a stereophonic recording, and the tape is reversed at the end and recorded on tracks 2 and 4 in the opposite direction. In *quarter-track quadraphonic* machines, all four tracks are recorded in the same direction.

Professional tape recorders using ¼-inch tape have gone through several historical generations, and several track formats. The earliest was the *full-track monaural* format, which used the entire width of tape for a single track. Next was *half-track monaural,* which used half the width, enabling the tape to be turned over at the end and recorded in the opposite direction. Finally came *two-track stereophonic,* recorder, which has become the professional standard. These different head formats are illustrated in Figure 3–3.2.

Crosstalk occurs when some of the signals recorded on one track of a multitrack tape recorder "leaks over" to an adjacent track. When all the

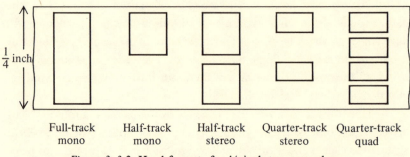

$\frac{1}{4}$ inch

| Full-track | Half-track | Half-track | Quarter-track | Quarter-track |
| mono | mono | stereo | stereo | quad |

Figure 3–3.2: Head formats for ¼-inch tape recorders.

[10]These figures are quoted by Strange, *op. cit.,* p. 102.

tracks on the tape are recorded in the same direction—as, for example, with half-track stereophonic or quarter-track quadraphonic machines—then the cross talk is less objectionable, because the sounds will mix within the playback environment anyway, although some spatial problems may occur. But when the crosstalk consists of signals recorded in the opposite direction, as with half-track monaural or quarter-track stereophonic machines, it can be quite disturbing.

From Figure 3–3.2 it is easy to see that half-track monaural and quarter-track stereophonic tapes may be played back on half-track stereophonic or quarter-track quadraphonic machines respectively, and that full-track monaural tapes may be played back on any other machine. In the latter case, it is best to use only one channel for playback, for the heads of the different channels may not be exactly aligned and phase cancellations between the tracks may result. Conversely, a full-track monaural tape recorder could be used to play back tapes recorded on any of the other head formats illustrated in Figure 3–3.2, but phase cancellations could also occur in this situation if the same signal is recorded on each track.

Half-track stereophonic tapes are not compatible with quarter-track machines, however, for the alignment of one head is not the same as the other, and it will be necessary to set the playback volume of one channel higher than the other, thus also increasing the amount of noise in that channel. A high noise level will also be present when smaller-width monaural tapes are played back on larger heads—as when half-track tapes are played back on full-track machines, for example.

Operating controls for the tape motion are usually mounted on the deck. These include *rewind, fast forward, stop, play,* and *record* buttons. The record button causes the machine to start recording on all tracks that are ready, and it must be hit either at the same time as the play button, or shortly thereafter, when the tape has started to move. The choice of tracks to be recorded is usually determined by a "ready" switch on the electronics. Sometimes there are separate record buttons for each track. Other operating controls may include switches for changing the speed of the capstan and for adjusting the tension to accommodate different size reels.

A separate set of electronics is necessary for each track of the tape recorder, and these are usually mounted in separate panels. The electronics contain *volume controls* for the recording and playback levels. The *VU meter,* illustrated in Figure 3–3.3, monitors the signal level. "VU" stands for "volume units," which are approximately equal to decibels. There are usually two scales on a VU meter: on top, the volume-unit scale, arranged logarithmically from −20 to +3 dB (negative values are marked in black and positive in red); below, a scale marked from 0 to 100, indicating percentage on a linear scale. When the pointer on the meter goes "into the red" (above 0 on the VU scale), the signal level is overloading the electronics, causing distortion. For this reason, the recording level should optimally be set to read 0 VU at the loudest portion of the tape. It is all right if the needle occasionally jumps into the red, but not if it stays there for more than a fraction of a second.

Selector switches for both the inputs and the outputs are located on the electronics. The input selector determines which one of the various inputs is to be used. Tape recorders generally have microphone inputs, with preamplifiers, as well as line-level inputs for signals already preamplified. The output selector determines whether the output that is monitored is taken from the playback head or from the signal going to the record head (the input signal). If the machine is equipped with selective synchronization (see below), this switch may determine whether the signal is played back from the playback head or from the record head, the latter in order to synchronize it with other signals that are performed live and recorded on a different track. Individual machines may determine these functions in any of a variety of different ways.

These items are only the essential components of a tape recorder. Individual machines may have several other features, some of which are discussed in detail below.

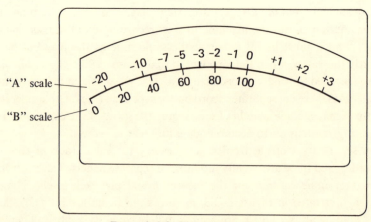

Figure 3–3.3: VU meter scales.

Tape-Recorder Accessories

SELECTIVE SYNCHRONIZATION

One problem that occurs very often in electronic music and sound-recording studios is that the several instrumental parts that constitute a musical passage must be played or modified individually as well as together. It is an easy matter to assemble these parts on separate tracks of a multi-track tape recorder and mix them down into the final result, but it is not possible to record over one track and play that back in synchronization with the other parts unless the machine is equipped with selective synchronization (abbreviated sel-sync). The reason for this is that there is a gap of approximately 1.3 inches between the record head, where signals are recorded on the tape, and the playback head, from which they are reproduced. This gap results in a delay of 0.175 seconds at 7½ ips (0.0875 seconds at 15 ips) between the tracks when they are played back later.

Selective synchronization allows sounds recorded on particular tracks to be played back from the *record head* rather than from the playback head. (The procedure for using selective synchronization is described below under "Overdubbing.") The most obvious limitation is the number of tracks on the tape recorder, and selective synchronization is most useful on machines with four or more tracks, although sometimes it is available on stereophonic machines.

SPEED VARIATION

Speed variation is a feature that enables the capstan motor to be driven at some rate other than its usual speeds, or to be changed during the course of a performance. Sometimes the speed of the motor is controlled by an external oscillator, on a separate device, and sometimes the speed is controlled internally.

It is essential to realize that speed variation always affects both the *pitch* and the *duration* of recorded signals uniformly. A doubling of the speed from, for example, 7½ to 15 ips raises the pitch of all frequencies recorded on the tape by an octave and halves the durations. Since this is a drastic result, which often makes the recorded material unrecognizable, speed-variation controls are most useful when they are capable of providing precise control of small deviations in speed, such as up to 15 per cent, for example. Although the duration of the music is also affected, a very small change in speed may allow a musical composition to be transposed to a new pitch level and remain recognizable in all its essential respects. Conversely, the duration of a piece may be slightly altered in order to fit an exact time slot, for example, from 9 minutes 50 seconds to exactly 10 minutes. Only with a *multiple-rotary-head tape recorder,*[11] an expensive device not generally available today, can the frequency or the duration of recorded signals be changed independently of one another.

Greater changes of speed, by ratios such as 2:1, are useful for some purposes in electronic music. For example, a musical passage that is difficult to synthesize may be recorded one octave down at half the speed and played back correctly. In this procedure, it is important to recognize that *all* frequency characteristics of the desired result, including filter settings and modulation frequencies, must be set down one octave in order to come out correctly.

REMOTE CONTROLS

Remote controls consist of a device incorporating all the operating controls for the tape recorder, including play, record, stop, rewind, and fast-forward buttons, at the end of a long cable. This allows the tape recorder to be operated from a more convenient location, at a distance from the deck. If the tape recorders cannot be physically located next to the synthesizing equipment in an electronic music studio, remote controls are more a necessity than a convenience.

NOISE-REDUCTION SYSTEMS

Noise-reduction systems are commonly referred to as "Dolbys," after the man who invented the first such system, one of the most important developments of the 1960s. Noise-reduction systems improve the quality of a tape recording in several ways. These devices can be used in any sound-reproduction system, but they are now usually marketed as accessories for tape recorders, and they are sold and packaged as part of the tape recorder. Individual units can also be purchased as "black boxes" for connection to older tape recorders.

More recently competing systems have appeared on the market, but the most common systems are still the "A-type" and "B-type" Dolby units. The A-type Dolby was the earliest, and was designed expressly for professional recording use. The B-type Dolbys are sold under the Advent trade name

[11]William S. Marlens, "Duration and/or Frequency Alteration," presented at the seventeenth annual meeting of the Audio Engineering Society, Oct. 11–15, 1965, preprint no. 412.

and are designed for home tape recorders and nonprofessional use. The two units are not compatible, and are in completely different price ranges.

Both systems employ the same general principle in order to improve the quality of the recording. Low-level signals are boosted before they are recorded, and attenuated in an exactly complementary way when they are played back. Whenever the loudness level of the input signal is below a certain threshold, the recording level is boosted; and when the loudness level rises, the recording level is reduced. The amount of noise reduction is, therefore, greatest for low-level signals, where it is most needed, for in this range the signal level approaches that of tape hiss. The system must be used both for recording and for playback, and it must be used when the original live recording is made rather than when a copy of a tape is made. *There is no way to eliminate noise from an existing tape* without also affecting the quality of the sound recorded on the tape.

The A-type Dolby system operates in four separate bands to reduce the noise over the entire audio spectrum. The B-type Dolby system, which operates only on the middle- to high-frequency portion of the audio spectrum, is designed only to reduce "tape hiss," which is the most annoying problem of home tape recorders.

Either type of Dolby system improves recordings in several ways. The signal-to-noise ratio is improved, allowing recordings with a greater dynamic range to be made. The amount of distortion is reduced as a result of the improved signal-to-noise ratio. A greater signal level can be recorded. The amount of signal-to-noise improvement with a B-type Dolby is from 3 to 10 dB, depending on the frequency; with an A-type Dolby, up to 15 dB. With A-type Dolbys, the print-through of a tape recording is also significantly reduced. Because of such improvements, slower tape speeds can be used, with such consequent advantages as greater recording time per reel. When B-type Dolbys are applied to standard cassette recorders, the resulting quality can be reasonably compared to open-reel tapes, whereas without them cassettes are really suited only for speech recordings.

Prerecorded tapes made with B-type Dolbys require the same systems in order to be played back correctly, but they are intelligible even when played back without them. The difference is that the low-level signals are boosted so that the dynamic variation is less and, of course, the tape hiss is still present.

The improvements brought about by noise-reduction systems require a period of adjustment on the part of the user, who must become accustomed to the greater dynamic ranges available and recordings without tape hiss.

Newer systems require an even greater adjustment, since their improvements are even more spectacular. Though these systems are presently much more expensive than Dolby systems, they can eliminate noise *completely,* and deliver a signal-to-noise ratio of as much as 110 dB (!), over 30 dB greater than A-type Dolbys. These systems allow the user to pick up sounds on a recording of which he is not even aware in his environment. The time will inevitably arrive when all recordings will be made with such devices, and many of the problems inherent in today's recordings will be things of the past.

4. COMPOSITIONAL TECHNIQUES USING TAPE RECORDERS

Overdubbing

Overdubbing, or *sound-with-sound,* is the name given to the procedure of building up a composition one track at a time on a multitrack tape recorder equipped with selective synchronization. The performer, according to the most conventional view of this procedure, regards himself as a sort of "one-man band," playing each separate "instrumental part" until the entire composition is generated. Not all applications of this procedure are so conventional, however, and at least some variation of this technique is indispensable when working in an electronic music studio.

At the beginning of a recording session, it is best to start by laying down a "click track" on one channel of the multitrack tape recorder. The click track consists simply of regular pulses to indicate each beat of the composition, and is used as a kind of metronome, to simplify the process of keeping all parts together. A click track can conveniently be made using a low-frequency pulse or sawtooth wave, which is so slow that it is heard simply as a series of clicks. In this manner the tempo can be kept absolutely precise. If a freer tempo is desired, the user can perform a series of tones for the click track. In many cases the best procedure is to play the separate parts of the composition onto their respective tracks, using only the click track as a guide to the music. (Other parts sometimes have a way of interfering with the performance of a given part.) On the other hand, just this kind of interaction may be desired, in which case all finished parts should be replayed when each new one is added.

Overdubbing is usually carried out on a tape recorder with a minimum of four tracks. Even with only four tracks, more than four parts can be recorded: after two tracks have been recorded, they can be mixed down into one track and re-recorded on a third track; then the two original tracks can be reused (hence the term *overdubbing*). It is also possible to combine one or more recorded tracks with the live part as it is played. If this technique is used, the ultimate spatial locations of the sounds must first be planned out, and each track then built up in accordance with the scheme (assuming, of course, that the end result is to be either a stereo or quad composition): whenever two tracks are mixed into one, both voices on the resulting track will necessarily receive the same spatial treatment. Also remember that the click track will always have to be kept free, since the clicks cannot be mixed with music; this reduces the number of available tracks by one. These considerations also show that the mixer is an indispensable part of the process of overdubbing.

Two stereophonic tape recorders with selective synchronization can be used together to achieve something like the same result as with a four-track tape recorder. (In this situation, however, a click track must be regarded as an unnecessary luxury.) The first and second voices are recorded on the two tracks of recorder 1, and then mixed down into one track on recorder 2, while the third voice is played live onto the second track. Recorder 2 now has three voices, two of which are distributed in one track and the third in the other. These can now be played back from recorder 2 and mixed down into one track on recorder 1, while a fourth voice is added on the second track. One advantage of this procedure is that every intermediate stage in the production of the final composition can be saved on a separate piece of tape, so that the whole thing can be reconstructed from the middle if it does not work out right. This procedure can also be used if only one of the two tape recorders has selective synchronization, provided that the tape that is played back is always placed on the machine without selective synchronization.

The disadvantage of overdubbing is that each time a track is mixed down there is a signal loss of approximately 6 db. The greater the number of overdubs, the greater the level of background noise. It is simply not feasible to carry out this procedure too many times, even though that limit is considerably extended by the use of a good audio noise-reduction system.

A more serious drawback of this procedure is simply its tediousness. Such techniques in electronic music synthesis had to be used in the past because of the limitations of the control equipment of electronic music synthesizers.

In the future, other alternatives ought to be made available, allowing the music to be generated in one pass, simply and correctly the first time.

Tape Reverberation

Tape reverberation or *tape echo* is a feedback process using two or more tracks of a multitrack tape recorder. A live signal is first recorded on one track of the tape recorder, and then fed back from the playback head of that track into the second track and recorded there. Since the signal is recorded at the record head of the first track but played back from the playback head, there is a delay between the two tracks equal to the distance between the two heads. This process may be continued through any number of tracks. In order to hear the effect of tape reverberation, all tracks must be monitored from the playback heads. The gain of each track must be carefully adjusted to avoid distortion, and if a microphone is used to record the material on the first track it must be situated so as to avoid acoustic feedback from the monitor system, which produces "microphone howl." The basic patch for two-track tape reverberation is illustrated in Figure 3–4.1.

The many varieties of tape reverberation result from the variations that may be made upon some aspect of this basic configuration. The most obvious variation is a change of speed of the tape recorder. The speeds available on professional tape recorders are usually 7½ and 15 ips. At these speeds the distance between the record and playback heads, usually 1.3 inches, works out to 0.175 and 0.0875 seconds respectively. On a tape recorder with speed variation, a continuous range of delay times between these values may be obtained.

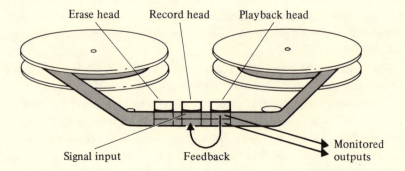

Figure 3–4.1: The basic patch for stereophonic tape reverberation.

Several tracks of a multitrack tape recorder can be employed to increase the delay time between a live and recorded signal, or between signals recorded on any two tracks of the tape recorder. For example, a tape-reverberation patch may be set up that feeds track 1 into track 2, 2 into 3, and 3 into 4, and then only track 4 can be monitored, resulting in a delay of 0.7 seconds between the live and recorded sounds at 7½ ips. Using variations of this patch, any multiple of up to 4 × 0.0875 or 0.175-second delay times may be achieved with a four-track tape recorder.

A more unusual kind of tape reverberation employs two tape recorders in succession in order to create very long delays between a live and recorded signal. Two tape recorders are mounted or placed in such a way that one tape can be placed on the feed reel of the first machine and strung to the take-up reel of the second machine. The signal is then recorded on the first machine and played back from the second. The delay is equivalent to the distance between the two machines, which may be several seconds in this situation. Further possibilities may involve setting up a stereophonic tape-reverberation patch on one or both of these machines, or by monitoring one or both of these machines in addition to whatever live sounds are present in the environment.

These variations are practically the only ones that may be accomplished with ordinary tape recorders. Some electronic music studios have constructed special machines that allow other variations in tape reverberation. Two of the most important special features are a means of varying the distance between the record and playback heads, and precise controls for many different playback speeds. Such facilities are not generally available, however.

One of the most interesting varieties of tape reverberation is the so-called "reverse echo." Reverse echo is accomplished by recording a tape with any kind of reverberation, including not only tape reverberation but also acoustic or electronically produced reverberation, and then reversing the tape and playing it backward so that the reverberation *precedes* the signal. Reversing the tape is the only means of producing such an effect, and it must be emphasized that *all* aspects of the recorded music are heard backward. The envelopes of all sounds will be reversed, so that short attacks and long decays will be heard as long attacks and short decays. If these facts are taken into account so that the envelopes and other characteristics are produced backward originally, the final tape will have these characteristics in their intended form.

In conjunction with the idea of reverse echo, it is good to know that there

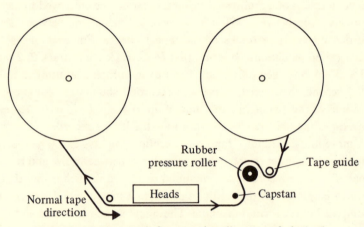

Figure 3–4.2: Tape path for reversing direction of playback.

is a method by which a tape may be played backward across the heads without reversing the reels on the feed and take-up hubs. This procedure will not work with all tape recorders—only those with three separate motors for play, rewind, and fast forward. The tape is wound around the rubber pressure roller in such a way that it passes in reverse direction between the roller and the capstan and around the back side of the roller (see Figure 3–4.2). While this method will work with most professional-quality tape recorders, it is recommended that you first try an experimental run with a worthless tape; always make certain that the tape is taut before starting the motor. Note that it is impossible to record on a tape threaded this way, because the tape passes the record and erase heads after the playback head.

Tape Loops

A tape loop is a simple thing to construct, and it has been one of the more frequently used devices over the history of electronic music. A length of tape is simply cut and its two ends are spliced together, creating a continuous loop. The loop is then threaded on a tape recorder without using take-up or feed reels, and held taut by means of guides placed behind the normal position of the feed and take-up reels, which can usually be adjusted to fit loops of various lengths. This configuration is illustrated in Figure 3–4.3.

Care must be taken when using a tape loop to insure that the tape tension

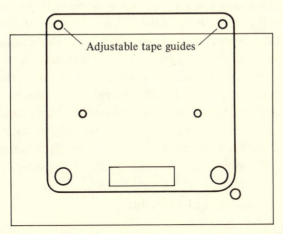

Figure 3–4.3: A tape loop. Note that there are no reels on the tape recorder.

is kept constant. If it is not, constant fluctuations will occur in the output signal. Tape loops produce ostinato effects, and they may be used as a source signal for further processing by other devices.

Reel Flanging

Reel flanging is a procedure that might be described as the "poor man's phase shifter." An audio signal is recorded on two separate tapes, and then played back simultaneously on two tape recorders and mixed into a single signal. The speed of one tape recorder is then varied very slightly by light hand pressure on the flange of the feed reel (hence the term *reel flanging*) or by a speed-variation device. The result is a kind of phase shifting, although with little control of the delay time. Nevertheless, since it is a real-time procedure, one can hear the results of the process immediately and adjust the speed in whatever way seems appropriate.[12]

Sound-on-Sound

Sound-on-sound is a feature formerly available on many nonprofessional tape recorders to enable a kind of synchronization between live and recorded signals, and which now appears to be disappearing in favor of the

[12]The author is indebted to the pamphlet "Countryman Associates Phase Shifters—How to Use Them," compiled and written by William Myers, for a description of reel flanging.

selective-synchronization feature. (*Sound-with-sound* is the term used to refer to recording on multiple tracks with selective synchronization.)

The sound-on-sound feature is essentially a mixer that allows one of the inputs on a two-track tape recorder to be mixed with the output of the other track and recorded on the second channel. The second track then contains the mixture of both the live and recorded signals. This process can then be repeated a few times, but there is a significant loss of signal quality in the previously recorded materials on each successive take, so that the absolute limitation is about five or six takes. This is undoubtedly the reason why the sound-on-sound feature is not generally produced any more.

"Classical" Compositional Procedure

The so-called "classical" electronic music studio is one without voltage-controlled synthesizing equipment, in which electronic music compositions are put together "by hand." This compositional procedure is indeed very tedious, but it is easy to describe.

Individual sounds are first recorded on separate pieces of tape and then cut into the appropriate lengths and spliced together into individual melodic strands. The duration of each tone is determined by the length of tape, which must be measured very carefully. This is not as difficult as it may seem, since ⅛ inch of tape represents only 0.0083 seconds of music at 15 ips. Silences should be inserted in the form of blank tape rather than leader or timing tape.

After many hours of tedious work, the several melodic strands constituting the composition exist on separate pieces of tape, ready to be mixed into the final result. In a classically oriented electronic music studio, the mixer is one of the most important devices, and must be centrally located, near the tape recorders, so that both may be operated simultaneously. The tape containing the first "voice" is played on one tape recorder and recorded onto the second track of the tape containing the second "voice." The resulting tape may then be played back through the mixer and recorded onto one track of the third tape, and so on, until the composition is completed. Other procedures, such as those described above under "Overdubbing," may also be employed at this stage in the compositional process.

As tedious as it may seem, the process of piecing together each individual melodic strand is often not as difficult as the process of producing the individual sounds desired in the first place. The oscillators in classical electronic music studios are often so unstable as to make it impossible to produce music with tempered pitches. Other devices may be difficult to control by manual methods.

Whether one feels disposed to employ this kind of compositional procedure is an entirely personal matter. It seems as useless to insist that people employ this method as it is to assert than nothing significant can be accomplished by it. Nevertheless, the use of advanced voltage-controlled synthesizers makes much of this kind of work unnecessary in more modern electronic music studios.

5. MISCELLANEOUS EQUIPMENT

Bulk Tape Erasers

A *bulk tape eraser* is a device for erasing an entire tape at one time. Bulk erasers are not expensive, and are a considerable convenience—but they must be used with caution.

Since bulk erasers are powerful devices, creating powerful magnetic fields, they must be operated at a safe distance from tapes and other equipment in the studio. Sometimes they draw an extraordinary amount of current, which may blow a fuse unless other equipment is turned off. Operators should remove wristwatches, even the "antimagnetic types." Even in storage, the bulk eraser should remain at a safe distance from tapes and equipment.

To operate the bulk eraser, place the reel of tape on the spindle and rotate it slowly, so that the entire surface passes over the demagnetizing area. Then turn the tape over and repeat this process.

Limiters

A *limiter* is a device that monitors an audio signal and attempts to prevent distortion if the level rises above an expected maximum. There are several ways in which this problem may be confronted, and the term *limiter* is not always used to describe the device in question. Furthermore, this is one area in which new products continue to appear, so that no "state of the art" standards can yet be agreed on.

Figure 3–5.1 shows three ways in which an original waveshape may be reduced in magnitude.[13] The first method is *attenuation*—simply turning the gain down. The second method is *compression*, which "squeezes" the waveshape into a smaller size. Whereas attenuation reduces the overall dynamic range of the sound, thus bringing it closer to the level of background noise, compression affects the shape of the waveform itself, thus introducing frequency components extraneous to the original signal. These components may not be significant enough to warrant concern, and may even be preferable to the alternative distortion. The third method, *clipping*, simply cuts out those waveform peaks greater than the acceptable limit, thus altering the waveform more drastically. From Figure 3–5.1, one can see that an exaggerated form of clipping may convert a sine wave into something resembling a square wave, which contains a very different harmonic spectrum.

When a signal is received at a level that would cause distortion if recorded or broadcasted unaltered, the choice of a solution is, in a sense, academic, because the signal would be distorted anyway. Some of the methods of

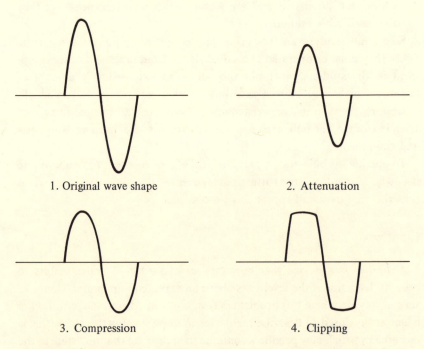

1. Original wave shape   2. Attenuation

3. Compression   4. Clipping

Figure 3–5.1: Methods of limiting a signal that would produce distortion.

[13]This figure is adapted from Strange, *op. cit.*, pp. 113–114.

limiting the signal introduce further distortion, thus making a bad situation even worse. The ideal limiter would simply cause the sounds above the maximum level to remain at that maximum level, thus destroying some of the dynamic differentiations at the high end but not causing distortion.

The hidden difficulty about limiters is that they are used all too often when we are not aware of it—for example, on almost all radio broadcasts and many commercial recordings, thus altering the dynamic characteristics of much of the music we are already listening to.

Test Equipment

Several devices, although used primarily by engineers and technicians who build and maintain audio equipment, are also useful in an electronic music studio. We will mention some of the more important ones here.

A *continuity tester* is simply a light bulb and battery with two leads. It is used to test whether a circuit is open or closed—i.e., whether an electrical connection actually exists between two points. One simply touches one lead to each of the points in question, and if the light goes on the connection is good. A continuity tester is especially useful for testing patch cords and cables.

The *volt-ohm meter* (VOM) and *vacuum-tube volt meter* (VTVM) are devices for reading the voltage levels, currents, or resistances that may exist in a circuit or component. There are many different scales on these devices, and it is important to use the scale appropriate for the range of values you are reading. These meters are useful primarily because they provide quantative data that may be necessary in setting or monitoring control voltages and other such signals in electronic music synthesizers.

An *oscilloscope* displays a graphic visual representation of a sound wave (or any wave motion) on a cathode-ray tube (CRT), which is a circular or square screen like a television picture tube. We will not explain here the technical details of the oscilloscope's functioning, but the user must understand that it displays only a portion of the complete signal, which would contain far too many cycles to fit onto a small screen. The portion shown is determined by the ratio between the frequency of the signal displayed and an internal time-base oscillator. By varying the internal oscillator, one can change the way in which the external signal is displayed.

In the normal use of an oscilloscope, the external signal is displayed as the vertical displacement of a light beam along a horizontal axis. Some oscilloscopes allow two inputs, affecting respectively the horizontal and the vertical displacement. While the graphic representation of a sound wave is an interesting thing to look at in itself, it does not provide as much or as musically relevant information about the signal as one can obtain simply by listening.

A *frequency counter* is a device that displays, in digital form, the frequency of an applied signal input. Frequency counters can be very useful for the purpose of tuning oscillators in an electronic music studio. By simply leaving an oscillator connected for a while, one can see the amount of drift that occurs over that time. Frequency counters are usually accurate only to within the last digit that they display. While a difference of one cycle may be insignificant at higher frequencies, at low or subsonic frequencies it could be crucial.

CHAPTER FOUR

Signal Generating and Processing Equipment

1. TYPES OF SIGNALS

Audio signal generating and processing equipment includes those devices on an electronic music synthesizer specifically concerned with generating *sounds* and modifying them in a variety of ways. These devices are distinguished from others that generate or process control information and other kinds of electrical signals that do not represent sounds. The term *audio signal* is often shortened to simply *signal,* and *control signals* are usually referred to as *control voltages.* Many signal-generating and processing devices are included on an electronic music synthesizer; these devices would be called *internal* to the system. *External* signals produced by a tape recorder, microphone, or preamplifier may also often be fed into and modified by the devices on a synthesizer. The terms *internal* and *external* may also refer to signals generated within or outside an individual device of an electronic music system.

In the organization of this book, Chapter 4 is devoted to signal generating and processing equipment and Chapter 5 to control equipment, but actually these two chapters concern different aspects of the same situation. Control devices determine the *operating characteristics* of signal generating and processing equipment—in other words, they *control* this equipment. An electronic music system normally includes a number of devices concerned exclusively with generating or processing control information, and it is for this reason that we have chosen to discuss these devices in a separate chapter.

Signal generating and processing equipment normally includes, in addition to audio outputs and inputs (see "Patching," below), a number of internal dials and switches and control inputs for external signals. In a sense, the versatility of the equipment can be measured by the number of properties that can be controlled by external control devices rather than by internal dials and switches. Keep these problems in mind as you read these chapters, and refer back and forth between them often. What kinds of controls are appropriate for each of the characteristics produced by the signal generating and processing equipment? This is a question of human engineering to which there are no simple answers.

The types of signals produced on electronic music systems are normally divided into three categories: *audio signals,* which represent sounds; *control voltages,* which determine the operating characteristics of the signal generating and processing equipment; and *triggers* or *timing pulses,* which start and sustain tones by providing an *attack time* and *duration.* A *tone* in this context is not necessarily restricted to its usual musical definition of "single pitch"; rather, *tone* refers to any event that begins and ends at times that are controlled by a trigger. We may wish to qualify our thinking further and define the *micro-note-level* as referring to events that go on within the time span of a given single tone or "note," and the *macro-note-level* correspondingly as referring to events that encompass two or more "notes" to define a particular characteristic.

These three types of signals are usually kept logically distinct within an electronic music system—that is to say, all of the connections between devices are between outputs and inputs of the same type of signal. In certain systems, however, it is possible that one kind of signal may actually be used in place of another. For example, on some synthesizers audio signals may be used as control voltages, or control voltages may be used as timing pulses. This is made possible by the fact that in some cases the electrical characteristics for the two kinds of signals are identical. When these signals are not compatible, special devices such as an envelope follower (*q.v.,* Chapter 5), for example, are necessary to convert from one form of signal to the other.

The reader must be warned that some electronic music systems may employ different terminology to describe these three types of signals. Sometimes even the signals themselves cannot be categorized in this manner; for example, the starting time and duration of a timing pulse may actually be controlled by two separate signals rather than by two properties of one signal. Worst of all, some systems may employ the *same terms* we have used here for different purposes on their equipment.

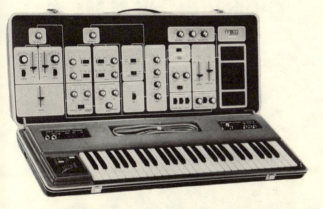

Above, The Moog Synthesizer 55, a large studio-type electronic music synthesizer. *Center,* The Moog Sonic VI, a two-oscillator duophonic portable electronic music synthesizer. *Below,* The Mini Moog, a compact perform-ance synthesizer.

Inventor Robert A. Moog tries out some of his instruments.

A large Buchla series 200 "Electric Music Box" studio-type electronic music system. *Below,* A small Buchla series 200 performance-type synthesizer.

A person working in front of a large Buchla system.

Facing Page, Top, A large studio-type ARP 2500 electronic music synthesizer. A unique feature of the model 2500 is the patching system, which is handled by the sliding switches at the top and bottom of the cabinets.   *Center,* The ARP 2600, a compact portable performance-oriented synthesizer. As in the ARP 2500, most patching is accomplished by means of sliding switches.   *Below,* The ARP Pro Soloist, designed to be used primarily as an accessory to an electronic organ, provides a very realistic simulation of live instruments.

A composer working at the SYNTHI 100, a large studio-type electronic music synthesizer manufactured by Electronic Music Studios (EMS) of London, Ltd. Patching on this synthesizer is accomplished at the two pin matrices on the front panel. (The person is shown in the act of making a patch.) The dual-manual keyboard at the right is also part of the instrument.

Three small performance synthesizers manufactured by EMS of London. At the upper left is the SYNTHI VCS 3 or "Putney" with its keyboard accessory. To the right is the SYNTHI A, containing the same devices as the VCS 3 but in a portable cabinet. At the lower left is the SYNTHI KB1, a complete instrument containing a built-in keyboard. Patching on all instruments is accomplished by the small pin matrices.

The original computer studio in Putney (London), England, showing a variety of instruments manufactured by EMS of London. The computer system itself is at the rear. The computer controls devices in the center racks that were built before the SYNTHI 100 at the right or the SYNTHI A in the foreground.

The descriptions of devices and other design considerations of electronic music systems are, in a general sense, covered in more detail in this book than they are likely to be in literature provided by individual manufacturers, who are, after all, interested in promoting their own equipment. Differences in the functions of signals may be omitted from a manufacturer's literature if his system does not categorize signals in this manner. The reader is advised to make absolutely certain that he understands the meaning of the terms used in the manufacturer's literature before comparing it to the terms used in this book.

2. PATCHING

In any electronic music system it is necessary to establish a method by which audio and control signals generated on one device may be connected to another device or perhaps through a number of other devices and eventually to a loudspeaker or tape recorder. The final audio-signal output of a series of devices is referred to as the *system output,* which is *monitored* by listening.

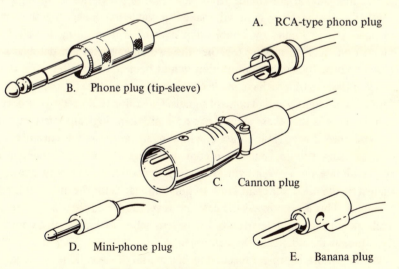

Figure 4–2.1: Common connectors.

The procedure for interconnecting separate devices on an electronic music system is called *patching,* and it normally involves connecting the *output* of one device to the *input* of another. When wires are used to make these connections they are called *patch cords* and they have *plugs* at each end that are inserted into *jacks* normally located on the front panels of the devices connected. Sometimes these jacks are located elsewhere, such as on a *patch panel* or central patching location to which all devices are connected, or on the rear of the device if the connection is to be made semipermanent. Patch cords almost always have the same kind of plug at each end. The types of plugs used by different systems include *phone plugs, miniature phone plugs, banana plugs, RCA plugs, cannon plugs,* and other kinds. (See Figure 4–2.1.)

Some systems do not allow the user to make different patches between the individual devices and employ instead some "standard" series of interconnections. Other systems substitute *switches* or a *pin network* to accomplish patching functions. The term *patching* is usually applied only when patch cords are used for these purposes. Still other systems employ a combination of these, in which, for example, a "standard" connection may be broken by the insertion of a patch cord. The question of which kind of patching is appropriate for a particular synthesizer is another problem for human engineering. In solving it designers have to consider the ease of operation and flexibility of connections that may be made with their system.

Patching is invariably made *from the output of one device to the input of another.* Sometimes a system will make it possible to connect together two outputs or two inputs by establishing a consistent meaning for such a connection, such as mixing together the two signals that are patched together. Normally, such a connection would be a contradiction.

All of the remarks we have made about patching are true for the patching both of audio signals and of control signals. One thing that needs to be borne in mind here is that these signals are normally kept logically distinct, but in some cases it is possible to use one kind of signal for a different purpose, such as using a timing pulse as a control voltage. If such a connection is not legitimate on a given synthesizer, this possibility is usually guarded against by the use of different kinds of plugs and jacks for the different kinds of signals. This is not always the case, however, and the reader is cautioned to check out the characteristics of his system before making such a connection since it may damage the equipment.

While a more complete discussion of patching connections is included below, it is necessary, before you read the following sections of this chapter,

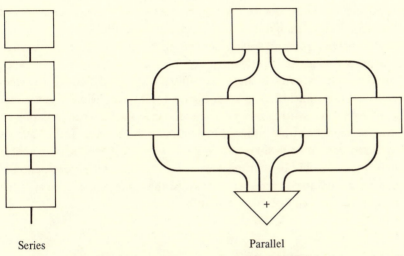

Series   Parallel

Figure 4–2.2: Series and parallel connections.

to know two kinds of connections that are frequently employed. Several devices are said to be connected in *series* if the output of the first device is connected to the input of the second, the output of the second to the input of the third, the output of the third to the input of the fourth, etc. Several devices are connected in *parallel* if the output of the first device is connected to the input of *each* of a following number of devices, whose outputs are then mixed together into a single signal. Each of these connections begins and ends with one signal. (See Figure 4–2.2.)

Sometimes it is necessary to connect the same output to more than one input. There is no difficulty in this procedure if the device has more than one jack for its output. If there is only one jack for the output, it is necessary to use a *multiple,* which is simply a group of jacks wired together. Patching a signal into any one of the jacks makes the signal available at all of the others. These jacks may then be connected to the desired inputs.

When *two* audio signals are patched into jacks connected as a multiple, the result is usually a mixture of the two signals with the relative levels determined by the ratio between their output impedances. Under special conditions of extremely low output impedance and high signal level, distortion will occur. This may cause *heterodyning* or "nonlinear" mixing, which introduces extraneous frequencies consisting of the sums and differences of the input frequencies, as in amplitude modulation. Some manufacturers have introduced safety features in their equipment to prevent this from happening. Generally, a mixer should be used when mixing is desired, and two audio signals should not be connected in a multiple.

When patching control voltages and timing pulses, it is sometimes desired to connect *two or more outputs* to *one input.* This procedure is called *paralleling* inputs, and it is not to be confused with signal processing devices connected in parallel, illustrated in Figure 4–2.2. (Paralleling inputs is not possible on some synthesizers.) It is useful, for example, when initiating an envelope generator from either of two timing-pulse sources. If the voltages paralleled consist of positive DC volts, the result of paralleling variable control voltages will be that the *highest input voltage* takes precedence. If the voltages paralleled represent AC volts, the result is the same as if the two signals were connected in a multiple.

3. OSCILLATORS

Oscillators are the basic signal-generating components of any electronic music synthesizer. They are distinguished by the characteristics of *frequency, amplitude,* and *waveshape* of their output signals, and sometimes they also produce *frequency modulation.* Sometimes each of these output characteristics is variable over a certain range; sometimes the waveshape and amplitude and, in rare cases, even the frequency of the oscillator are constant.

Oscillators can be distinguished in a more important sense by the variety of controls that can be used to determine each of their variable characteristics, particularly frequency. Oscillators designed more as electrical test equipment than as basic components of an electronic music synthesizer may have only a dial, or a combination of dials and switches, to control frequency. Most oscillators on electronic music synthesizers allow frequency to be controlled either entirely by external control voltages or by a combination of control voltages and internal settings.

When considering the frequency controls available on a particular oscillator, one must keep in mind the individual characteristics of pitch that are structured in musical compositions: the octave relationship and the equal-interval property. How easy or difficult is it to obtain equal-tempered pitches and octave transpositions in a given system? The answers to this question will determine much about the variety of music that can be generated on that system. Some systems employ a *rotary switch* to provide octave transpositions. Very often a *frequency vernier* is included to allow precise tuning of individual pitches. In other cases, the entire frequency-controlling mechanism is an external element, such as a keyboard, which is patched into the oscillator.

Frequency modulation is produced on most oscillators by taking some external audio signal and patching it into a control input. This input usually has an amplitude control, which is necessary to control the bandwidth of modulation, and it is then added to some other constant value that sets the center frequency. For systems in which audio signals and control voltages are compatible, there is no particular difficulty with this patch; but for systems in which they are not compatible, a special input on the oscillator or external device is required to convert the modulating signal into a control voltage capable of driving the oscillator. Usually this device is built directly into the oscillator, the only unfortunate aspect then being that it cannot be detached from the oscillator and used as a separate device.

Other important properties of an oscillator's frequency characteristics are the *frequency stability* and *tracking response*. The frequency stability refers to the amount that an oscillator will "drift" in pitch after it has been adjusted to a particular frequency. This was a major problem on earlier electronic music synthesizers, which easily became "out of tune" and were impossible to use over long periods of time for compositions that had any very demanding pitch relationships, such as equal-tempered intervals(!). The frequency stability of oscillators on electronic music synthesizers has improved greatly in recent years.

The tracking response of a group of oscillators is a measure of the degree to which they will all stay in tune on different frequencies after having initially been tuned to a single frequency. Another unfortunate characteristic of early oscillators was that they would all produce different frequencies upon receiving the same control-voltage input. This problem has now been solved on some systems by allowing control-voltage inputs to be processed in such a way that the same input can affect two devices to a different degree. If this possibility can be provided on all the sine-wave oscillators on a given system, then it would be possible for the group of them to function as a *harmonic generator (q.v.)*, in which case each oscillator would be tuned to a separate harmonic partial of a given fundamental frequency, which could be determined by a control-voltage input. This application would also require, of course, the most demanding frequency stability.

The *amplitude* of an oscillator, when it is a variable characteristic, is most often controlled simply by a potentiometer. On many systems, however, the amplitude output is constant, and it can only be controlled by being patched through a mixer or voltage-controlled amplifier. This restriction is not as inconvenient as might be imagined, for almost all signals on electronic music synthesizers are patched through some amplitude-controlling device such as an envelope generator or mixer before going to the system output.

A more important characteristic of an oscillator to be made variable is the waveshape. Many oscillators provide separate waveshape outputs of the same frequency, and some provide variable waveshapes as well. The most basic waveshape output of an oscillator is a *sine wave,* which consists simply of a *single frequency with no overtones.* Fourier's theorem states that *any signal* may be broken down into a *sum of sine waves* of various amplitudes and phases. The reverse—that any signal may be generated by a sum of sine waves of various amplitudes and phases—is, of course, true. This is called *additive synthesis,* but it is not always practical to consider synthesizing any signal in this manner. Of particular relevance in this context is Helmholtz's idea that phase is not a perceptible characteristic of a complex sound,[1] which has been verified by subsequent observations. (See our discussion of phase in Chapter 2.) This would mean that the wave*shape* of a signal would not be as important a piece of information as a list of the frequencies and amplitudes alone. We will return to this point later, but for the moment let us note that the sine wave is a signal of unique importance in this application.

Other frequent waveshape outputs of electronic music oscillators include the *sawtooth, square,* and *pulse waves.* These waveshapes each consist of a theoretically infinite series of harmonic partials of the fundamental frequency determined by the period of the waveshape, and are distinguished by the harmonic partials that are present and their relative amplitudes. (Phases are all uniform for these signals.) A sawtooth wave consists of *all harmonic partials* in the amplitude ratios of the *reciprocal of the partial number:* for a given harmonic partial *n,* the amplitude is $\frac{1}{n}$. Thus, the higher the partial, the less the amplitude. A *square wave* has the same amplitude *ratios* as a sawtooth wave, but consists only of *odd-numbered* partials.[2] A

---

[1]Hermann von Helmholtz, *On the Sensations of Tone,* trans. Alexander J. Ellis (New York, 1954), pp. 124–127.

[2]Some synthesizer manufacturers have attempted to delude their customers into thinking that they are providing a new signal by asserting that they have a waveshape consisting only of *even-numbered* partials to contrast with the square wave. A tone consisting of even-numbered partials is simply an octave higher than the given tone, and is thus available on any system.

"pure" pulse wave—"pure" in the sense that the length of the pulse is almost nonexistent—consists of *all harmonic partials at equal amplitudes.* Thus, higher harmonic partials are present at considerably greater amplitudes than for sawtooth or square waves. (See Figure 4–3.1.)

Other less common wave shapes include the *triangle wave* and the *ramp wave.* A triangle wave consists of *odd-numbered* partials, like the square wave, but the amplitude of a given partial is $\frac{1}{n^2}$ instead of $\frac{1}{n}$. Also, every other odd partial has a phase of 180 degrees in a triangle wave. A ramp wave is a name for any intermediate shape between a sawtooth wave and a triangle wave, and its precise spectrum and amplitude characteristics are different for each shape.

The ramp wave brings us to a consideration of the *variable waveshape* controls on oscillators. As Figure 4–3.1 suggests, it appears quite simple to imagine a change between a square wave and a pulse wave or between a sawtooth wave and a triangle wave, with the ramp wave including intermediate values in this latter change. Many synthesizers include such variable waveshape controls; another common variation is between a sine wave and some other waveshape. Although such changes in waveshape produce quite attractive shapes when displayed on an oscilloscope, their musical value is certainly less significant than changes in timbre produced by filters. Different waveshape outputs are provided primarily to allow contrasting signals to be fed into a filter. Because all waveshapes with a "sharp edge" or discontinuity in the shape produce an infinite series of harmonic partials, they sound "raspy" or "buzzlike" and are usually not suitable for use in a composition unless filtered. Thus the change between one amplitude ratio of harmonic partials and another is a less distinguishable feature of the final sound than changes produced by a filter. This is not to say that the change is not important, only that it is relatively mild, and it leads us to two final observations about the value of different waveshapes: first, the change from a sine wave to another shape is inevitably the most contrasting variation, for the other waveshape contains all the overtones of the fundamental represented by the sine wave; second, the pulse wave is probably the most useful complex waveshape available, because the entire harmonic spectrum of the sound can be controlled by the settings on the filters, and when the difference between the center frequency of the filter and the fundamental frequency of the oscillator increases, the amplitudes of the overtones within the range of the filter do not decrease, although there are more overtones per octave.

When a tone is produced by being generated on an oscillator and processed through a filter, it is said to be produced by *subtractive synthesis.* Most tones in electronic music are produced in this manner.

4. HARMONIC GENERATORS

A *harmonic generator* is a signal-generating device that contains either separate outputs or separate controls for each of a certain number of the *harmonic partials* of a fundamental frequency. The most basic characteristic of a harmonic generator is the *number of harmonic partials* it produces in its output signal. Other characteristics include the *amplitude* of each partial and how it is controlled and the frequency control for the fundamental frequency, which can sometimes be controlled to produce *frequency modulation.* The *waveshape* of each partial should naturally be a *sine wave.*

The simplest construction of a harmonic generator provides just several separate outputs that can be patched into additional devices for control of the amplitude of each partial. If a fixed amplitude is needed for each partial, the easiest solution is to patch each output into a mixer and adjust the amplitude individually. If variations in amplitude are required, then each output may be patched separately to a voltage-controlled amplifier *(q.v.),* which can then be controlled by an envelope generator *(q.v.).* If not as much variation is required, a group of outputs can be mixed into a single signal and then patched to an amplifier.

There is no a-priori way of determining what would be a sufficient number of harmonic partials for a harmonic generator. The most logical divisions of the overtone series occur at the octaves. Perhaps eight partials would be a minimum and sixteen or even thirty-two would be optimum. The higher the series continues, the more harmonic partials are contained in the octave.

Since the design of a harmonic generator requires most of the circuitry of separate oscillators for each harmonic partial of the output signal, and since its controls are necessarily complex in their operation, many manufacturers have shied away from building harmonic generators, preferring instead to require the user to purchase separate oscillators for each of the partials he wishes to control, if indeed the oscillators are stable enough to allow this application. This is an unfortunate circumstance, for a harmonic generator provides a different kind of control over musical timbre than what is presently available on most systems, and the following paragraphs enumerate some of the advantages of harmonic generators.

A harmonic generator provides the most feasible method for creating musical timbres related by *waveform transposition*. The only alternative available on most systems is to use the raw, unfiltered waveshapes of the oscillators, such as square waves and sawtooth waves. By waveform transposition, in this context, we are referring to signals of different frequency that have the same overtone spectrum. To produce timbral relationships with filters would require changing the frequency response of each filter in accordance with the frequency of the input signal.

Another advantage of a harmonic generator, when it provides a separate output for each partial of the output signal, is that it allows much more accurate control of dynamic variations in the amplitude of the partials during the course of a tone. Many researchers have stressed the importance of such controls in order to make accurate electronic reproductions of live sounds.[3] Although this application is available through additive synthesis using separate oscillators for each partial, tuning the oscillators precisely enough is often so difficult as to be impossible in practice.

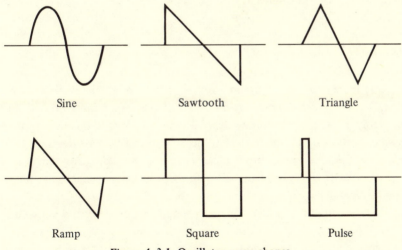

Sine   Sawtooth   Triangle

Ramp   Square   Pulse

Figure 4–3.1: Oscillator wave shapes.

[3]See, for example, James W. Beauchamp, "A Computer System for Time-Variant Harmonic Analysis and Synthesis of Musical Tones," in Heinz Von Foerster and James W. Beauchamp, eds., *Music by Computers* (New York, 1969), pp. 19–62.

5. NOISE GENERATORS

Noise is a kind of audio signal that contrasts sharply with the periodic or cyclic outputs of audio oscillators. *White noise* is produced by random fluctuations, and it contains equal energy at *all frequencies* in the audible range. It is called "white" by analogy with white light, which is a mixture of all colors. *Pink noise,* a recently developed adjunct to white noise, contains an equal amplitude distribution per octave, and is often claimed to be more useful in music. White noise sounds somewhat like hissing steam, whereas pink noise sounds more like distant thunder.

Noise generators usually have just outputs and no controls. Sometimes they have an amplitude control, and sometimes they have a selector switch for white or pink noise.

Noise generators are often used in the production of random control voltages, and for this purpose a sample-and-hold device is usually also included. These devices are discussed in Chapter 5.

Noise is an important element in percussive sounds, and it can also be filtered sharply to produce a definite pitch.

6. AMPLIFIERS

Amplifiers in an electronic music system generally have two functions: first, they *amplify* a sound, providing control over its *loudness.* Second, and probably more important, they *apply a control voltage* to the amplitude of a sound, allowing the amplitude to be determined by an external signal, which is frequently the output of an envelope generator. Amplifiers are, therefore, used for practically all sounds produced on electronic music synthesizers.

When an amplifier is used for the second function described above it is often called a *gate,* especially in systems where the electrical characteristics of control voltages and audio signals are different. *Gate* is a standard electrical term used to describe devices that have two or more inputs and one output, the value of which depends in some predefined manner on the inputs. In the particular case of an "amplifier gate" or voltage-controlled amplifier, the amplitude of the output depends on the voltage level of the control-voltage input. Other types of gates, called "logic gates," are discussed in Chapter 5.

Amplifiers frequently have a manual control for the *gain,* which is the *ratio between the output and input signals.* On a voltage-controlled amplifier (often abbreviated VCA) the gain is controlled by an external control voltage. Amplifiers thus do not control the level of a signal in an absolute sense, but rather in a relative one.

There is often a complication in the operation of gain controls on voltage-controlled amplifiers, which comes from the relationship between the internal dials on the device and the control-voltage input for determining the gain. On some systems, turning up the gain has the effect of opening the gate, so that the sound never drops to silence when the control-voltage input drops to 0. This occurs when the dial is placed in parallel with the control-voltage input. The opposite situation occurs when the dial is placed in series with the control-voltage input. The output level is the result of both the control setting and the input signal, so that the dial is a kind of "volume control" for the output, and the level never rises above the maximum of either source.

Sometimes amplifiers will have a *mode switch* with positions for *linear* and *exponential* response modes. In the linear mode the gain follows the control-voltage input precisely, whereas in the exponential mode a change of equal voltage produces a change of equal ratios in the output. The mode switch thus determines the "shape" of the gain. Figure 4–6.1 illustrates the difference between a linear and exponential amplifier. It can be observed that an exponential shape makes proportionally greater changes as the gain approaches unity, whereas the linear shape always changes by equal amounts. A mode switch might alternatively be included directly on the envelope generators rather than on the amplifiers, in which case the amplifier would require only a linear mode of response.

The two main functions of amplifiers, then, are the application of envelopes and other control signals to audio signals, and the control of amplitude or loudness. A third function is generating *amplitude modulation* or *tremolo,* which is obtained merely by applying an appropriately varying control-voltage input much in the same manner as frequency modulation is obtained from an oscillator. (See our discussion of the characteristics of modulation in Chapter 2.)

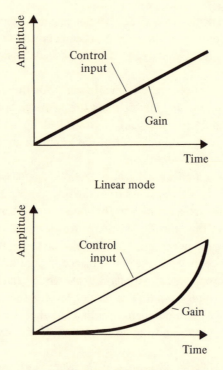

Figure 4–6.1: The difference between the linear and exponential response modes of a (hypothetical) voltage-controlled amplifier. In the linear mode, the gain and the control-voltage input are identical, whereas in the exponential mode the gain changes by equal ratios as the control input changes by equal amounts.

7. MIXERS

A *mixer* is a device that simply *adds* or *combines* two or more input signals into one or more outputs. Differences in mixers arise primarily from the number of inputs and outputs they contain and the controls available for each.

Mixers are generally named "*x*-in, *y*-out," where *x* and *y* are the number of inputs and outputs respectively. A "10-in, 4-out" mixer thus contains 10 inputs and 4 outputs. On such a mixer it is usually standard that each of the 10 inputs can be fed into each of the 4 outputs in any proportion. The easiest visual layout for such a panel consists simply of a 10 × 4 rectangular matrix of dials with the inputs next to the long side and the outputs on the short side of the rectangle. Almost all mixers have volume controls for their inputs, and sometimes an additional "master gain" control is provided for each of the outputs.

Sometimes mixers that are components of electronic music synthesizers allow the volume levels of the inputs or outputs to be determined by a control-voltage input. Such a device would be called a "voltage-controlled mixer" and it thus combines the function of a gate with that of a mixer. On most systems these functions would be controlled by separate devices.

Some mixers, especially the large console mixers at the center of commercial recording studios, may also have *microphone preamplifiers* on some of the inputs, allowing these inputs to be taken from microphones. These mixers also contain such additional features as "echo send" and "echo return"—reverberation units that can be connected to the inputs or outputs —and they usually employ *sliding potentiometers* rather than dials for the volume levels. Since they are at the center of the studio, these mixers often have a built-in patch panel or other means of interconnecting various devices in the studio together. Such features are less common in electronic music studios.

Finally, some mixers may have an assortment of switches next to each of the inputs that determine to which outputs the inputs are connected. In this design frequently only a single volume control is provided for each input, and it is connected to each of the outputs selected at the same level.

8. FILTERS

The operation of a *filter* must be understood in relation to the *frequency continuum,* which is the total range of frequencies audible to the human ear. The filter's function is to *resonate* (increase) or to *attenuate* (decrease) the amplitudes of any frequencies within some particular area of the frequency continuum. Filters are also described as *passing* or *rejecting* certain frequency areas.

A *low-pass filter* is a filter that cuts out high frequencies, thus *passing* low frequencies. A *high-pass filter* is the reverse of a low-pass filter, because it cuts out low frequencies and passes high frequencies. The frequency at which the attenuation of the low-pass or high-pass filter begins is called the *cutoff frequency*. A *band-pass filter* is a filter that resonates only one particular area of the frequency continuum. The mid-point of this area is called the *center frequency*, and the *bandwidth* is the area on each side of the center frequency that is resonated.[4] A *band-reject filter* or "notch" filter, the reverse of a band-pass filter, rejects one particular frequency area and passes frequencies on each side of that area. The response characteristics of these filters are shown in Figure 4–8.1.

The *rate of attenuation* or *slope* of a filter is usually indicated by a figure that expresses some number of decibels attenuation per octave, such as 24 dB per octave. This figure indicates that frequencies one octave above the cutoff frequency are down 24 dB over those at the cutoff frequency, those two octaves above the cutoff frequency are down 48 dB, etc.

Filters are most often used when the input signal consists of a fundamental frequency and its harmonic partials, so that the filter affects the timbre of a single tone. One should bear in mind, however, that a filter will operate indifferently upon any collection of frequencies. It is therefore meaningful to speak of the "timbre" of a chord or of an entire musical passage, and the use of a filter should not be restricted to any particular application. Furthermore, the filter does not change any of the component *frequencies* of the input signal; it affects only their *amplitudes*, so that all of the pitch components of the input signal remain intact unless they are filtered out completely.

Electronic music systems offer a variety of filters, which are highly individual and hard to generalize about from system to system. Probably the most common type of filter available is the *low-pass filter*, which often has a voltage-controlled cutoff frequency. Since it is an experimentally validated characteristic of sounds produced by brass instruments that an increase in the amplitude of a sound is correlated with the entrance of higher harmonic partials,[5] a voltage-controlled low-pass filter that is controlled by the envelope of the sound is often described as producing "brasslike" sounds. An

[4]Terms used with *pass* and *band* are frequently combined into a single word: *lowpass, highpass, bandpass,* and, of course, *bandwidth* and even *bandreject.* With the exception of *bandwidth,* we will not follow this convention in this book.

[5]Jean-Claude Risset, *Computer Study of Trumpet Tones* (Murray Hill, N.J., 1968).

envelope generator may be patched into the control input of the low-pass filter to produce this effect.

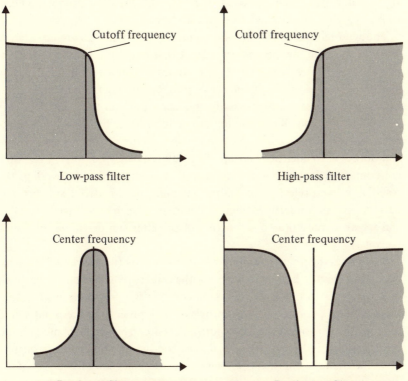

Figure 4–8.1: Filter response curves. Each of these curves plots *amplitude* (or, more appropriately, *gain*) on the vertical axis and *frequency* on the horizontal axis. The band-pass and band-reject filters can be formed by combining a high-pass and a low-pass filter in series or in parallel, respectively. The darkened portions of the curves show the frequency areas of the input signals which are *passed* by the filters.

Some systems have developed an interesting modification of the voltage-controlled low-pass filter: a "resonance" control changes the mode of the filter from low pass to band pass, with the center frequency of the band-pass filter at the cutoff frequency of the low-pass filter, which is controlled by the control input. In this mode, if the input signal consists of a series of harmonic partials, the precise partial at the cutoff frequency is greatly emphasized. If the cutoff frequency is moved very slowly from low to high, each of the partials of the harmonic series will be resonated one at a time. If the cutoff frequency is moved more rapidly, the filter produces effects similar to vocal diphthongs like "wa-wa" or "yeow."

Though high-pass filters are less common, their controls are usually the same as those on low-pass filters, except that they do not have the "resonance" feature described above. Sometimes the mode of a filter can be alternated between high-pass and low-pass, but it is more common to find both a low-pass and a high-pass filter incorporated in the same device or connected by a switch or coupling device to produce band-pass and band-reject filtering. When a high-pass and low-pass filter are connected in series and the cutoff frequencies overlap, the result is a band-pass filter; when they are connected in parallel and the cutoff frequencies do not overlap, the result is a band-reject filter. Individual differences between systems and devices amount primarily to which characteristics can be voltage-controlled and whether more than one function of the filter can be employed simultaneously.

Sometimes the frequency characteristics of a filter (i.e., the cutoff frequencies of low-pass or high-pass filters, or the center frequency and bandwidth of a band-pass filter) have inputs or controls for *frequency modulation.* Usually such a control also has provisions for processing the input signal in some manner so that the bandwidth and center frequencies of modulation are controlled independently. (*N.B.,* the bandwidth and center frequency of *modulation* are different from the bandwidth and center frequency of the filter. See our remarks about modulation in Chapter 2.)

Some filters have a control for the "Q," which allows the slope of the resonating frequency to become so sharpened that the filter acts like an oscillator and can be used as a tone generator. In order to understand adequately exactly what is happening when a given device is used in this mode, it will be necessary to check the specifications provided by the manufacturer.

Many systems provide a "fixed filter bank" consisting of a series of filters of fixed frequency characteristics contained in one panel. A single input signal is divided into a series of frequency bands whose amplitudes may be controlled independently. In some cases the amplitudes must be controlled by a separate device, such as a mixer, while in others a volume control for each band is included on the device. Each band must be available at a separate output if one desires to vary dynamically each of the amplitudes over the course of a single tone (without resorting to manual variation of the individual volume controls). In this application separate outputs are patched to separate amplifiers.

The elaborate instrument known as a *vocoder* contains two fixed filter banks among its components. The vocoder is a device for extracting the spectral variations of an input signal and imposing these upon another sound. It is divided into an *analysis portion* and a *synthesis portion.* Each portion contains an identical fixed filter bank. The input signal is patched

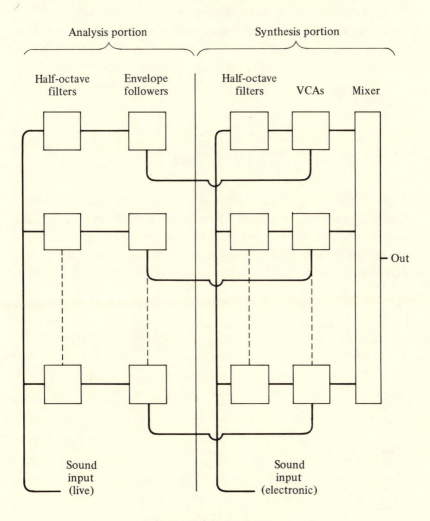

Figure 4–8.2: A vocoder.

into the fixed filter bank of the analysis portion of the vocoder, and each of the outputs of the filter bank is connected to an envelope follower (*q.v.,* Chapter 5). The signal upon which the characteristics are to be imposed is patched into the fixed-filter-bank input of the synthesis portion, and each of these outputs is patched into a voltage-controlled amplifier (VCA). Each of the VCAs is controlled by the envelope follower of the corresponding output of the analysis portion, and the outputs of all of the VCAs are patched into a mixer or to system output. The design of a vocoder is illustrated in Figure 4–8.2. Interesting spectral variations can be obtained by patching the outputs of the envelope followers into noncorresponding VCAs on the synthesis portion. Note also that a vocoder can be assembled out of the appropriate modules on a large electronic music synthesizer.

Another kind of filter, called a *comb filter,* is discussed below under "Phase Shifters."

9. ENVELOPE GENERATORS

The function of an *envelope generator,* which is also referred to as an *attack generator,* is to control the growth and decay characteristics of a sound. Envelope generators require some kind of trigger or timing-pulse input in order to initiate their cycle, and their output consists of a control signal used to vary the amplitude (or any characteristic) of an audio signal.

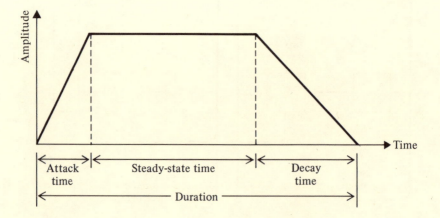

Figure 4–9.1: A simple linear envelope.

The controls on an envelope generator vary the times or, more precisely, durations of the various components in the envelope.

A *simple envelope* consists of three portions, illustrated in Figure 4–9.1: an *attack time, steady-state time,* and *decay time.* The sum of these three times is the *duration* of a given note. Another characteristic of an envelope is its *shape* of amplitude variation over each component time segment. A *linear* change in amplitude varies by equal differences over equal durations, and an *exponential* change in amplitude varies by equal *ratios* over equal durations. (See Figure 4–6.1 for an illustration of these shapes.) In Figure 4–9.1, the attack and decay times are linear in shape, whereas the steady-state time shows no variation in amplitude.

Complex envelopes are called *contours,* and they are indicated in terms of pairs comprising the amplitude level and the duration over which the amplitude is to vary from one level to the next. The first amplitude level of the next segment in a contour is always the last level of the previous segment. Figure 4–9.2 indicates a four-position contour. In these terms, a simple envelope is a *three-position contour.* Contours actually include a broader range of events than envelopes because they may begin and end with any amplitude, whereas envelopes normally begin and end at 0 (unless two notes in succession are "tied" together, in which case the last level of the first is the same as the first level of the next).

Envelope generators in electronic music systems are highly individual and may vary greatly from system to system. The simplest kind of envelope generator encountered usually has controls only for the attack and decay

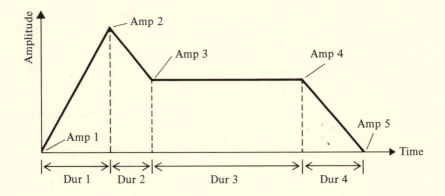

Figure 4–9.2: A complex envelope consisting of a four-position contour.

times of a tone. A third control may be provided for the duration, or the duration may be taken from the duration of the trigger input. *Duration* in the latter case usually indicates the duration of the attack and steady-state times, with the decay time commencing as soon as the trigger is released. The manner in which different systems indicate the length of a trigger may also be different, so that it is difficult to generalize about this mode of operation. Usually the duration of the trigger is determined by the length of time that the user depresses a key with his finger.

On some systems the four-position contour illustrated in Figure 4–9.2 is taken to be a kind of "standard" envelope, and the envelope generators thus include more controls. In this case the four segments are customarily labeled "attack time," "initial decay time," "sustaining level," and "final decay time." These envelope generators can thus be used to place a sharp accent at the beginning of a tone, but there is no way of altering the basic contour of the envelope.

The shapes of envelopes produced on electronic music systems are usually either linear or exponential, since these shapes are easy to produce. Sometimes the shape of all envelopes is linear, and the conversion into an exponential shape is provided by a feature of the amplifier that is controlled by the envelope generator. (If one desires to use the envelope generator to control some property other than amplitude, however, no control is available.) It should be pointed out that *exponential* envelope generators on electronic music synthesizers normally produce an "inverted" exponential

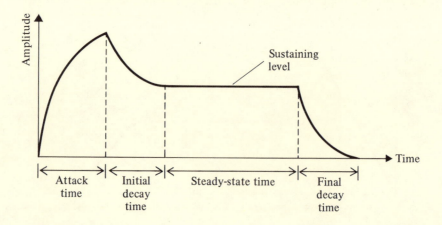

Figure 4–9.3: The amplitude output of a typical "exponential" envelope generator.

shape during the attack time, for the reason that this kind of circuit is easier to construct than one with a normal exponential attack shape. (See Figure 4–9.3.)

Some envelope generators also provide an additional control for *delaying* the attack of an envelope by a certain duration. (Sometimes this feature is provided by means of another device called a "trigger delay.") This control is useful particularly when initiating a series of attacks from a single trigger.

One of the most sophisticated kinds of controls available on some envelope generators is a control-voltage input for note duration. In this mode, each of the time segments of the envelope is taken to indicate a *relative* duration, and the entire shape is compressed or expanded to fit the duration indicated by the control input. A great range of variation is thus available from a single device.

More complicated envelopes can be obtained by processing the outputs of two or more envelope generators. Figure 4–9.4 illustrates how a six-position contour similar to the envelope shown in Figure 4–9.2 can be obtained by adding the outputs of two envelope generators initiated by the same trigger. This same patch can be effected by processing the same input by two envelope generators and mixing the result, so that it is not even necessary to have a device that adds control voltages. Since this kind of processing is always available, it is hard to understand why some manufacturers have put additional contour portions on their envelope generators. Instead of having all these features on one device, there could be more devices with fewer controls, and the versatility of the system would be extended.

Finally, it should be mentioned in the context of this discussion that some

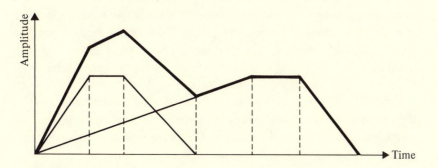

Figure 4–9.4: A six-position contour produced by adding the outputs of two envelope generators.

systems make it possible to use the output of a pressure-sensitive keyboard directly as an envelope. (See our discussion of pressure-sensitive keyboards in Chapter 5.) Though such an application is completely intuitive and simple to use, it is not susceptible to the same range of control provided by an envelope generator.

10. REVERBERATORS

The function of a *reverberator* is simply to reverberate an input signal. Reverberation is, however, a very complicated characteristic, as we pointed out in our discussion in Chapter 1. For most inexpensive reverberators, it is impossible to know exactly what the characteristics of an individual device may be, but it is certain that any two reverberators will be different. For this reason, each reverberator will have its own characteristic "sound," which is a result of its reverberation time and of the loop times of its component feedback circuits. (See our discussion of phase shifters, below.)

Currently, analog devices employ several methods for producing reverberation: spring reverberators, electronic delay circuits, and reverberation chambers, as well as acoustic or room reverberation. More than one of these methods may be combined in one device. Another method, so-called "tape reverberation," was discussed in Chapter 3.

Spring reverberation is produced by mechanically stimulating one edge of a spring and sensing the vibrations produced at another edge. Since the spring contains a certain degree of mechanical inertia, there is a delay between the signal that stimulates the spring and that which comes off the other end, and reverberation is produced. This is the most inexpensive method of producing reverberation, but it is also the most difficult to calibrate in any precise way, since the inertia of the spring depends on such factors as the material it is made from, its thickness, length, and other properties. The reverberation time for this type of reverberator can be controlled by mechanically changing the location on the spring that senses the vibrations, but this kind of control is provided only rarely, so that the reverberation time is usually constant. This is the type of reverberator that is most commonly employed for electronic instruments.

A second method of producing reverberation involves using one or more *digital delay lines*. This type of reverberation unit starts with a time-delay circuit and then provides feedback from the output to the input. The overall circuit then has a comb response (see "Phase Shifters," below). The important distinction is that this type of unit has *electronic* time delay, as opposed to the electromechanical time delay of a spring.

A third method for generating reverberation is a *reverberation chamber*. The chamber consists of a large box (several cubic feet in volume) containing plates of springs. There appear to be different ways in which the plates may enter into the production of reverberation. A reverberation chamber is a very expensive device, but it creates the most complex kind of reverberation available with analog devices.

Sometimes an entire room may be set aside for the purpose of generating reverberation. The room would be set up with a loudspeaker at one location and a microphone at another. This facility is ideal for producing the kind of reverberation that occurs during the performance of a composition in a natural acoustic environment.

Any analog reverberation unit may contain an additional control variously described as "reverberation mix" or "depth." This control is usually just a mixer that determines the proportion of the reverberated signal that is contained in the output. At 0 the output is entirely "dry," and at maximum it is entirely reverberated; intervening positions contain some proportion of each signal. It is important to remember that this control does not affect any of the characteristics of the reverberation, but only the proportion of reverberation mixed into the output.

11. RING MODULATORS

Ring modulation is a special case of amplitude modulation that contains only the sum and difference frequencies of two input signals. If two input signals have frequencies x and y, the output signal consists of $x + y$ and $x - y$. Regular amplitude modulation contains the carrier frequency as well as the sum and difference frequencies. However, not all of these components are present at the same amplitudes. (See our discussion of modulation in Chapter 1.) Two input signals consisting of single frequencies would necessarily be sine waves, so that the result for any other kind of input signal would be more complicated; and the output would consist of all of the sums and differences of all of the input frequencies. Since the output of a ring modulator is thus quite a complicated signal, it remains a somewhat mysterious device to many composers, and it has sometimes been regarded simply as a device that produces a crazy sound out of two simple ones.

One of the inputs to a ring modulator is sometimes referred to as the "program input" or "signal input" and the other as the "carrier frequency." Technically, there is really no need for this distinction, for ring modulation is produced simply by multiplying the two input signals. Nevertheless, the distinction is useful when some kind of further processing is applied to one of the inputs and not the other.

Sometimes a ring modulator may contain a control labeled "squelch" or "noise suppressor." This control suppresses the output of the ring modulator unless the amplitude of one or both of the input signals is above a certain minimum level. A "squelch" control may also be provided through some external device such as an envelope follower. Sometimes no control is visible on the device, but one of the inputs is marked "high rejection." In this case little or no sound will "leak" through the modulator when a signal is patched only into that input.

Ring modulators can be used to produce amplitude modulation by mixing one of the inputs with the output of the ring modulator. Ring modulation can also be produced on some systems by mixing a given signal with the same signal after it has been processed by a voltage-controlled amplifier that is modulated by another signal, and adjusting the amplitudes appropriately.

Ring modulators are frequently combined with other devices into a kind of comprehensive signal-processing module, which may contain various other fancy controls not necessarily related to ring modulation. It will be necessary to check out the precise characteristics of your system in order to understand exactly how these devices work.

12. FREQUENCY SHIFTERS

A *frequency shifter*[6] is a signal-processing device similar to a ring modulator, which contains two audio signal inputs, or in some cases only one input. One of the inputs is usually called the "signal input" or "program input" and the other is the "carrier frequency." If the device has only one input, it is normally for the program input, and the carrier frequency is generated internally. The output consists of all of the frequencies in the input signal

[6]The "Klangumwandler" is a frequency shifter.

shifted up or down by an amount determined by the carrier frequency. Shifting is uniformly applied to all frequencies in the input signal so that the frequency shifter is not a transposing device, but a device for producing complicated sounds usually containing frequency components that are not harmonically related. Often there are separate outputs on the frequency shifter for both the sum of the carrier frequency and the input signal, which is shifted up, and the difference, which is shifted down.

In order to clarify the relationship between the inputs and outputs of a frequency shifter, let us consider some examples. Suppose that the input signal consists of the first five harmonic partials of the fundamental frequency 100 cps, thus containing the frequencies 100, 200, 300, 400, and 500 cps. Now suppose that the carrier frequency consists of a signal of 40 cps. The sum output of the frequency shifter would thus contain the frequencies 140, 240, 340, 440, and 540 cps. Thus the frequencies in the output signal are no longer harmonic partials of a fundamental frequency of 100 cps, but they have coincidentally become the seventh, twelfth, seventeenth, twenty-second, and twenty-seventh partials of a new fundamental frequency of 20 cps. Since this frequency is so low that it is nearly the bottom limit of audio frequency discrimination, it is questionable whether the fundamental frequency of 20 cps would be perceived as the "pitch" of the output.

Suppose now that the carrier frequency were changed to 43 cps, thus producing frequencies of 143, 243, 343, 443, and 543 cps. The lowest common fundamental of this collection of frequencies would be 1 cps, which is below the lower threshold of frequency discrimination and thus would certainly not be perceived as a distinct pitch. Either each of the component frequencies would be heard separately, or the entire collection would be heard as a complex, "clangorous" sound.

Now let us return to the previous example of a carrier frequency of 40 cps and an input signal consisting of the first five partials of a 100-cps fundamental, but take the difference output of the frequency shifter instead of the sum. Here the output frequencies will consist of 60, 160, 260, 360, and 460 cps. The lowest common fundamental for these frequencies would again be 20 cps, as in our first example, but in this case the frequencies would represent the third, eighth, thirteenth, eighteenth, and twenty-third partials.

If the sum and difference outputs of the frequency shifter are mixed together, the result is the sum and difference frequencies of the two input signals, thus containing all of the same frequencies as a ring-modulated signal of the same two inputs. Note also that the fundamental frequency of

20 cps is greatly reinforced in this particular example, since all the frequencies are overtones of this fundamental. This kind of coincidence is likely to occur only when great control is exercised in the choice of the input frequencies.

Suppose that we take the difference output of the frequency shifter but that we change the carrier frequency so that it is greater than some of the frequency components of the input signal. For example, suppose that the carrier frequency consists of 280 cps and the input signal, as before, consists of 100, 200, 300, 400, and 500 cps. Here, the difference output would contain the frequencies −180, −80, 20, 120, and 220 cps. Negative frequencies are actually completely audible but are 180 degrees out of phase with the same positive frequency, so that the result here would be the first, fourth, sixth, ninth, and eleventh harmonic partials of a fundamental of 20 cps.

A frequency shifter is a very useful device when the relationship between the input and output signals is properly understood. It produces signals that cannot be produced on live instruments and that cannot really be duplicated in any other manner, so that its "sound" is unique to the electronic medium.

13. PHASE SHIFTERS

As we pointed out in Chapter 2, the *phase* of a sound is not a perceptible characteristic in the sense that the amplitude and frequency are, although differences in the phase of the same signal arriving in different ears at slightly different times play an important part in our ability to recognize sound locations. For this reason, the function of a device that affects the phase of a sound must be thought of as producing changes in other characteristics of the sound, and the relationship between the controls on the device and the changes in the sound must be explained carefully.

A *phase shifter* is a device that delays an input signal for a certain controlled duration, typically some very small fraction of a second, such as a couple of milliseconds. Usually there is also a mixer built into the device, so that the delayed signal may be combined with the original signal. The phase shifter has many applications and produces many different effects.

When the output of a phase shifter is mixed with its input signal, the result is *ipso facto* a *comb filter*. As illustrated in Figure 4–13.1, it can be seen that a mixture of this sort will have the effect of resonating every input

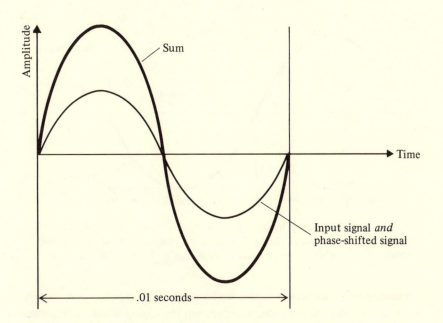

Amplitude

Sum

Time

Input signal *and*
phase-shifted signal

←————— .01 seconds —————→

Figure 4–13.1: A delay mixture produced by a phase shifter resonates every frequency that is an integral multiple of the basic frequency determined by the duration of the delay. This particular loop will resonate frequencies that are multiples of 100 cps.

frequency that is an integral multiple of the basic frequency determined by the duration of the delay or *loop time,* which is the reciprocal of the delay. When exactly one cycle, or *n* cycles, of a signal fit into this duration and the result is added together with the input signal, it will double the amplitude of that frequency. The opposite situation occurs when the duration of the phase shifter equals exactly one half of a cycle, or *n* + ½ cycles, of an input frequency. In this case the entire signal is canceled in the output, as illustrated in Figure 4–13.2. The frequency response of the comb filter will thus have peaks at each of the multiples of the reciprocals of the loop time and troughs between these peaks; it acquires its name because the response curve resembles a comb.

Many discussions of phase shifting are expressed in terms of *degrees* shifted rather than duration. While this may clarify the results for certain frequencies, such discussions have meaning only in relation to these specific frequencies. The combination of phase in degrees and frequency is equivalent to duration, but without the knowledge of frequency, phase in degrees

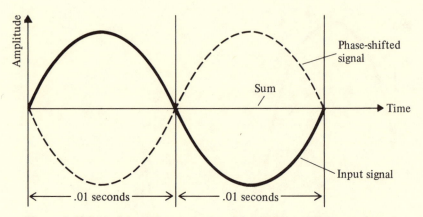

Figure 4–13.2: A delay mixture produced by a phase shifter cancels any frequency that is exactly one half, or $n + \frac{1}{2}$, of a cycle of the basic phase-shifted signal. This loop will cancel frequencies of 50, 150, 250, etc., cps.

is meaningless. Furthermore, the controls on phase shifters are usually expressed in terms of duration. If this is not the case, further information is required to understand the nature of the device.

If the duration of the phase shifter can be changed dynamically during the course of a sound, the result is *phase modulation,* which is similar to frequency modulation. In phase modulation, the frequency deviation is proportional to the derivative of the modulating signal; in frequency modulation, the frequency deviation is proportional to the modulating signal itself. Thus, for example, if an audio tone is phase modulated with a 6-cps triangular wave, the result is a trill, but if it is frequency modulated with the same 6-cps triangular wave, the result is a vibrato.[7]

"Stereophonic" effects are produced with a phase shifter by placing a sound in one speaker and the phase-shifted equivalent in another. While this produces the same result as the comb-filter network described above, the mixing in this case takes place in the air between the speakers and the listener, and the signal is subject to environmental interference and acoustic reverberation. The effect of this process is to change some aspects of the listener's perception of the location of the sound. Many devices are being marketed today that produce this "pseudostereo" effect from a monaural signal.

A phase shifter thus produces many complicated effects, which may alter

[7] I am grateful to Robert A. Moog for this example.

the frequencies or the amplitudes of certain frequencies of the input signal.

14. SPATIAL LOCATORS

Spatial locators are devices that feed some proportion of an input signal into two or more output channels to achieve the effect of locating the sound in and moving it through some illusory space. The space is "illusory" because nothing moves physically; the only change is in the amplitudes of signals in different speakers. Note also that a spatial locator produces no Doppler effect, which is always present when a sound-producing device is moved physically. A spatial locator usually has a single input signal and two or more outputs. When a spatial locator has several inputs, it is usually a multiple device consisting, in effect, of several spatial locators, in which the appropriate proportions of the input signals are mixed together into each output channel.

Spatial locators must be considered in relation to an actual or imagined playback situation in which precise control over the placement of loudspeakers is possible. It is thus not normally used in connection with sound-with-sound procedures on a multitrack tape recorder, but would be used to process the sum of these channels into a final composition.

Most playback situations employed in electronic music today are either stereophonic or quadraphonic. In a stereophonic playback environment it is possible to locate a sound either isolated in one loudspeaker or at any location between the two loudspeakers. In a quadraphonic playback environment, it is possible to locate a sound at any point in a two-dimensional space if the loudspeakers are situated in the four corners of a room,[8] and it is possible to locate a sound at any point in a three-dimensional space if the loudspeakers are arranged as the four corners of a tetrahedron. Figures 4–14.1 and 4–14.2 illustrate these playback situations.

Spatial locators are thus either stereophonic or quadraphonic, and frequently they incorporate several separate devices connected to a mixer to provide several paths of traveling. One of the most useful controls provided on some spatial locators is the so-called "joy stick" or "panpot," the correct

[8]It is actually possible to locate a sound anywhere in two dimensions with only three loudspeakers, but three-channel playback systems are a rarity.

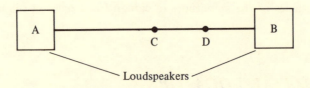

Figure 4–14.1: A stereophonic playback environment. A sound can be located at point A or point B by being isolated in either loudspeaker. A sound can be located at point C by being evenly balanced between the two speakers, and at point D by having three fourths of its amplitude in speaker B and one fourth in speaker A.

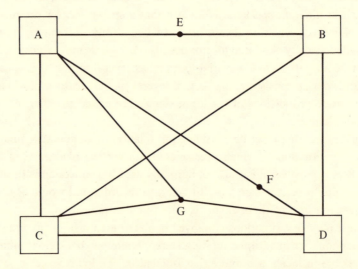

Figure 4–14.2: A quadraphonic playback environment. A sound can be located at any of the points A, B, C, or D by being contained in only one speaker. It can be located at point E by being balanced between A and B and at point F by being placed between A and D, with more amplitude at D. Placing some amplitude at C could move it to point G, but this movement could be offset by placing some amplitude at B. If A, B, C, and D are arranged as the four corners of a tetrahedron, the sound would move in three dimensions.

name for which is actually "two-dimensional potentiometer." This control consists of a stick that can be moved either up and down or back and forth simultaneously, and it can be used to make sounds travel in a circle or in a variety of continuous paths. (See our discussion of potentiometers in Chapter 5.) Sometimes the path of traveling can be determined by a control-voltage input, which makes it possible to use external devices to make the sound travel and to co-ordinate the traveling with other characteristics of the sound. The ability to locate a sound spatially is another unique characteristic of the electronic medium, which is generally impossible to control with the same range of variation in live music, although composers sometimes specify the locations of their performers.

15. PREAMPLIFIERS

The function of a preamplifier is to take an audio signal from some device external to an electronic music system and amplify the signal in such a way that its electrical characteristics are compatible with those of other audio signals in the system. There are generally two types of devices that are used together with preamplifiers: microphones and electric musical instruments such as guitars and electric pianos. A third category of devices, including tape recorders, phonographs, radios, and other components of a "hi-fi" system, does not require some special device on an electronic music synthesizer, because the "hi-fi" system itself usually contains the necessary preamplifier. The signal characteristics of most electronic music systems are compatible with tape recorders, so that signals can readily be recorded and played back.

Preamplifiers are distinguished by two characteristics: the impedance and the signal level of the input signals they accept. Impedances are usually classified as "high" or "low." Low-impedance signals (600 ohms) require less signal level than high-impedance signals because they are less susceptible to strong electrostatic pickup. This is why *all* high-quality microphones have low-impedance outputs, and microphones have the lowest signal level of any audio source. High-impedance signals (anything from 10K to 200K ohms, where K is an abbreviation for 1,000) may not be carried great distances, but may be extremely low-level signals. Within certain limits, two high-impedance lines that are connected do not have to match each other in impedance. Low-impedance inputs on preamplifiers often employ three-prong XLR cannon plugs. High-impedance signals are employed by electric instruments, contact microphones, and other sources, and high-impedance preamplifier inputs usually employ phone plugs. (These connectors are illustrated in Figure 4–2.1.)

Signal levels are usually indicated in terms of dB (decibels) at some impedance. Signals of the same impedance but different levels may be employed simultaneously on the same system; lower-level signals simply sound softer.

Once a signal is patched into a preamplifier, it may be used just as any other audio signal in the system. The preamplifier usually contains a gain control to adjust the volume of the signal, and it may also contain "treble" and "bass" filters.

16. COMBINATION DEVICES; PROGRAMMING SIGNAL PROPERTIES

A combination device is a single device incorporating many signal generating and processing functions in one package. As electronic music synthesizers have been developed and refined over recent years, more and more such devices have appeared. The advantage of combination devices is that they eliminate the necessity for patching together many separate modules that are frequently used in various applications. The disadvantages of combination devices are that it is frequently difficult or impossible to use the individual devices within the combination separately, and, more importantly, it is possible to use a combination device without really understanding the way in which the component parts of the device contribute to the total sound.

Recently there have been entire synthesizers built according to the principle of a combination device. All patching is eliminated in favor of certain "standard" arrangements. All signals are processed through the same series of devices; but usually it is possible to eliminate any device by switching it out or turning its volume to 0. When a device is switched out, it is lost to the system and cannot be used by another patch, for there is no patching. Experimentation with "nonstandard" patching is either discouraged or impossible. Worst of all, users of these synthesizers may learn only to produce "canned" or "prepackaged" sounds, which are in no sense a demonstration of the sonic depth and breadth of the electronic medium.

Nevertheless, combination devices and synthesizers with standard patching interconnections are likely to proliferate and become popular, because they are usually simple to construct and to operate and may cost less than more complex systems. It is therefore important that the components of the combination device be understood in their operation. While it is unlikely that every useful device and combination would be included in a combination synthesizer, it is certainly possible that many of the most important items could be included; and while some patching connections and devices are not available, the users are encouraged to experiment with others that are available. Many things can be learned from this kind of system.

One of the most important things that must be learned by someone who uses an electronic music synthesis system is how to program the sounds he wants on the available devices. He must be able to break down his sounds into their constituent properties and learn how these properties are controlled on his equipment. Each of the separate signal generating and processing devices discussed above controls the audible properties of sounds in a unique manner. In fact, there has been considerable effort by manufacturers of electronic music equipment to invent devices that control each audible property of sound separately. There is still much speculation concerning the nature of sound, and as new properties are discovered new devices will undoubtedly be invented to control them.

We have not introduced a notation for patching in this chapter. Every user of a synthesizer should learn to write down his patching connections in a "patch chart" to which he can make reference later. Many different patching notations have been invented by different users. We will introduce a form of symbolic notation for flowcharting instruments when we discuss computer sound generation in Chapter 8. The same kind of notation can be used for analog equipment, even though it will, of course, also have to take into account control equipment, which is discussed in Chapter 5.

CHAPTER FIVE

Control Equipment

1. VOLTAGE CONTROL

The concept of voltage control was a very important—perhaps the most important—development of early electronic music synthesizers. Voltage control is the principle by which the *operating characteristics* of the various devices on the synthesizer, including both signal generating and processing equipment and control equipment, may be determined by an externally applied signal or by the combination of an externally applied signal and manual controls on the device. Since the voltage level of the external signal is the property that is used for the control, these external signals have traditionally been called "control voltages." By using the principle of voltage control, the characteristics of individual devices can be dynamically controlled and varied without the composer having to intervene manually, and the compositional versatility of the system is greatly increased.

The earliest electronic music studios consisted of much of the same signal generating and processing equipment now found on most electronic music synthesizers, with one major difference: this equipment was not voltage controlled. A studio of this type used to be called a *classical* electronic music studio; today this term seems to be disappearing. Most of the equipment in classical studios was not designed for use with music, but as electronic test equipment. Much of it was not really suitable for music, because it could not be adequately controlled.

Voltage control is the characteristic that enables the output of a device to be determined by another device, and hence our attention is now directed to these other control devices and their manner of operation, and to human engineering considerations in the construction of a system. Before turning to this subject, it is relevant to discuss the electrical characteristics of control voltages and how they may relate to other signals in electronic music systems.

A fundamental decision must be made early in the design of an electronic music synthesizer about whether the electrical characteristics of audio signals and control voltages should be the same or different. While this decision is not so important from the viewpoint of the operation and understanding of the system, it vitally affects the circuitry of the devices and ultimately such aspects as the cost and specific operating principles. Both kinds of systems have been constructed, and both can be extremely versatile. It is not the object of this discussion to "evaluate" either design. The user must always be aware of the different functions of the various signals in his equipment.

While the specific subject of this chapter is voltage control, it is important to remember that there is a third kind of signal used in electronic music synthesis, namely the *timing pulse.* In the context of this discussion, it is relevant to consider timing pulses together with control voltages rather than with audio signals, for very often timing pulses are generated or used as inputs on the same devices as control voltages, but not as audio signals. The function of a timing pulse is the initiation and continuation of "events" in a piece of music, thereby controlling such properties of the music as the starting time and duration of a note; viewed in a compositional sense, timing pulses are certainly "controls."

Another fundamental decision that must, therefore, be made early in the design of an electronic music synthesizer concerns the electrical compatibility of timing pulses and audio signals or control voltages. In this regard manufacturers have tended to opt for the alternatives of either making audio signals and control voltages compatible but not timing pulses, or making control voltages and timing pulses compatible but not audio signals. A third alternative is that none of the three kinds of signals are electrically compatible. At the present time, the author knows of no system in which timing pulses are compatible with audio signals, nor is there any intuitive reason for such compatibility.

The electrical compatibility of various kinds of signals in an electronic music system allows for the possibility of interconnecting one type of output to another type of input. At first, such a connection may seem illogical, but upon closer consideration it may not only be logical, but may also allow for the production of events that would not be possible otherwise. In order to know whether such a connection makes any sense, the user must have precise knowledge of the electrical characteristics of each signal. Therefore, a detailed consideration of the use of timing pulses as control voltages or of audio signals as control voltages must be deferred to a discussion of specific systems and devices.

2. OPERATIONS ON CONTROL VOLTAGES

When a control voltage is patched into a device, the device responds to the voltage level of the signal and adjusts its characteristics accordingly. At this point it would seem relevant to consider voltage levels in quantitative terms. However, since these characteristics are different for each electronic music system, and since we are not considering individual systems in this book, let us instead direct our attention to some of the musical purposes for which control voltages are used and to the controls required for these purposes.

The most demanding application of control voltages is to oscillators for the control of frequency or pitch. If we assume that the total range of variation of an oscillator covers the entire range of audible frequencies, which represents approximately ten octaves, and that we can perceive changes by an amount as small as a fraction of a semitone, then obviously very small changes in voltage may produce perceptible changes in pitch. It is clear, therefore, that some device is required to change the range over which the oscillator will respond to the input voltages. Such a device is called a *control-voltage processor* or *attenuator,* and it raises the question of the kinds of operations we need to perform on control voltages in order to effect desired changes in the pitch of the oscillator.

The first kind of operation we can perform on a control voltage is an arithmetic operation such as addition, subtraction, multiplication, or division. The voltage may be regarded simply as a number (of volts), which we process by another number. The addition or subtraction of a voltage that is acting as a control input for an oscillator would *transpose* the pitch of the oscillator up (for addition) or down (for subtraction).

Multiplication and division of control voltages are more complicated than addition or subtraction, because they must be considered in relation to the definition of 0 volts in the system. If a synthesizer has a control-voltage range of, for example, -3 to $+12$ volts, the way in which it would treat control voltages would have to be much different from a synthesizer with a range of from 0 to $+15$ volts, even though the total span of voltage is the same. For the sake of simplicity, let us assume that we are dealing with a system that has a voltage range of from 0 up to some quantity. In this case, the division of a series of voltages that range from +1 to +15 volts by 2 would produce a series of voltages ranging from ½ to 7½ volts. In addition to altering the lowest output voltage, division or multiplication of voltages have the effect of *compressing* or *expanding* the range of response.

Control-voltage processors often incorporate all of these operations in a single device. Systems in which control voltages are compatible with audio signals often do not include separate control-voltage processors. In these instances, audio-signal-processing devices such as mixers or amplifiers must be used instead. While this might not seem appropriate from the viewpoint of the function of the signals, it provides the same range of control as a separate control-voltage processor.

Control-voltage processors are used most typically when the range of voltages produced by a control-voltage source affects too great or too small a range of response in the device controlled. Returning to our example of the oscillator above, compressing the range of input voltages from a control-voltage source would change the range of response of the oscillator from extending over the entire audible-frequency spectrum to a smaller, more manageable musical interval, such as one or two octaves. However, within this range the input voltages would then control much finer distinctions between successive pitches than when the voltages were spread over the entire audible-frequency range.

The same operations are useful for most devices on electronic music systems. It is not always the case, however, that both positive and negative processing is necessary. Devices like oscillators and filters, which control characteristics relating to frequency, have a clear and useful purpose for both positive and negative processing—that is, above or below a given input range. Devices like amplifiers, for which a zero value would have some special meaning such as silence, usually require processing that extends only from 0 or a given value up to the maximum. Many devices on recent electronic music systems contain control-voltage processors built directly into their control inputs, in order that frequently used and appropriate processing operations are readily available.

3. MANUALLY OPERATED DEVICES

In this section we will cover the manual controls found on electronic music devices—and, for that matter, on almost any devices operated by human beings. These controls will be found both on the front panels of the individual units as well as on the controllers that automatically operate these devices. Often the actual operating characteristics of the equipment are determined by a combination of these controls, which may interact with one another.

In deciding what types of controls are appropriate for a particular device, it is necessary to bear in mind the purposes for which the device is to be used or, more importantly, the perceptible musical characteristics controlled by the device and the type of structuring or measurement appropriate for those characteristics. Whether or not these considerations are borne in mind by the designers of electronic music equipment, the actual decisions that they make vitally affect the applications for which the equipment can be used. Many of the deficiencies of "classical" non-voltage-controlled equipment are highlighted by these considerations. For example, if we describe the perceptible musical characteristics of pitch as the "higher than" relationship, the "equal interval" property, and the octave relationship, then it is readily apparent that an oscillator that provides only a control that produces equal changes in frequency (not pitch) is not adequate for the control of the equal-interval property and the octave relationship. On the other hand, if early oscillators had been designed with a series of push buttons that produced transpositions by octaves and semitones, then they might have been so useful that designers would not have been stimulated to develop external keyboards—an eventuality that, in retrospect, seems equally disastrous!

Push Buttons, Switches, and Potentiometers

A *push button* is probably the simplest manual control that exists. Everyone is aware of the characteristics of a push button from operating doorbells and elevators. But note that a push button is an extremely intuitive device from which to initiate a timing pulse; it starts the pulse as soon as the button is depressed and sustains it as long as it is held down. For other applications, a push button is an effective on-off switch. Some types of push buttons remain "on" after they are pushed, and are turned off in some other manner.

Often, several push buttons are mounted adjacent to one another on a panel, where they control a property that requires only that one button be depressed and sustained at a time, so that when one button is pressed any other buttons that are in control are shut off. In such a circumstance it is a good idea that there be some visual indication of which button is currently in control. Such an indication can be provided either by a button that remains depressed at a deeper level than the other buttons, or by a light on the button.

A *switch* is an object that can assume only one out of a *discrete number of positions* at a given time. The simplest kind of switch is the *on-off* switch, with which we are all familiar from turning the lights on and off. Such switches are made in a variety of shapes and sizes. One advantage of the on-off switch is that it is easy to recognize which position the switch is in. Similar switches are available that can assume any of three, four, or even more positions. A *rotary switch* may also assume a greater number of positions than an on-off switch.

A *potentiometer* (abbreviated "pot") is technically a device for controlling the electrical potential in a circuit, but in context of the controls we have been discussing it provides a *continuous range* of values that are usually determined by turning a knob. This kind of potentiometer is called a *rotational* potentiometer. One important aspect of potentiometers is that it is often not possible to calibrate the positions on the knob accurately— not because the potentiometer cannot actually produce certain values, but because the amount that it has to be turned is not always directly proportional to the change it produces. Of course, this depends on the quality of the potentiometer, but often those that are used in electronic music devices are not the most expensive. Most potentiometers in electronic music synthesizers make only one complete rotation between the minimum and the maximum values, but potentiometers are available that make two or more rotations before spanning their entire range.

Potentiometers themselves are actually components of electronic circuits that remain behind the front panel of the devices to which they are attached, and a knob or dial is attached to the front. Although the knob is the only visible portion, the quality of the potentiometer cannot be judged from the knob.

Linear or *sliding* potentiometers have the same electrical function as rotational potentiometers but are controlled by moving a knob up or down in a straight line. Sliding potentiometers are usually more expensive than rotational potentiometers, and are often found on large console mixers.

All the potentiometers we have considered so far are *one-dimensional*—which is to say that they produce only one discrete value at a time. *Two-dimensional* potentiometers, also called *joy sticks,* consist of a lever that can be moved in two directions at the same time: up or down, and left or right. Joy sticks are ideal controls for the spatial movement of sounds through four speakers, since there are four poles and movement must be continuous. For other applications, it must be remembered that the joy stick has two separate voltage outputs, and each must be patched to a separate input.

Perhaps the most sophisticated manual controller currently available is the *three-dimensional potentiometer.* This consists of a large cube containing a ball, usually attached to a stick, which can be moved in any of three dimensions simultaneously: up or down, left or right, and to or fro. Devices of this kind have not yet been manufactured in any great quantities, and are not usually available except under special circumstances.

Twelve-Tone Keyboards

Perhaps the most popular manually operated controller, certainly for the control of frequency or pitch, is the *twelve-tone keyboard* or *piano keyboard.* Most people are familiar with the pattern of white-and-black keys and with the location of certain pitches on conventional keyboard instruments, but electronic music controllers of this kind are quite different from the keyboards on mechanical musical instruments. The most confusing aspect of operating many electronic music synthesizers with these keyboards is that they contradict some of our expectations of their modes of operation.

Keyboard controllers in electronic music systems are sources of two separate controls simultaneously: both timing pulses and control voltages. As such, the keyboard is both a rhythmic controller and a pitch controller. A timing pulse is initiated as soon as any key is touched, and is sustained as long as that key is depressed. This aspect of the keyboard's operation is in accordance with our previous experience. A control voltage proportional to the position of the key selected in the overall range of the keyboard is also produced. Let us deal with each of these aspects separately.

First, consider the keyboard as a frequency controller. There are two rationales for using a device in the shape of a twelve-tone keyboard: first, we expect it to produce *equal* musical *intervals* between each successive key;

and second, we expect it to produce *octaves* between corresponding keys in each register, or after every twelve semitones. Actually, in certain circumstances *neither* of these expectations may be satisfied. The most common discrepancy is that the keyboard can be tuned to some form of equal temperament other than twelve-tone temperament. In this case, equal intervals will still be produced between successive keys, but octaves will not be found in their customary locations.

Occasionally keyboards will not produce equal intervals between successive keys. Sometimes there are special-purpose devices to make this possible. Historical tuning systems such as just or meantone temperament may be produced in this manner. In other cases, mistuning is more likely to indicate some kind of malfunctioning either of the keyboard or of the oscillator it controls. In order to troubleshoot this problem it is necessary to remember that the keyboard itself is just a source of voltage. The principle according to which it produces equal intervals requires either that it generate equal changes in voltage between successive keys, or that it produce a series of unequal voltages that nevertheless produce equal changes in the response of the oscillator. The oscillator itself may be the cause of the problem.

Most twelve-tone keyboards sustain the voltage level produced by the last key depressed when it is released. Sometimes this does not happen, however, or whether it does or does not is determined by a switch. If the last voltage is not sustained, what usually happens is that it drops to a very low or 0 value. In some cases this may create problems with the oscillator being controlled, as it may produce a subaudio frequency.

Most keyboards contain a number of processing controls that affect the control-voltage outputs of the keys. The first of these is usually a *transposing* or *range* control, which transposes the output of the keyboard up or down uniformly. This means that given keys on the keyboard are rarely associated with fixed pitches, as they are on mechanical keyboard instruments. The next is a *scale* control, which compresses or expands the outputs of the keyboard, creating equal-tempered scales of any number of notes. The keyboard may also contain an *external input,* which may allow these functions to be controlled from an external device. Finally, keyboards may contain more exotic types of processing controls such as a frequency-modulation or vibrato control. Since electronic music synthesizers have several independent oscillators, the keyboard usually has an external input for this purpose rather than an internal oscillator. In using these controls, it is important to remember that they affect the output of the keyboard and are usually in *addition* to other similar controls on the oscillators affected.

Many keyboards have a *portamento* control, which allows glissandos to be produced between two keys on the keyboard. At the 0 or "normal" position, the change between one key and the next is instantaneous. As the portamento control is increased, the keyboard takes a longer and longer amount of time to reach the pitch determined by the new key, and the oscillator controlled by the keyboard makes a glissando between the two pitches. At the highest position on the portamento control, the keyboard takes a very long time to reach the new key—so long that it may appear never to get there. The portamento control thus affects the *duration* between two successive key depressions on the keyboard.

The portamento control is produced simply by inserting a capacitor into the output circuit of the keyboard. Many designers have not yet produced them, but capacitors could be inserted between the outputs of *any* electronic music controller to produce this kind of delay in reaching the next value. It is not a very accurate control, however. Further devices of this type are mentioned below under "Logical Devices."

It is in its capacity as a rhythmic controller that the electronic music keyboard differs most markedly from mechanical musical instruments. First, many of the keyboards on electronic music synthesizers are *monophonic*. This means that they can produce only one output at a given time. When two keys are depressed, then there is some standard result, such as that the lower key or the last key depressed takes precedence. This fact does not mean that the keyboard can control only one oscillator at a time, but it does mean that it has only one voltage output available at a time, so that if it is used to control two or more oscillators they would have to move up or down by proportional amounts when new keys are depressed. Nevertheless, the monophonic aspect of the keyboard often results in the keyboard being used to control only one tone at a time, and this means that polyphonic compositions require elaborate mixing or overdubbing on multi-track tape recorders.

An intermediate design between a monophonic and polyphonic keyboard consists of a keyboard divided into two or more portions, each of which produces a separate single output. People who perform at these keyboards must learn complicated and unusual techniques of stretching the fingers between two sections and employing both hands simultaneously, and usually it is still not possible to control many events with any dexterity. Fully polyphonic keyboards are very rare for analog electronic music synthesizers, however, since they require a separate oscillator for each key on the keyboard. In addition to the fact that such a solution would be extremely expensive, it would place great emphasis on the signal-generating aspect of the synthesizer at the expense of signal processing. Such an instrument would be more comparable to an electronic piano or organ than a synthesizer.

Polyphonic keyboards of a limited number of voices can be constructed for electronic music systems using sample-and-hold devices. In this manner, the sample-and-hold device can actually be an entirely separate module from the keyboard, and devices of this kind are discussed below. Quite simply, the manner in which this combination would work would be to send both the control voltage and timing-pulse outputs of the first key depressed to the first sample-and-hold outputs, the second to the next, and so forth. The first such keyboards to be manufactured for electronic music systems have operated in a cyclical fashion—which is to say that after each *n* keys the output is returned to the first sample-and-hold. This creates a confusing situation for people familiar with other keyboard instruments, for even if one key is "sustained" while others are released, it is overriden by the *n*th key to be depressed. If this problem can be worked out of future keyboards, it will be a major advancement in making the synthesizer a more versatile performing instrument.

Linear Controllers

A *linear controller* or *analog controller* or *ribbon controller* is a device that consists of a measured length of ribbon or a touch plate that produces a control-voltage output proportional to the *location* where it is touched in relation to the overall length of the ribbon. Continuous changes in the control-voltage output of the device can be achieved by sliding the finger back and forth along the surface of the sensitive portion of the controller. Voltages cannot generally be produced in accurate steps as with the twelve-tone keyboard; this is the primary distinction between the two types of controllers.

Linear controllers often have a *scale* control, which compresses or expands the range of voltages produced by the device. They may also have a *transposing* or *range* control, *vibrato* control, or *external inputs,* as twelve-tone keyboards. These controls may not be found on systems where individual control inputs contain processing controls, however.

Linear controllers usually produce trigger outputs as well as control-voltage outputs. Sometimes the trigger outputs are initiated whenever any portion of the sensitive length of the controller is touched, and sustained as long as the finger is kept down. Sometimes, however, there is a separate portion of the controller that is touched for the trigger output, in order to give independent control over both outputs of the device. Usually these portions are adjacent, in order to allow both outputs to be initiated with one hand or finger.

Linear controllers are necessarily *monophonic* devices, since the output must be variable over the entire range. In order to achieve a kind of polyphonic capability, however, several of them can be mounted adjacent to one another, so that each can be operated separately.

Since pitch discrimination is very sensitive, linear controllers are often used to control devices such as filters, voltage-controlled amplifiers, and sound locators rather than oscillators. The interchangeability of function of the controller is, again, simply an aspect of the overall power of the principle of voltage control.

Touch-Sensitive and Miscellaneous Keyboards

Touch-sensitive keyboards include a variety of manual controllers whose outputs vary depending on the manner in which keys are touched.

Pressure-sensitive keyboards provide control-voltage outputs proportional to the pressure applied on the key. Actually, these devices do not respond to pressure in the sense of the number of pounds exerted per square inch, but to body capacitance, which is more often a response of the surface area of the key covered by the finger. Each individual key is called a *touch plate* and has its own sensitive area. One disadvantage of pressure-sensitive keyboards is that the voltage output may vary greatly depending on very minor changes in finger pressure; such a variation may affect the entire range of response of the device controlled unless the output is processed carefully. Another disadvantage is that each person has a unique skin resistance that may affect the voltage output, so that performance directions about the manner in which such keys should be touched may not be meaningful for different performers.

Velocity-sensitive keyboards consist of keys that must be depressed below the surface of the keyboard, like a piano keyboard, but that produce an individual control-voltage output proportional to the striking force applied to the key. This output is in addition to the control-voltage output proportional to the position of that key in the range of the keyboard, and hence it may be used to control some other property of the sound produced. Intuitively, by analogy with the piano, such an output might be used to control loudness; but, of course, according to the principle of voltage control, it could determine any property.

Depth-sensitive keyboards, like velocity-sensitive keyboards, also consist of keys that must be depressed below a common surface height, but in this case another control-voltage output is produced that is proportional to the vertical depth to which the key is depressed. This kind of keyboard is available on only a few synthesizers, and obviously it requires extremely sensitive actions on the part of a performer.

A *memory keyboard* is not a touch-sensitive keyboard in the sense of any of the three discussed above, but a keyboard consisting of a number of keys or touch plates that merely *select* a *stored*-voltage output whenever the appropriate key is touched. The stored-voltage output is normally adjustable by means of an individual potentiometer. This type of keyboard may contain individual indicator lights on or adjacent to the keys to indicate which keys are currently in control. Each key on the keyboard may have several separate adjustable outputs. This type of keyboard is similar to a sequencer (see below), except for the fact that keys are manually selected and do not have to be activated in any particular order.

Whereas pressure-, velocity-, and depth-sensitive keyboards are often organized as separate additional outputs of individual keys on a twelve-tone keyboard, memory keyboards are entirely separate devices. There is no reason why memory keyboards cannot be fully polyphonic, with separate outputs for each key. Alternatively, memory keyboards may be monophonic in design, with only one output available at a given time. Memory keyboards may also have pressure outputs, but do not usually have velocity or depth outputs; keys that must be depressed below a given surface are normally found only on twelve-tone keyboards.

Any of these keyboards may also initiate *timing pulses* in a variety of ways. Pressure-sensitive keyboards, for example, may initiate pulses when the pressure reaches a certain level. Likewise, velocity- or depth-sensitive keyboards may initiate pulses in ways unique to these devices. Trigger outputs are also a function of the number of separate voices controlled by the keyboards—that is, whether they are monophonic or polyphonic.

Combination Controllers

Combination controllers are devices that combine two or more of the operating principles discussed above into a complex performing device. Often, one operating characteristic may be used to modify another, so that the control-voltage output is a function of both characteristics; alternatively, each kind of output may be available separately in order to control different devices.

For example, consider a sliding push button—at the moment, a purely hypothetical device. This could control one characteristic depending upon where the sliding control was positioned and another depending upon whether the button was depressed. Or, alternatively, it could control only one device, with an operating characteristic proportional to the position of the sliding mechanism, but only if the push button were on.

The most intuitive type of combination controller is the pressure- or velocity- or depth-sensitive twelve-tone keyboard. Actually, most keyboard controllers on electronic music systems are combination devices. Performing on these keyboards may require a technique of unprecedented complexity, but on the other hand they may be extremely powerful performing instruments.

Designers of electronic music systems must make several decisions about the nature of the manual controlling devices in their systems that seriously affect the performance capability of their instruments. Unfortunately, it is not apparent that much consideration has been given to musical-performance criteria in existing electronic instruments. Otherwise, designers would probably have spent more effort in perfecting polyphonic keyboards. Little attention has been paid to the characteristics of mechanical musical instruments and their performance technique.

Nevertheless, there are some aspects of mechanical musical instruments that do not provide a very good model for electronic music controllers. One such characteristic is the fact that, on mechanical musical instruments, certain operating principles always control the same musical qualities. For example, on the piano, velocity always controls loudness, to within limitations qualified by the pedals. On electronic instruments the principle of voltage control obviates the necessity of any such correlation. The musical qualities controlled by the performer's actions can be entirely a matter of his own individual programming, as determined by the patchings and control settings on the devices he uses. Designers should be encouraged to maximize the programming possibilities of their systems, rather than to limit them by analogy to mechanical musical instruments.

4. AUTOMATIC DEVICES

Automatic controlling devices are devices that can operate and control other devices in an electronic music system autonomously, usually in accordance with preset conditions. Obviously, such controllers are of great importance to the power of an electronic music system, and offer the opportunity of extending the range of control beyond what the user of the system can operate manually. However, up to the present time these have not been developed to any degree of complexity, and those currently available have various limitations (described below). Devices of this kind are currently being developed in conjunction with nearly every major electronic music system, and the shape of the field is changing even as these words are being written. Therefore, a separate section is devoted to the subject of the control of an electronic music studio by means of a digital computer (see Chapter 9, "Hybrid Systems"), the most important kind of controller presently under consideration. This section of the present chapter will be devoted to devices already available in many familiar designs.

Sequencers

A *sequencer* or *sequential-voltage source* is basically a device that generates a series of control voltages, which can be preset and used to control any devices in the system. Generally, several associated control-voltage outputs are available simultaneously, and the rhythm of the sequence can also be preset and varied. The sequencer returns to the first position in its series after the last, producing a circular pattern in its outputs.

Most sequencers consist of two distinct components, which are sometimes packaged as separate devices in the system. One is a *timing-pulse generator* or *pulser* or *clock,* which automatically generates timing pulses or triggers that advance the sequencer from position to position; the other is the *sequencer* itself, which can be envisioned as a matrix of preset controls that advance from position to position when the unit receives a timing-pulse input. We will consider each of these components separately.

The *timing-pulse generator* is basically an oscillator that produces timing pulses instead of audio signals as its output. The rhythm of the timing-pulse generator is determined by a *period* control, which varies the *duration between successive pulses.* Since period is the reciprocal of frequency, when the period increases the rate of pulse outputs decreases. Some pulsers also provide *pulse-length* or *pulse-width controls,* which determine the *duration of each pulse,* which must be distinguished from the duration between each pulse. The pulse length may be set either as a percentage of the period or as an absolute duration; the former design is somewhat easier to operate because it does not get out of phase with the period when either control is changed. Usually the period and pulse-length controls can be determined by external control voltages in addition to or instead of the internal controls; this is the way in which the rhythm of the pulser can be changed.

Timing-pulse generators often provide a number of different outputs, which allow different rhythms to be produced simultaneously. All pulses may be available at certain outputs; alternate pulses may be available at others. More elaborate rhythmic effects may be achieved by a *pulse matrix* in which individual pulses may be programmed. Such devices are not commonly available, however.

Pulsers may contain a variety of additional controls. The functions of *start* and *stop* buttons are self-explanatory. Sometimes, timing-pulse inputs may control the same properties. *Single-pulse buttons* cause the pulser to generate pulses only when the button is pressed; these may be used to advance the sequencer manually when setting the preset controls.

The pulser, in the context we have been considering, is basically a device to advance the sequencer from position to position. For this reason, it is often mounted on the same panel as the sequencer. The pulser can also be used to control any other devices that accept timing-pulse inputs, such as envelope generators, random-voltage sources, or sample-and-hold devices. Conversely, other devices that generate timing pulses can be used to advance the sequencer from position to position. These devices may include keyboards or envelope followers, for example.

Some sequencers have been developed that do not include a device like a pulser but that enter timing information into the sequencer in some other manner. For these devices, the above remarks about the controls on timing pulse generators do not apply.

The *sequencer* itself is basically a memory bank of control voltages that may be selected only in a given order. The control voltages are usually preset by a matrix of potentiometers, and an indicator light tells which position is currently in control. An individual location in the sequence is referred to as a *position;* a typical sequencer may have three or four voltage outputs or *stages* at each position. The principle of voltage control allows each output to control any device in the system, including even the pulser that advances the sequencer. For example, three- or four-note chords could be produced by controlling separate oscillators with each output of the sequencer; alternatively, the outputs could control the frequency, amplitude, and duration of a single tone.

Sequencers often have additional outputs or controls of various kinds. Each position in the sequence may have an associated *timing-pulse output* that is activated only when the sequencer is at that position. Each position may have a *timing-pulse input* that sends the sequencer to that position, overriding the normal sequence of events. Some sequencers have a control-voltage input for this purpose instead of a timing-pulse input. Switches may be included that skip an individual position or stop the sequencer at that position. More elaborate controls may enable the sequencer to take each output individually instead of in associated groups of three or four outputs, thus converting, for example, a three-stage eight-position sequencer into a one-stage twenty-four-position sequencer (but see our remarks below, under "Logical Devices," that explain how this may be accomplished by a relay network and another sequencer). Another control may enable two or more sequencers to be attached, converting two three-stage eight-position sequencers into one three-stage sixteen-position sequencer. These controls may be housed in a separate module, or they may come as part of the sequencer itself. All of these controls increase the power of the sequencer at the expense of operational simplicity; there is inevitably a trade off between these two quantities in any device.

The most important limitation of a sequencer is the size of its memory, in either dimension: the number of positions, the number of stages, or both. Sequencers are available that have as few as five positions and four stages or eight positions and three stages up to as many as 256 positions and four stages. Smaller sequencers may be played with in a number of ways to produce sequences of pitches that are repeated, in the manner of a loop, or altered on each occurrence, producing patterns of various sorts. The idea of a series is important in much music, and the smaller sequencer allows many opportunities for experimenting with such ideas. Larger sequencers are powerful devices for presetting the controls for an entire composition or portion of a composition, which may then be generated automatically in real time by the sequencer.

The experience that many users of electronic music systems have with sequencers seems to suggest the desirability of expanding the number of positions or stages on the sequencer as the solution to a fully automatic electronic music controller. Some studios have invested a great deal of money in systems of this nature, and they have achieved a level of control undoubtedly greater than is possible with manually controlled systems or with smaller sequencers. Most of these systems were developed before the idea of using a small digital computer as a controlling device became a practical possibility. At the present time, the cost of expanding the number of sequencers in a studio, which may exceed the cost of a small computer system, is not commensurate with the amount of control acquired. Computer-controlled systems are still in infancy, and exactly what they will be able to do and how they will operate is not yet clear; but these systems offer much greater potential control than a sequencer bank.

5. OTHER DEVICES

In this section we include a number of devices that produce control-voltage outputs but that are not manually operated or automatic controllers in the sense of the equipment described above. Individual electronic music systems may have other devices that are not covered in this chapter. Sometimes these devices are subcomponents of equipment covered here, such as devices that connect sequencers together or that modify the outputs of keyboard controllers.

Random-Voltage Sources

A *random-voltage source,* sometimes called a "source of uncertainty," is a device that produces a voltage output that is not controlled except with regard to the range in which it occurs (and sometimes even that is not controlled). What this means is simply that the output is unpredictable, but that it will be a signal that has the appropriate characteristics of a control voltage.

A *stored* or *held* random-voltage source produces a new voltage whenever it receives a timing-pulse input, and sustains that voltage until it receives another timing-pulse input. Sometimes this device will contain an internal *clock* or timing-pulse generator, which produces the triggers that cause it to generate new random voltages.

A *fluctuating* or *interpolating* random-voltage source generates random voltages in the same range as a stored random-voltage source, but produces an interpolation between successive voltages so that the output is always changing. Since an interpolating random-voltage source always requires at least two voltages to be able to produce the interpolation, it usually has its own internal timing-pulse generator, or input from an external pulser, the period of which may then be controlled by another external control-voltage input.

The output of a random-voltage source is, initially, a voltage that may be anywhere within the range of control voltages acceptable to the system. This voltage is usually produced by sampling a noise generator, the output of which fluctuates in a random manner. If the noise generator produces *white noise,* then the range of output voltages will be distributed uniformly over the spectrum.

The random-voltage source may contain a control-voltage processor on its output, which is used to bring the output voltages into the range required by the devices being controlled. Alternatively, these controls may be found on other modules in the system, or on the inputs of the devices affected.

Random-voltage sources may contain a variety of additional controls or components. Since a stored random-voltage source contains a sample-and-hold device on its output, this component may be capable of being extracted from the device and used separately; and since a fluctuating random-voltage source contains an interpolating device, this component may also be capable of being used separately. Sometimes a random-voltage source may contain a *correlation control,* which determines the maximum that the next voltage may deviate from the present voltage. And finally, random-voltage sources may contain white-noise outputs as part of the same device, since these are required in any case.

Sample-and-Hold Devices

Sample-and-hold devices are basically *memories* for control voltages. They are used in conjunction with a variety of different applications in electronic music and, therefore, may come in a number of different physical configurations that reflect the intended use of the device. We will not attempt to describe every application of sample-and-hold devices, but merely to show the basic idea of a sample-and-hold and the kinds of decisions that must be made in its design.

A sample-and-hold has a control-voltage input and output. Its function is to store the current value of the input when a special command is received, and to hold this value at the output until the next command is received. In this manner, the input may fluctuate but the output will be sustained until the device is told to change. The simplest design for a sample-and-hold has a *timing-pulse input* associated with the control-voltage input. When the unit receives a timing pulse, it stores the value of the control-voltage input at that instant and holds it until another timing pulse is received. Thus, the control-voltage input may change, but the output will hold until another timing pulse is received.

One type of design complication of a sample-and-hold can occur when the timing-pulse input is replaced by some other device, such as a threshold detector or envelope follower. For example, the sample-and-hold may change its value only when a control-voltage or audio-signal input reaches a certain value. Fortunately, most systems incorporate these functions in additional modules that provide timing-pulse outputs when these conditions are present rather than including them directly within the sample-and-hold.

Another type of design complication of a sample-and-hold occurs when some other property of the timing-pulse input, such as the *pulse length,* affects the value of the output. For example, the output of the sample-and-hold may be allowed to vary while the pulse sustains, and then hold the last value after the pulse is released.

Another type of design complication of a sample-and-hold is a *polyphonic adapter.* A polyphonic adapter consists of several sample-and-holds or *voices* that are grouped together and selected in some order as determined by a single timing-pulse input and control-voltage input. When the first timing-pulse input is received, the value of the control-voltage input is sent to the first control-voltage output. When the next timing-pulse input is received, the control voltage is sent to the second output, but the first is unaffected. A timing-pulse output may be associated with each control-voltage output, indicating the attack time and duration of each voice.

Sample-and-holds are logically subcomponents of other devices in electronic music systems, and often they are not available as separate modules. This is unfortunate, because it is only when they can be used separately that the user can experiment with their many applications.

Envelope Followers

An *envelope follower* or *envelope detector* is a device that tracks an audio-signal input and produces a control-voltage output proportional to its *amplitude*. At low frequencies it follows the *instantaneous* amplitude of the input signal, producing an output that tracks all the variations of the waveshape of the input signal. At higher frequencies the envelope follower tracks the peak-to-peak amplitude of the individual cycles of the input signal, producing an output that "follows" the envelope of the signal; this description explains the reason for the device's name. (See Figure 5–5.1.)

Envelope followers thus produce a variable output that traces all of the complex variations present in a live signal. They usually also produce timing-pulse outputs that are generated when the amplitude exceeds a given threshold or sensitivity level and sustained as long as the amplitude remains at that level. The threshold can sometimes be varied by a potentiometer. The timing-pulse output may be used to trigger an envelope generator that starts at the same time as the signal input to the envelope follower.

There may be a number of controls on an envelope follower, and these must be studied carefully, for there are several different ways in which they might work. One kind of control is a *threshold detector,* which inhibits the output of the device unless the amplitude of the input signal is greater than a certain variable value. Sometimes a *decay-time control* will be available

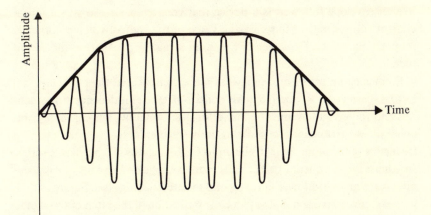

Figure 5–5.1: The output of the envelope follower is shown by the heavy line, which traces the peak-to-peak amplitude of the input signal.

as an adjunct to the threshold detector. When the amplitude of the input signal falls below the amount determined at the threshold, the output of the envelope follower does not instantaneously drop to 0, but decays to 0 over a preset duration. This function is useful particularly when using the output of the envelope follower directly as an envelope.

A more complicated kind of control allows the user to vary the *frequency* at which the envelope follower stops tracking the variations of the wave-shape and begins to track the peak-to-peak amplitude of the input signal. For systems in which control voltages are compatible with audio signals, there is little reason for a device that tracks the waveshape of the input signal, for the input signal itself could be used for this purpose.

A very interesting application of the envelope follower involves the storage of control signals on analog tape, which are converted to control voltages by the envelope follower as the analog tape is played back.[1] Audio signals recorded on analog tape are played back through an envelope follower and converted to control voltages and timing pulses that automatically generate a portion of a composition. For systems in which audio signals are compatible with control voltages, there is never a problem about storing control voltages on analog tape, but the envelope follower may be used to generate timing pulses.

Frequency Followers

A *frequency follower, frequency detector,* or *pitch-to-voltage converter,* like an envelope follower, is a device that converts an audio signal into a control voltage, but in this case the value of the control-voltage output is proportional to the *frequency* of the input signal rather than to the amplitude.

Frequency detectors are somewhat more complicated than envelope detectors, because most audio signals consist of several independent frequencies and some method must be found for discriminating among these components. A frequency follower usually responds to the fundamental frequency of the input signal if the input signal consists of a harmonic series. In other cases, frequency detection is more complicated and may be inaccurate. A frequency follower may respond to zero crossings (see Figure 5–5.2), but zero crossings are not always a clear indication of the pitch of the signal.

[1]This application is described by Morton Subotnick in his article "The Basic 'Patch' for *Sidewinder," Synthesis* II, 6–9.

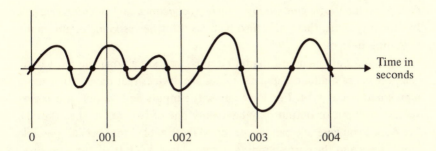

Figure 5–5.2: The output of the frequency detector is a control voltage proportional to the frequency of the audio-signal input, as determined, in this instance, by the zero crossings of the signal. This frequency produces ten zero-crossings or approximately 4.5 cycles in 0.004 seconds, which represents a frequency of 1,125 cps.

A frequency detector usually contains a *sensitivity* or *threshold* control, which determines the minimum frequency to which it will respond. It may also produce a *timing-pulse output* when the input frequency reaches a certain value, which may be affected by the threshold control. Finally, there may be *audio-signal outputs* of various descriptions. Of these, the most important is a sine or square wave which tracks the *fundamental frequency* sensed by the frequency detector.

Frequency detectors normally do not respond to the complete range of audible frequencies, but to within certain limits which may possibly be varied by controls on the device.

Frequency detectors are not yet available for all electronic music systems, but devices of this kind are currently under development. Especially for systems in which audio signals and control voltages are not electrically compatible, frequency detectors may have many important applications.

Logical Devices

"Logical" devices include a variety of special-purpose items that are simply components of the electrical circuits of certain control devices, and may be selected to accomplish various functions. Most of these items were originally standard or nonstandard circuit components that were not made available on early voltage-controlled electronic music synthesizers until it was recognized both that they could serve some important purposes and that their inclusion in a patch should be at the option of the user. These devices include *logic gates, relays, diodes, capacitors,* and *Schmitt Triggers.* In future systems, there may also be a need for newer kinds of automatic switching devices.

Logic gates are standard digital circuits, and are among the most basic components of digital computers. Gates are devices that have two or more inputs and one output. For logic gates, the inputs and outputs are *binary values;* an input or output may have only one of two values (i.e., 0 or 1). For each logic gate one can construct a "truth table" that lists all possible input states and the corresponding output states. Each truth table, in turn, can be represented by a Boolean statement. Boolean algebra, named for the nineteenth-century logician George Boole, is a branch of mathematics specifically concerned with logical operations of this sort.

An AND gate produces an output value of 1 if, and only if, the input values A and B are both 1. An OR gate produces an output value of 1 if at least one of the input values is 1. A NOT circuit produces the opposite value of its input. A NAND (meaning "not and") gate produces an output value of 1 unless both of the inputs are 1. A NOR (meaning "not or") gate produces an output value of 1 only if both inputs are not 1—that is, if

AND

A	B	Output
0	0	0
0	1	0
1	0	0
1	1	1

NAND

A	B	Output
0	0	1
0	1	1
1	0	1
1	1	0

OR

A	B	Output
0	0	0
0	1	1
1	0	1
1	1	1

NOR

A	B	Output
0	0	1
0	1	0
1	0	0
1	1	0

NOT

A	B
0	1
1	0

Figure 5–5.3: Truth tables for logic gates.

neither A nor B is 1. The truth tables for these logic gates are illustrated in Figure 5–5.3.

Logic gates in digital circuits operate simply by recognizing a certain voltage, such as 5 volts or more, as a value of "1," and anything below as "0." A circuit of this type would be said to employ "5-volt logic." It is important to realize that this is identical to the manner in which electronic music synthesizers recognize *timing pulses.* This is to say, timing pulses are the natural "logic" elements of electronic music synthesizers. Most of the applications of logic gates are in relation to timing pulses, although some have to do with control voltages as well.

For example, suppose that in a certain patch a composer wanted to have a certain note present only if two other notes were also present. He could employ an AND gate that had the timing pulses that initiated the other two notes as inputs, and the output of the gate would provide the timing-pulse input for the third note.

A *relay* is essentially an *on-off switch* that can be turned on by a trigger. Relays can be of particular value when they are used in conjunction with control voltages: when a timing pulse is present, the associated control voltage is allowed through the switch; otherwise not. A relay network can be constructed to convert a three-stage eight-position sequencer to a one-stage twenty-four-position sequencer, in conjunction with a second sequencer, which is used for control. The "control" sequencer is set to have three positions, and it is moved to the next position when the other sequencer, the "master" sequencer, loops back to its first position. The timing-pulse outputs from each of the three positions of the control sequencer are patched to the trigger inputs of three relays, and the control-voltage outputs of the eight-position sequencer are patched to the control-voltage inputs of the relays. The outputs of the relays are paralleled, forming the final control-voltage output. Now when the sequencer loops back to its first position, the control sequencer moves to its next position, shifting to the next relay, which allows the next stage of outputs through. This patch is illustrated in Figure 5–5.4. Many other such applications are possible.

Another type of "logical" device is a *diode.* A diode allows electric current to pass in one direction only. Normally when a patch cord is connected from the output of one device to the input of another, current can flow in either direction. This may create problems when inputs or outputs are paralleled. Figure 5–5.5 illustrates a patch in which two timing-pulse sources are used to drive two envelope generators. Timing-pulse source 1 is supposed to drive *only* envelope generator 1, but timing-pulse

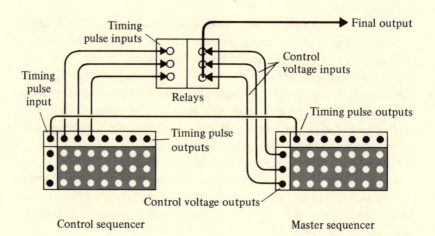

Figure 5–5.4: Use of three relays and a "control" sequencer to convert a three-stage eight-position sequencer to a one-stage twenty-four-position sequencer.

source 2 is supposed to drive *both* envelope generators. The trouble is that current flows backward from the input of envelope generator 1 to the output of timing-pulse source 2 and accidentally sets off envelope generator 2 whenever timing-pulse source 1 produces a pulse. This problem is solved by placing a diode into the patch between timing-pulse source 2 and envelope generator 1. Now current can flow *only* from timing-pulse source 2 to envelope generator 1 and not in the other direction.

Another useful circuit component is a *capacitor,* which is placed following the output of a control-voltage source. This type of component is identical to the portamento control on many twelve-tone keyboards *(q.v.),* and produces a gradual change from one control voltage to the next. When it is available as a separate component, the capacitor can be used to create this effect for any control-voltage source.

A *Schmitt trigger* is a device containing an input signal (either a control-voltage or audio signal) that produces a timing-pulse output when the input reaches a certain level. Schmitt triggers are logical subcomponents of devices such as envelope followers and frequency followers. Sometimes they are available as separate components.

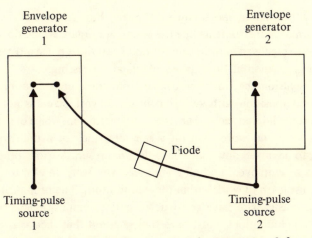

Figure 5–5.5: Use of a diode to prevent envelope generator 2 from being driven accidentally by timing-pulse source 1.

6. CONCLUSION: COMPOSITION WITH VOLTAGE-CONTROLLED SYNTHESIZERS

Now that we have surveyed all of the control devices of present electronic music systems, it is possible to draw some conclusions about the current state of the art. A synthesizer is a performing instrument, just like other musical instruments, operated by a person with special skills to create music in real time. Basically, there are only two ways in which a musical instrument may be optimized: either with respect to the maximum number of separate events that an individual performer can achieve, or with respect to the maximum amount of control that can be exercised over an individual event. Up to this point, the term "synthesizer" has usually been employed to designate an instrument of the second variety, although occasionally it has been used for some of the first variety and some compromises between the two.

There are valid reasons for believing that it may never be possible to design an electronic music synthesizer that achieves any greater optimization of live-performance capability (without, of course, resorting to automatic computer control). An individual performer has but two hands and two feet with which to operate the synthesizer. Furthermore, it is clear that live-performance instruments like the piano and organ, which do allow the performer to create an entire composition in real time, place most emphasis on signal generation at the expense of signal processing.

The conclusion that must be drawn from these considerations is that real-time composition with voltage-controlled synthesizers is not possible except in some limited sense. The user can generate one voice of a composition at a time and store each on a separate track of a multitrack tape recorder, to be mixed down later into the final result. Various other procedures can be employed, and all composers who work in electronic music studios must learn to work within these limitations. The proponents of live electronic music, who have constructed entire compositional procedures around these limitations, must nevertheless admit that their conception of *music* is rather different from past conceptions, and from those of most composers active at the present time. The vision of a composer sitting at a keyboard or any kind of manually operated console and producing an entire composition in real time is still, and may always be, a fantasy.

In order to generate a complete composition, some method of *storing* all of the composer's specifications and controlling sounds with all the necessary precision must be found. In order to achieve this goal, we must turn to the use of computers, which is the subject of the next part of this book.

One final remark about the current state of the field is in order. Early electronic music synthesizers were designed before the musical requirements of the users were fully understood. Many mistakes were made on early equipment that have led to unnecessary limitations in the music that could be produced. Today systems are being designed that will overcome many of the problems of the devices described above. Nevertheless, it is impossible to predict when these improvements will benefit the ordinary user. Research of this kind, and, more important, production, require extensive financial backing that cannot easily be raised by musicians. The older equipment will still be in use for many years.

CHAPTER SIX

How to Design
an Electronic Music Studio

Many people who read this book will undoubtedly want to consider setting up an electronic music studio, either for themselves or for an institution with which they are connected. While many considerations relevant to studio design have been pointed out in the chapters above, a separate chapter is nevertheless included to summarize this information, in order that new studios may profit from some of the mistakes and good fortune of the past.

While some of the points made below may conceivably apply to any studio, it must be emphasized that different studios may stress different compositional procedures and approaches and may, therefore, desire to employ different designs. Some people are fortunate enough to be able to afford their own private studios at home, where they do not have to worry about other users; institutions, however, must establish policies and procedures that will allow a large number of people to work together in harmony.

The first design consideration is the choice of the room itself. This should be large enough to accommodate all of the equipment planned in addition to leaving space for future expansion as well as a few visitors. While it may be useful to hold small classes in the studio, large classes are best held elsewhere, since it is not possible to demonstrate equipment or techniques except to a small group, which must often look over the shoulder of the instructor.

Temperature and humidity control are paramount, and if the room selected is not presently air-conditioned, it is best to choose a room in which window units can be mounted. On the other hand, noise control is also important, and if the site is near an airport or a road on which heavy traffic passes, the room is best located in a basement or other area away from the outside noise. Furthermore, the studio should be situated in a place where noises made by users are not going to disturb people in adjoining rooms, though this problem can sometimes be avoided by using earphones. Windows in the room are unnecessary except as places for mounting air conditioners, and the outside view can be distracting, although one may enjoy being distracted at times.

The electric power required to run the equipment in the studio is usually not more than 20 amps, or what would be found in an ordinary room. If air conditioners are included, more power is needed, of course. Also, if computer equipment is planned for the studio, additional power will be required. While the central processing unit itself normally does not consume much electricity, the peripheral equipment may.

Good lighting is essential to an electronic music studio. Overhead fluorescent lights are very good, if the transformers, which emit a constant 60-cycle hum, can be located elsewhere.

Many of the customary accouterments of a classroom or office are useful in an electronic music studio. These include a blackboard, instructor's desk, tables, bookcases, coat racks, storage and filing cabinets, bulletin board, telephone, wastebaskets, etc.

Soundproofing in the studio itself is essential. If the studio can be made completely "dead," although not quite like an anechoic chamber, users will find it much easier to hear very minor "clicks" or other problems on their tapes, which will often not be noticed when the tape is played back in a normal acoustic environment. The studio is a working facility, not a concert hall. If soundproofing materials cannot be installed by a contractor, it is possible to paste objects with rough, pock-marked surfaces on the walls to cut down reflections. Egg crates, for example, are ideal for this purpose.

For people working on tapes, the listening area is crucial. Therefore, loudspeakers should be situated in such a way that the main working location is in the center of the stereophonic or quadraphonic environment. Obstructions in front of the speakers should be avoided, and for this reason it is often convenient to mount the speakers on the wall or on top of tables or stands. Ideally, loudspeakers should stand at about the same height as the listener's head, and they should never be placed on the floor (unless there are legs on the speakers), adjacent to the ceiling or in a corner where three sides of the room (two walls and either the floor or ceiling) converge.

The general layout of the equipment in the studio should be planned and not allowed simply to accumulate in a random manner. There should be a central working area where all of the main controls are within an arm's reach of a single user. These controls should include the on-off power switch or emergency switches, the patch panel of the studio or central mixer from which connections are made, a multitrack tape recorder or remote controls for operating the tape recorders, and the synthesizing equipment. A U shape is often preferred for this reason. Items such as microphones, graphic displays, or areas where tape splicing is carried out can be located farther away, especially if the tape recorders have remote controls. Earphone jacks for sound monitoring without disturbing other users should be located throughout the studio.

The equipment should be placed on top of tables or benches, which allow it to be operated conveniently while standing. Some people prefer to sit while working, but standing usually offers the greatest flexibility. A height of 29 to 35 inches is most convenient for this purpose. Tape recorders should be mounted horizontally or placed on tables or benches, since this simplifies editing and the placement of loop guides. Console cabinets for tape recorders are usually lower than 29 inches, but they are still convenient to work at. Tables and benches should be sturdy enough so that they do not sway or vibrate while in use.

All equipment should be mounted in such a way that it can be serviced without ripping the studio apart. Aisles should be left between the equipment and the wall so that repairmen can get behind the equipment easily.

Wiring is best located under a false floor, if this luxury can be afforded. If not, special conduits can be installed so that users and visitors will not rip out vital connections if they trip on cables. If these cannot be afforded, all wires in the same direction should be taped together into a single strand and affixed to the floor with masking tape, which is also useful for attaching wires to the walls. Excess wiring, which is sometimes necessary to allow the studio to be assembled in different ways, should be kept under the tables or benches and away from areas in which users may put their feet.

The studio should be cleaned regularly, since a clean working environment encourages respect for the facilities. Carpeting is even recommended, and it should be pointed out that carpeting absorbs sound well. Heavy security should be maintained for the studio, since it contains expensive equipment. It is best if an employee can remain in or near the studio at all times, both to lock it and unlock it and to assist users.

A log book can be kept in the studio for users to sign in and out and to report any problems they encounter. Assignment of time to work in the studio seems to be most productive when each user is given a regular weekly appointment. If the facilities become overtaxed, it is convenient to have a couple of small, portable synthesizers which can be carried to other rooms for users who are just beginning. Consumable supplies such as splicing blocks, razor blades, and even empty reels and boxes can be provided by the studio, but users should purchase their own tape, since this will discourage waste.

A tape library of compositions created in the studio, plus other music that the instructors may wish to encourage users to listen to, should be kept in the studio, so that users can hear what others have accomplished with the same facilities. Books and manuals are also handy for reference, especially in case problems develop, but the studio should not be made into a library, since users will generally prefer to work alone and will be distracted by people who come there to read.

The director of the studio, or the person who is responsible for co-ordinating whatever teaching is carried out in the studio, should prepare a number of documents and even manuals describing particular features of the installation. There are usually very many special points that are different for each studio, and the only way anyone will ever keep track of these things is if they are written down. Another item that should be prepared for each studio is a master "patch chart" diagram of the equipment in the particular arrangement of the studio, on which users can record patches and control settings that they want to preserve.

Regular policies should be established concerning problems such as the use of tapes left lying around, or patchings and control settings left after a user is finished working. Users' rights should be respected, and it creates an especially unpleasant situation if the studio personnel bump other users to do their own work, unless a clear emergency exists.

These are some of the pointers that the author has acquired over many years' experience in studio design and management. Other people undoubtedly have other ideas and different experiences to draw upon, and may disagree with some of these recommendations. Many problems may nevertheless be avoided by following these recommendations.

PART 3

Computers
and Electronic Music

CHAPTER SEVEN

Basic Concepts of Computer Music

INTRODUCTION TO DIGITAL COMPUTERS

1. The Design of Digital Computers

In this section we will present some of the basic terms and concepts dealing with digital computers. Most of this material is readily available in books and reference manuals about computers that are often published by specific computer manufacturers. We do not intend this section to be comprehensive; we will introduce only a minimum amount of information necessary for a musician to understand the various applications of computers to electronic music, which we discuss in detail below. This information should be supplemented by specific details about individual computers for people who intend to use a particular system.

The basic design of a typical modern digital computer is illustrated in Figure 7–1.1. The components consist of a *central processing unit* (abbreviated CPU), which is the basic controlling mechanism of the computer. The CPU normally contains or has the ability to access a number of *registers* in which operations such as arithmetic are carried out. The CPU also accesses the *memory* or *storage* of the computer, which consists of a large number of individual locations in which numbers can be stored and retrieved at a very high speed. Each individual storage location has its own unique *address,* which is a number indicating its position in the memory. The address must be distinguished from the *contents* of the location, which is the number that is stored there.

The amount of memory and the memory-access time are important in-

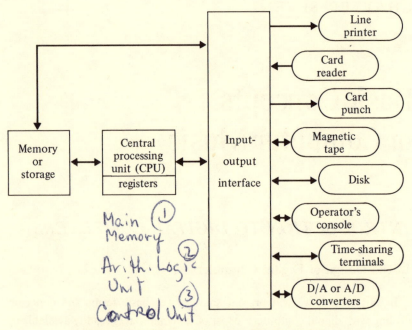

Figure 7–1.1: Design of a typical digital computer.

dicators of the size and flexibility of the computer. Memory sizes are usually indicated by a figure such as NK, where K is normally 2^{10}, which equals 1,024 or approximately 1,000, and N is the number of units of K of memory. For example, 256K memory means 256 times 1,024 storage locations, or · exactly 262,144 locations. The confusing factor is that different computer manufacturers use different quantities to indicate memory sizes. Most manufacturers indicate memory sizes in words; the memory of the IBM System/360,[1] which is actually an entire line of different models of the same basic computer, is indicated in bytes. (See section 2, below.)

The memory-access time of a computer indicates the length of time that it takes the computer to store or retrieve a number in its memory. Since these times are very fast, it is necessary to know some of the terms in which these times are normally indicated. One *millisecond* is $\frac{1}{1,000}$ second, or 0.001 second. This time is slow enough actually to be useful to indicate some of the events that may occur in music, such as attack times. (See Chapter 2.)

———

[1]This section was written before the System/370 series had appeared. The System/370 is functionally identical to the System/360.

One *microsecond* is one *millionth* of a second, or $\frac{1}{1,000,000}$ second, or $\frac{1}{1,000}$ millisecond. Such a speed is beyond the scope of human comprehension, as far as musical functions are concerned, but it is a typical time for computer operations. One *nanosecond* is one *billionth* of a second, or $\frac{1}{1,000,000,000}$ second, or $\frac{1}{1,000}$ microsecond. Some modern computers are so fast that their memory-access times must be indicated in nanoseconds.

To give some typical computer memory-access times, the **IBM** System/360 model 65 takes approximately 1.30 microseconds to load a word in a general register from a memory location. The model 91 has a basic memory-access time of 60 nanoseconds. This means that the model 65 could take 1.3 seconds to load 1 million words from its memory, or that the model 91 could take 1 second to load over 16 million words.

Arithmetic operations carried out by a computer normally take times in the same range as the memory-access time, with operations such as multiplication and division taking slightly longer. We can see that computers can carry out in a few seconds operations that would take human beings a lifetime. Not all of the computer's time is taken up with such operations, however. Much of its time is devoted to *input-output* operations.

Input-output operations refer to operations by which the computer transfers information between its memory and external devices, or in more general terms, operations by which the computer communicates with the outside world. A *read* instruction refers to a transfer from the external device to the memory, and a *write* instruction refers to a transfer in the opposite direction. Since these operations usually consume much more time than arithmetic or memory-access operations, they are connected to the computer through a device called an *input-output interface,* which contains special processing hardware of its own. Input-output operations are controlled by the CPU usually through what is called a *priority-interrupt* system. Such a system works in the following way: when an input-output device is ready to transfer data, it sends an "interrupt" message to the CPU. As soon as the CPU can respond, it suspends whatever it is doing and turns its attention to the input-output device. All that the CPU has to do is to start or terminate an input-output operation; once the operation is in progress, it is controlled by the interface, and the CPU can return to its original task. Thus, the CPU can have several different input-output operations in progress simultaneously and still be devoting most of its time to computations. It often happens, however, that the CPU has to wait for an input-output device before it can continue processing, for it needs data from the device to use in current calculations. Waiting of this kind is substantially reduced by a multiprogramming operating system. (See section 4, below.)

Familiar input-output devices available on most computers include a *card reader*, which reads standard 80-column punched cards; a *card punch*, which punches the same kind of cards; a *line printer*, which prints output on 11-by-14-inch pages in characters that include usually just capital letters, numerals, and special characters, all of which are $\frac{1}{10}$ inch in size; a *magnetic-tape unit*, which reads or writes information on magnetic digital tape; and a *disk*, which is another kind of magnetic input-output device like a tape but which has a different physical configuration. (Magnetic tapes and disks will be discussed in detail in section 3.) A computer also has an *operator's console*, a special device at which the operator types instructions into the computer.

Computers may also contain special-purpose input-output devices. These include *digital-to-analog* and *analog-to-digital converters*, which are necessary for producing or analyzing musical sound. (These devices are discussed in section 6.) Sometimes the computer will be equipped with *time-sharing facilities*. These enable a number of different users to be connected to the computer simultaneously at individual stations called *terminals*. The time-sharing controller is illustrated in Figure 7–1.1 as an input-output device because it actually spends most of its time doing just that; the computer's time is "shared" between the users by transferring between them as rapidly as possible. Usually this is sufficient for none of the users even to notice, for the computer is much faster than all of them together. In this manner the time-sharing system allows each terminal to function as a minicomputer as far as each user is concerned.

The fact that input-output operations are much slower than normal computations and that they are handled by priority-interrupt procedures means that *real-time* operations on a computer are very difficult to achieve. This fact is especially important when dealing with music and other functions of time, which cannot wait for other instructions to finish before proceeding. It makes the programming for musical functions very difficult and sometimes impossible to achieve except under limited conditions.

2. Binary Numbers: Bytes, Words, Integers, and Floating-Point Numbers

The numbers that are stored and operated on inside computers are of a very special kind. Rather than the numbers we are familiar within everyday life, which are decimal numbers, computers deal exclusively with *binary numbers*. Binary numbers are numbers in which each binary digit or *bit* can assume only one of two values, which are indicated as 0 or 1. Decimal numbers can assume any of ten values, which are indicated as 0 through 9. Binary numbers require many more bits to express quantities than decimal numbers. Figure 7–2.1 indicates several binary numbers and their decimal equivalents.

Binary	Decimal	Binary	Decimal
0	0	1111	15
1	$1 = 2^0$	10000	$16 = 2^4$
10	$2 = 2^1$	100000	$32 = 2^5$
11	3	1000000	$64 = 2^6$
100	$4 = 2^2$	10000000	$128 = 2^7$
101	5	100000000	$256 = 2^8$

Figure 7–2.1: Some binary numbers and their decimal equivalents.

Although binary numbers are more difficult for us to recognize than decimal numbers, they are much easier to construct and more accurate for recording data. Since a bit can contain only one of two values, there is less likelihood of error in reading or writing it than there would be with a decimal number, which could assume any of ten different values. To record binary numbers, many magnetic devices can be constructed which simply magnetize a small quantity of material in either a positive or negative direction, and there is almost no possibility of error in reading the result (unless the material comes accidentally into contact with a magnet!).

In reading decimal numbers we recognize that each successive digit to the left of the decimal point represents a power of 10. The number in each position represents a value that is multiplied by the appropriate power of 10 to determine the value of the total number. For example, in evaluating the decimal number 543 we add $(5 \times 10^2) + (4 \times 10^1) + (3 \times 10^0)$. In evaluating binary numbers we perform exactly the same procedure except that we use powers of 2 instead of powers of 10. For example, to evaluate the binary number 10,101 we add $(1 \times 2^4) + (0 \times 2^3) + (1 \times 2^2) + (0 \times 2^1) + (1 \times 2^0) = 21$. Each successive bit to the left of the binary point represents a greater power of 2. Decimal numbers are said to employ a base of 10; binary numbers employ the base 2. The greatest number that can be represented in a quantity of n bits is $2^n - 1$. This actually gives us 2^n different values, since 0 is one of the values.

All numbers used by digital computers are represented internally in binary form. For one thing, this means that all numbers are represented as explicit quantities; there is no possibility that a number could be halfway between one quantity and another. This does not mean that computers cannot handle fractional quantities, however; all that is needed is a convention concerning where to locate the binary point, or how to represent fractional quantities.

For another thing, computers do not deal arbitrarily with binary numbers of any length. Certain decisions about the magnitude of numbers that the computer can handle are made by the manufacturer when he designs the computer. In this regard, it is necessary to know some terms that represent binary numbers of various magnitudes. A *byte* is a binary number of *eight bits.* Many modern computers, including particularly the IBM System/360 and the XDS Sigma-5, -7, and -9, employ the byte and multiples thereof as the basic unit of information. On these computers, a *word* is a quantity of *four bytes.* (Note, then, that both bytes and words denote binary quantities in which the number of bits is a power of 2.) The *word* is the basic quantity in which most operations are carried out inside most computers. That is to say, almost all instructions involving arithmetic operations on numbers or the transfer of data between memory and the registers in the CPU are carried out on complete words at a time, even when the magnitude of the numbers being used does not require as much precision. Other quantities are *halfwords,* which are two bytes in length, and *doublewords,* which are eight bytes in length.

Since binary numbers are so long and clumsy to recognize, computer manufacturers have developed other ways of indicating them. Of these, the most important is the *hexadecimal number system,* which uses the base of 16. Since 16 is a power of 2, there is a direct relationship between numbers represented in this system and the binary system. Each hexadecimal digit translates exactly into a four-bit binary number. Figure 7–2.2 illustrates the sixteen hexadecimal digits and their binary equivalents. Since sixteen symbols are needed to distinguish the digits, the letters A through F are used for 10 through 15. It is awkward to think of FC as a number, but it denotes a specific quantity (252) without ambiguity. Hexadecimal numbers, therefore, represent binary numbers in one fourth the number of digits. A byte translates into two hexadecimal digits, and a word into eight.

The numbers stored and manipulated inside computers do not always represent numerical quantities. Computer manufacturers have developed a method of representing *alphanumeric data* in numerical form. Alphanumeric data include the letters of the alphabet, the numerals 0 through 9, and

Decimal	Hexadecimal	Binary	Decimal	Hexadecimal	Binary
0	0	0000	8	8	1000
1	1	0001	9	9	1001
2	2	0010	10	A	1010
3	3	0011	11	B	1011
4	4	0100	12	C	1100
5	5	0101	13	D	1101
6	6	0110	14	E	1110
7	7	0111	15	F	1111
			16	10	10000

Figure 7–2.2: Hexadecimal numbers and their binary equivalents.

other characters such as punctuation marks and special symbols. The fact that computers can represent data of this kind means that, in addition to the more familiar numerical operations, computers can deal with verbal and abstract concepts, and they can compose poetry and music or analyze sentence structure. Alphanumeric data are usually represented by a convention that assigns a unique value of a single byte to each character. The two most widely used eight-bit conventions are the EBCDIC (Extended Binary-Coded-Decimal Interchange Code) and ASCII–8 (American Standard Code for Information Interchange) conventions. Tables indicating the interpretation of these codes are printed in many computer manuals.

For the IBM System/360 and XDS Sigma-5, -7, and -9 computers, a word contains thirty-two bits. Two entirely separate kinds of numbers are often represented in words. The first of these is called an *integer,* and it is the most familiar kind. An integer is a whole number, one containing no fractional part. Each successively greater value represents a greater quantity. The leftmost bit is reserved as a *sign bit,* which indicates whether the number is positive or negative. The highest value that can be represented in an integer is, therefore, $2^{31} - 1$.[2]

Integers do not allow us to represent fractional quantities unless we simply make some agreement about where to locate the binary point. The binary point is the same thing as a "decimal point" except that the bits to the right of the point are binary numbers instead of decimal numbers and, therefore, represent binary quantities. For example, if we allow just two bits to the right of the binary point then each fractional quantity represents ¼,

[2]Negative numbers are represented in these computers in a special manner called "2's complement form." We have passed over this detail for simplicity.

since there are four separate values in a two-bit quantity. Numbers of this kind are called "fixed-point binary numbers," but this is not the usual way in which fractional quantities are handled in computers.

Fractional quantities are normally represented as *floating-point numbers* in computers. A floating-point number contains three separate quantities: a *sign,* an *exponent,* and a *fraction.* To simplify, let us assume for the moment that we are using decimal numbers instead of binary or hexadecimal numbers. The sign indicates whether the number is positive or negative. The fraction is the value of the number, represented to the six most significant digits. The exponent indicates where the decimal point is to be placed, and the exponent itself could be either positive or negative; a negative exponent would indicate that the decimal point is to be moved to the left and zeros copied into vacant positions. Figure 7–2.3 indicates a floating-point decimal number in this fashion.

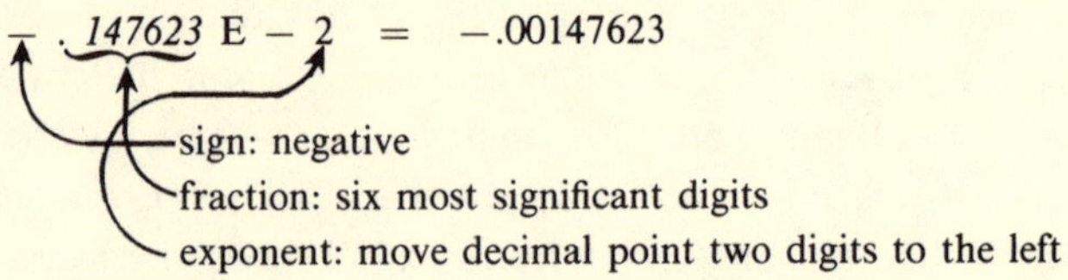

$$-\ .147623\ \text{E} - 2\ =\ -.00147623$$

sign: negative
fraction: six most significant digits
exponent: move decimal point two digits to the left

Figure 7–2.3: A floating-point number with components indicated in the decimal-number system.

The floating-point numbers that are actually used by the IBM System/360 and XDS Sigma-5, -7, and -9 computers are identical in form to the number shown in Figure 7–2.3 except that the individual digits are represented in the hexadecimal number system rather than the decimal number system.[2]

The only problem that must be kept in mind when dealing with floating-point numbers is that they are not absolutely accurate, and floating-point arithmetic often introduces minor errors into computations. The reason for this is that numbers are represented only to the six most significant (hexadecimal) digits. In the decimal system, we can see that if we add together two numbers such as 100,000. and 1.02, the result, when reduced to six significant digits, will be 100,001.; in other words, a small amount of precision is lost in the result. Some of this error may be eliminated if we use more than six significant digits, and in fact this is the solution provided by

[2]Floating-point numbers are not actually identical in these two machines. All negative numbers for the Sigma-7 computer are stored in 2's complement form, whereas for the IBM System/360 negative floating-point numbers are not.

double-precision floating-point numbers, in which two words are used to store the result instead of one, providing fourteen significant (hexadecimal) digits of precision. But all of the error cannot be eliminated because of the fact that certain values, such as the decimal quantity ⅓, can be represented only by repeating decimals in floating-point form (.3333, etc.). A certain quantity will always be lost in floating-point arithmetic involving such fractions. Nevertheless, the amount that is lost is very small, and the results are accurate enough for most purposes.

It is customary to indicate integer quantities as numbers with no decimal point and floating-point quantities as numbers with a decimal point, even if there is no fraction after the decimal point. Thus, 1, 14, and 924 are integer quantities, whereas 1.0, 1., 14., and 924.9 are floating-point quantities. When a floating-point number is converted to an integer, the part after the decimal point is truncated unless the user adds .5 in order to round off the number. Thus, 924.9 would become 924 when converted to an integer unless .5 is added before the number is converted, in which case the result would be 925. When an integer is converted to a floating-point number, the fraction is always 0.

3. Digital Data Storage

In this section we will cover some of the explicit details about the way in which data is recorded on magnetic digital tapes and disks. While some of these details are the kinds of things that are usually covered in highly technical computer-manufacturer's manuals rather than in beginning textbooks, they are important for understanding some of the limitations of computer sound-generating systems. The explicit details we will introduce here concern specifically the devices for the IBM System/360 computers. Since IBM is unquestionably the major computer manufacturer, most other manufacturers have developed devices that are compatible with IBM equipment. Even when they are not compatible, these devices usually employ the same general principles.

Magnetic digital tape units generally employ magnetic tape that is ½ inch in width. The width of the tape is divided into either seven or nine parallel tracks. Data is always read or written in quantities that access all of these tracks simultaneously—i.e., seven or nine bits. One of the bits is called a parity bit and is reserved for error checking, so that six or eight bits are for data. Thus, nine-track digital tapes transfer byte quantities, which are very appropriate for the IBM System/360 computers.

The manner in which data is written along the length of the tape is indicated by the *density* of the tape, which is expressed in *bytes per inch* (abbreviated BPI) for nine-track tapes or *characters per inch* for seven-track tapes. (A character is a six-bit data quantity.) Nine-track tapes normally employ densities of either 800 or 1,600 BPI, and seven-track tapes employ densities of 200, 556, or 800 characters per inch. Thus, a 1-inch record on a nine-track 800-BPI tape would contain 800 bytes, or 6,400 bits of data.

Data is written on digital tape in quantities of a fixed number of bytes or characters called *physical records.* Following each record is an *inter-record gap* (IRG), which is 0.6 inches on nine-track tapes and 0.75 inches on seven-track tapes. The length of each record is called the *blocksize,* which is simply the number of bytes in the record. Each block may be divided into a number of *logical records,* which are packed together within the record. The *record format* indicates the manner in which logical records are blocked in the record. Figure 7–3.1 illustrates the way in which data is written on magnetic tape.

Using the figures given above for the density and record-gap sizes, we can calculate the length of tape necessary to contain a specific quantity of data. These factors are summarized in the following formula,

$$\text{INCHES OF TAPE} = (\frac{\text{BLKSIZE}}{\text{DEN}} + \text{GAP}) * \text{NRECS}$$

where BLKSIZE is the number of bytes per physical record, DEN is the number of bytes per inch, GAP is the interrecord gap size, and NRECS is the number of records of data. For example, 20 records at 2,000 bytes per record at a density of 800 BPI would occupy 62 inches on a nine-track tape.

After all the data for a particular purpose is written onto a magnetic tape, it is followed by an *end-of-file* mark. Further data may then be written on

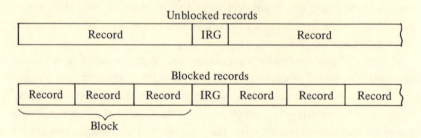

Figure 7–3.1: Recording of data on magnetic tape.

the tape following the end-of-file mark until the last file, which is indicated by a double end-of-file. Each end-of-file mark occupies 3.75 inches. Each quantity of data on a single file is called a *dataset*.

In order to calculate the maximum amount of data that may be written on an individual reel of tape we must, of course, know the length of the reel. Most digital tapes come in reels of 1,200 or 2,400 feet in length. From this amount we must subtract 30 feet from the tape to allow a 15-foot leader and trailer at the ends of the tape. The tape is not actually written along its entire length, but only between reflective indicators called beginning-of-tape and end-of-tape sensors. The reason for this is that since data is packed so densely along the length of tape, a speck of dust along the surface may be mistaken for a bit of data. Therefore, the portion of tape used to record data is never handled by the operator or exposed to the polluted air.

Magnetic digital tapes are *sequential access* devices, which means that data must be read or written one record at a time. In order to read a particular record from a magnetic tape, the tape must first be positioned at that particular record. This property makes it impossible to edit digital tapes by inserting a corrected record into the middle of the dataset; the entire tape must be copied up to and after the corrected record.

Magnetic disks, on the other hand, are *direct access* or *random access* devices, which means that any location on the disk may be accessed as rapidly as any other. A disk contains a number of round, flat, rotating cylindrical surfaces that are coated with magnetic oxide like the surface of a magnetic tape. These surfaces or "disks" are situated vertically with

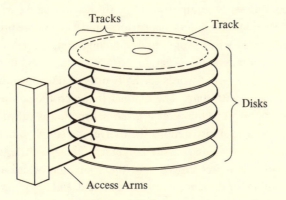

Figure 7–3.2: Physical configuration of a disk drive.

respect to one another. The disks are divided into many *tracks,* each defined
by the circumference of the recording surface. Related tracks are arranged
vertically with respect to one another. Data is read or written from the disks
by means of a number of access arms containing read-write heads. Any
track on the disk can be accessed in the time that the disk makes one
revolution and the access arms are positioned on the track. Figure 7–3.2
illustrates the physical configuration of a disk drive.

We will not cover the precise capacity of a disk or the manner in which
space is allocated on direct-access devices. These details vary from model
to model, and this information is readily available from computer manuals.
The data-transfer rates for disks are usually much faster than for tapes, but
the volume capacity of a tape is greater than a disk. Tapes are also conveniently dismounted and transported from place to place, whereas disks may
or may not be capable of being dismounted, and even when they can be
dismounted they are large and bulky. The essential difference between
magnetic tapes and disks is the access method.

4. Computer Instructions and Programming

In computer terminology, a *program* is a series of instructions to a
computer that causes it to perform a particular task. Writing the program
for a particular problem is a very important job, and much work has been
invested in discovering the most efficient procedures or algorithms for
solving specific problems. Since the program may be changed from run to
run, it is categorized under what is called the *software* of the computer; the
hardware comprises the equipment itself. In this section we will cover the
kinds of instructions computers can perform and some of the problems that
must be confronted when programming a computer.

In modern computers, the program that causes the computer to execute
its operations is a series of words (or halfwords or doublewords) stored in
the memory along with data. The manner in which the computer selects
which instruction to execute after a given instruction is called *instruction
sequencing.* The actual instructions themselves are simply binary numbers
that have a special meaning to the computer. Binary instructions in this
form constitute an *object program* to the computer, which requires no
special translation for the computer to understand. But object programs and
binary numbers in general are very difficult for human beings to understand,
and, therefore, the original program that is written for the computer is

written in a *source language,* whose terms are more easily comprehended, and *compiled* or *assembled* into the object language. The compilation itself is executed as a special program on the computer whose input consists of the statements in the source language and whose output is the object program. The normal manner in which a program is executed on the computer consists of three stages: *compilation,* in which the source program is translated into an object program; *link editing* and *loading,* in which the object program is loaded into the memory of the computer; and *execution,* in which control is transferred to the program in memory and the instructions are carried out. For the user, it is important to realize that errors may occur during any of these stages. Finding the errors in a program and making it execute properly is a process that has been dubbed *debugging* in "computerese."

A program may be broken down into several *subprograms,* each of which carries out a different part of the program's overall task. Execution begins in the *main program,* from which a subprogram may be *called.* A subprogram may also call other subprograms, and when the task of a subprogram is finished it *returns* to the program that called it.

Every computer has what is called an *operating system* or *supervisor,* which controls the compilation, loading, and execution of all programs that are run on the computer. The operating system takes over when the user's program is finished, and it simultaneously controls all operations being carried out on the computer. Sometimes the operating system can manage to allow several programs to be run simultaneously on the same computer through *multiprogramming.* Actually, only one program is executed at a time, proceeding until it makes an input-output interrupt, and then the system transfers control to another program while the input-output operation is carried out. Since all this happens so rapidly, the programs appear to be running simultaneously. *Systems programming,* which involves maintaining the operating system, is one of the most advanced levels of programming.

In a *batch-processing* operating system, jobs are read into the computer individually from a card reader or terminal and executed either one at a time or several at a time if the system allows multiprogramming. A *job* refers to a single stream of input run in this fashion. The output of the job is printed following its completion, and the user receives it later. Batch processing thus always involves a delay from the time the job is read into the computer and received by the programmer. The alternative to a batch-processing system is a *time-sharing* system, where several users are simultaneously connected to the computer through individual terminals, which create the illusion of each user working at his own minicomputer. Actually, the computer alternates processing between each user so quickly that he is usually unaware of the others. This switching between users occupies a significant portion of the computer's time, so that less overall computing is accomplished, although from the viewpoint of an individual user the response is immediate. It is important to note that the type of processing is determined by the operating system, although special hardware is required for each system. Some computers support both time sharing and batch processing simultaneously, and they may allow jobs to the batch-processing system to be input from the time-sharing terminals.

One of the amazing things about modern computers is that since the instructions to the computer are simply binary numbers stored in the memory, they can be operated on and altered just like any other data. The program has the capacity, therefore, of *altering itself* in order to adapt to appropriate conditions it encounters in the course of executing a program. One of the simple ways in which a program can alter itself is through the use of *branching instructions,* which are instructions that affect the instruction sequencing of the program. Normally, the computer takes its instructions sequentially out of adjacent locations in the memory. A branching instruction causes the computer to *jump* to some different location, either backward or forward. Often, the branching instruction may be dependent on a series of conditions that are established in the course of the program's execution. For example, the computer can test some data variable and branch to a special location only if it is a certain value. In this manner the computer is capable of making *conditional decisions.*

Perhaps the most common kinds of instructions that computers execute are concerned with *fixed-point arithmetic.* These instructions include not only the more familiar mathematical operations of addition, subtraction, multiplication, and division, but also instructions that transfer data between the registers in the CPU and memory. The normal manner in which a fixed-point instruction such as the addition of two numbers would be executed involves three operations: first, one of the numbers is loaded into a register from the memory; second, the other number is added to the register; and finally, the result is stored in a memory location. Fixed-point arithmetic normally applies only to integer variables (see section 2, above), although the numbers that are operated on in this manner may represent any symbolic quantity. Other instructions also considered part of the repertoire of fixed-point arithmetic include the comparison of two numbers, testing a number for whether it is positive, 0, or negative, or converting a number to a positive or negative form. (Shifting instructions will be covered below under "logical operations.") Fixed-point operations are normally carried out on full-word quantities, but they can also be carried out on bytes, halfwords, or doublewords.

Another group of instructions closely related to fixed-point arithmetic includes *floating-point arithmetic.* Floating-point arithmetic includes exactly the same operations as fixed-point arithmetic except that they are carried out for floating-point numbers instead of for integers. Normally floating-point numbers are full-word quantities. *Double precision* floating-point numbers are doubleword quantities. Sometimes the floating-point instructions are executed in special registers reserved for floating-point calculations, and sometimes they are carried out in the same registers as the fixed-point calculations. Usually the floating-point processor for a computer is a special option that must be purchased at extra cost. Almost all machines used for scientific purposes, however, are equipped for floating-point arithmetic.

Logical operations include a variety of instructions used for various purposes. What distinguishes logical quantities from arithmetic quantities is that logical quantities normally do not have a sign bit and do not represent positive or negative numbers but symbolic quantities. One category of logical operations is *shifting instructions.* A shifting instruction moves the number in a register to the right or to the left some number of bits. Vacated bits are filled with zeros unless the shift is circular, in which case bits shifted off of one end reappear at the other. An arithmetic shift, which is a shift instruction that does not change the sign bit, is equivalent to multiplication or division by a power of 2, and is often faster to execute than an integer-multiply or -divide instruction. A logical shift is often used to pack different quantities into a single word, or to position a number within a word.

Another category of logical operations is that of *Boolean operations,* which include the operations AND, OR, and exclusive OR. These operations are also called the logical product, logical sum, or modulo-two sum respectively. These operations are always carried out on pairs of bits. The logical product of two bits is 1 only if both are 1; it is 0 in all other cases. The logical sum is 1 if either is or both are 1; it is 0 only if both bits are 0. The modulo-two sum is 1 if either of the two bits is 1, but not if both are or neither is 1. These operations are used to test for the presence of bits in a number, to put them there or to change them under any of the circumstances above.

Other operations that are part of the instruction repertoire of a computer include input-output operations, conversions, and other special operations that we will not consider in detail in this book. For any operation on a computer, it occasionally happens that the user makes a mistake in his program and tells the computer to do something that it cannot do. Such an instruction causes an *exception* or *interruption* in the instruction sequencing of the program, and it either results in the program being terminated or some sort of standard error result being given for the operation. Usually this condition also causes an error message to be printed along with the user's output, but it occasionally does not, and when it does not the user must puzzle over incorrect results.

INTRODUCTION TO COMPUTER SOUND SYNTHESIS

5. Sampling and Quantizing

As we have see in Chapter 1, sound is the continuous displacement of particles in an elastic medium, or a continuous change in pressure in the air. The manner in which the pressure changes determines all of the characteristics of the sound. The pressure is transmitted to the air by a vibrating body, such as human vocal cords, the sounding board of a piano, or the diaphragm of a loudspeaker. Sound is perceived when the changing pressure in the air is sensed by the eardrum. Vibrations that are perceptible to the human ear as sounds begin from frequencies that are slightly too fast to hear as individual pulses and extend upward to approximately 16,000 cps, the upper limit varying considerably with the individual listener.

A graph of the manner in which the pressure in the air changes is called a *sound-pressure waveform,* and an example is illustrated in Figure 7–5.1. Represented in this form, sound has only two dimensions—*amplitude* and *time.*

Sounds are continuous changes in pressure, or *analog* signals, whereas computers are capable of handling only discrete numbers, or *digital* quantities, at a time. In order for a computer to deal with a sound, we must find a method of representing an analog signal in digital form. Such a method is provided by *sampling* the sound.

Sampling a sound is achieved by taking the *instantaneous amplitude* of

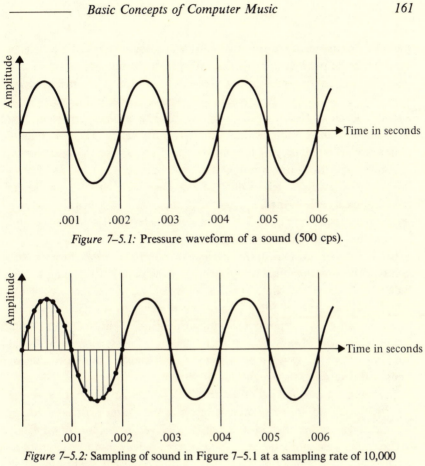

Figure 7–5.1: Pressure waveform of a sound (500 cps).

Figure 7–5.2: Sampling of sound in Figure 7–5.1 at a sampling rate of 10,000 samples per second.

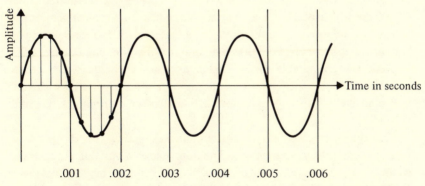

Figure 7–5.3: Sampling of sound in Figure 7–5.1 at a sampling rate of 5,000 samples per second.

the sound-pressure waveform at successive and equally spaced intervals of time. These amplitudes are called *samples,* and the number of samples in which we choose to represent one second of sound is called the *sampling rate.* Figure 7–5.2 illustrates sampling the sound shown in Figure 7–5.1 at a sampling rate of 10,000 samples per second. The resulting representation will thus contain 20 samples per cycle of this frequency. These individual numbers can thus represent the analog signal of 500 cps in digital form.

Figure 7–5.3 illustrates sampling the sound in Figure 7–5.1 at a sampling rate of 5,000 samples per second. In this case there are 10 samples to represent each cycle of the frequency of 500 cps, which is less accurate than the representation in Figure 7–5.2 but nevertheless still a reasonable approximation of the analog waveshape.

Each of the dimensions in the original sound-pressure waveform is contained in the sampling: time is represented by the sampling rate, and amplitude is represented by the magnitude of numbers or *quantization* of the samples. If the representation in these two dimensions is sufficiently accurate, a sound can be represented without perceptible distortion in digital form. There will always be a certain amount of distortion in a digital sampling of an analog waveform, and the limitations of these two dimensions will determine the magnitude of distortion.

The sampling rate and quantization which are actually used to represent a particular sound are more often a result of the characteristics of equipment available rather than ideal conditions. Nevertheless, it is not difficult to determine what minimum specifications are needed for musical purposes.

The minimum number of samples needed to represent a vibration of R cps is 2R samples. Thus, to provide a minimum representation of a sound of 15,000 cps a sampling rate of 30,000 samples per second is required. Since 15,000 cps is nearly the upper limit of human hearing for most people, this would be a minimum sampling rate for a system used to represent music. Actually, it is probably more than a minimum, for while sounds above 8,000 or 9,000 cps are audible to the human ear, they are seldom regarded as essential characteristics of music and are more often associated with such things as clicking of fingers against keys and other by-products of sound production.

The other approximation used in sampling a sound wave is the quantization of the amplitude dimension. The numbers used for this purpose can contain only a limited number of digits, or actually binary bits inside computers. In order to determine what limitations are necessary in this dimension, we must know how much distortion is present, or what the *signal-to-noise ratio* is, in a given numerical representation. The approximate signal-to-noise ratio inherent in a given number of digits equals the maximum number expressible with the digits divided by the maximum error in representing any number. For example, with two decimal digits the maximum number expressible is 99 and the maximum error is .5. $\frac{99}{.5}$ equals approximately 200. The relationship between this number and decibels is shown by the formula

$$dB = 20 \log_{10} amp.$$

Thus, 200 "amplitude units" equals approximately 46 dB. Three decimal digits would correspond to a signal-to-noise ratio of $\frac{999}{.5}$, or approximately 66 dB. Since computers use binary numbers, it is also helpful to know the figures for various binary numbers. Ten bits can represent decimal numbers from 0 to 1,023, or approximately 66 dB as above; twelve bits provide a signal-to-noise ratio of 78 dB; fifteen bits provide about 93 dB.

Since most analog tape recorders are not capable of recording sound with a signal-to-noise ratio greater than approximately 60 dB, it would appear that ten bits would be sufficient. Actually, this is not so, for this figure represents the signal-to-noise ratio for a single sound only, and most musical passages contain many sounds. Furthermore, since it would represent a loss of signal quality, it is undesirable to use less than 60 dB for the softest passage in a musical composition. Therefore, this quantization level of approximately 1,000 amplitude units would be the minimum amplitude level used. Fifteen or sixteen bits is a standard quantization figure used today, and twelve bits is considered a minimum.

To summarize, the sound-pressure waveform can be envisioned as being projected onto a grid of a limited number of points, in which the actual values of the waveform are plotted in terms of two co-ordinates, one representing time and the other amplitude. The terms in which these dimensions are measured are the sampling rate and levels of quantization, and the accuracy of representation depends upon the magnitude of these two dimensions. For musical purposes, a sampling rate of 30,000 samples per second and an amplitude quantization of fifteen bits is sufficient.

6. Digital-to-Analog Conversion; Smoothing Filters; Analog-to-Digital Conversion

Digital-to-analog conversion is the process of transforming a sequence of digital samples into an analog signal. This process is carried out by a device called a digital-to-analog converter (abbreviated DAC). Fortunately, this process is easily carried out, and a variety of commercial equipment is available.

While a DAC is a normal output device of a computer, not all computers have DACs, for they are always extra, optional features. Unlike other output devices, DACs must operate in real time and cannot be interrupted at will by the system. For this reason, the programming for a DAC is very complicated, and it is not always feasible to attach a DAC to any computer. Often, the computations that generate a tape for conversion to sound by a DAC are carried out by a large general-purpose computer, and the DAC itself is attached to a small special-purpose computer that is not costly to tie up for long periods of time. In other circumstances, the same computer is used for both processes. It is also possible to construct a digital-to-analog conversion system *off line,* not involving any computer but simply a digital tape drive, controller, and buffer, along with the smoothing filters and other hardware discussed below. Such a system has to be designed and constructed specially, however.

One of the difficulties in programming the operation of a DAC has to do with the manner in which digital data is stored on magnetic tapes or disks, which is in quantities of bytes called physical records, separated by record gaps. The difficulty is that while there are gaps on the digital tape, there are not supposed to be any gaps in the music. In order to eliminate the gaps, the records are read from the digital tape into two *buffers* in the computer's memory. Samples are converted continuously out of one buffer until it is empty, and then out of the other. While samples are being converted from the second buffer, the next record off the digital tape is read into the first buffer. When the second buffer is empty the computer switches instantly to the first buffer and refills the second buffer at the same time.[4]

Since the highest frequency that can be generated at a sampling rate SR is ½SR,[5] no frequencies higher than this value can actually be part of the signal being converted into sound by a DAC. Such frequencies are often produced as a by-product of the switching elements within the converter. While these switching transients can be eliminated or improved in various ways, their elimination is never completely assured. For this reason, the

[4]Some converting programs may use only one buffer or more than two, but we will not consider these details here.

[5]The frequency of ½SR is also called the *Nyquist frequency.*

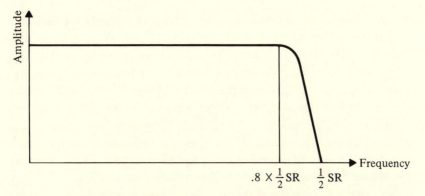

Figure 7–6.1: Frequency response for smoothing filter.

output of the DAC is processed by a *smoothing filter* before it is recorded on analog tape. The smoothing filter is simply a low-pass filter that has a very steep slope and that cuts off at ½SR. The frequency-response curve for a typical smoothing filter for a DAC system is illustrated in Figure 7–6.1. Ideally, all frequencies below ½SR would be passed uniformly and those above would be rejected completely. In practice it is not possible to achieve these conditions, so the cutoff slope generally begins at about 80 or 90 per cent of ½SR.

An entire system for digital-to-analog conversion is illustrated in Figure 7–6.2. The components consist of a digital magnetic tape or other high-speed input-output device, a computer or special-purpose buffer, the digital-to-analog converter, smoothing filter, and analog tape recorder.

Sometimes there are additional components in the DAC system. Often the sampling rate is set by an external oscillator that is extremely stable and easily controlled. Sometimes the sampling rate is set by an internal clock that is part of the computer and that cannot be manipulated except by programming. Sometimes an oscilloscope is attached to the system to provide visual display of the signals generated. Finally, there are always ear-

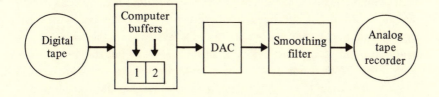

Figure 7–6.2: Digital-to-analog conversion system.

phones or loudspeakers enabling the operator to monitor the signal as it is generated by the DAC.

One fact that should be apparent from our discussion of digital-to-analog conversion is that, while the process of conversion to sound takes place in real time, the process that generates the digital tape does not have to take place in real time. Usually this process takes a greater amount of time than the duration of the music itself, although there is no fixed relationship between these two time scales, for the amount of computer time that it takes to generate the music depends entirely upon the complexity of the music at every point. What is apparent is that the conversion process takes only a short amount of time, and that the digital tape must be prepared in its entirety before conversion can begin. The composer, therefore, does not spend much time at all actually operating the computer, or rather the tape recorder at the end of the conversion process. (Usually there are special operators who run the computer.) Most time is spent in preparing the input to the program that generates the digital tape, and there is a considerable delay between the time that the piece is conceived and the time it is converted to sound and heard. There is no way of eliminating some of this delay as long as this method of sound production is employed. Therefore, it is impossible to carry out improvisation or other spur-of-the-moment procedures using the computer in this manner. In Chapter 9 we will discuss another application of computers to electronic music when we consider the computer control of analog sound-generating and -processing equipment. While that application operates in real time and provides instantaneous response to the composer's directions, it involves a totally different kind of computer and associated peripheral equipment.

Analog-to-digital converters (abbreviated ADCs) are input devices to computers that sample an analog signal and produce digital output which can then be written on digital tape or another storage medium. ADCs are used for a variety of purposes having to do with music. One application involves creating digital tapes of known analog signals in order to analyze their components by a computer. Another application is the production of digital recordings of live signals to be processed or combined with other signals generated by the computer. An ADC system uses the same components as the DAC system illustrated in Figure 7–6.2, but the path of flow from device to device is exactly the reverse: smoothing filters are applied to the signals from the analog tape recorder before they are transmitted to the ADC, etc. Because of design complications, ADCs usually contain fewer quantization bits than DACs.

7. Foldover

Since it requires a minimum of two samples to produce a vibration, the highest frequency that can be produced at a given sampling rate SR is ½SR. At a sampling rate of 10,000 samples per second, the highest frequency would be 5,000 CPS. What happens when we attempt to generate a frequency higher than ½SR?

Figure 7–7.1 illustrates a frequency of 15,000 CPS, which is shown on a time scale indicating ten thousandths of a second, the points at which samples could be generated at SR = 10,000. Each of the appropriate amplitudes for the frequency of 15,000 cps is generated, but the result is not 15,000 cycles, but 5,000 cps as illustrated. These two frequencies happen to coincide exactly at the points where samples are generated at a sampling rate of 10,000 samples per second.

Whenever we attempt to generate a frequency higher than ½SR, the resulting frequency is "folded over" at ½SR. The formula showing the foldover frequency is,

$$FOLD = SR - F$$

where F is the frequency we attempt to generate. To understand this formula it is necessary to realize that negative frequencies are identical to positive frequencies except that they are 180 degrees out of phase, and that

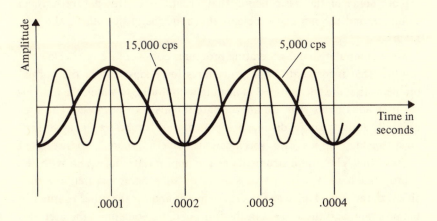

Figure 7–7.1: Attempting to generate a frequency of 15,000 cps at SR = 10,000. The resulting frequency is "folded over" at ½ SR producing a frequency of 5,000 cps.

foldover also occurs at multiples of the sampling rate, so that when the formula yields a result like − 16,000 cps this needs to be corrected to 4,000 cps by adding multiples of SR.

Foldover tends to occur unexpectedly when tones containing harmonic partials higher than ½SR are generated. For example, if we generate a tone of 1,500 cps with four harmonic partials at a sampling rate of 10,000 samples per second, the fourth partial should be 6,000 cps. However, it will be folded over to 4,000 cps, and this tone is no longer harmonically related to the fundamental frequency of 1,500 cps. Once foldover frequencies are present in a signal, it is impossible to remove them by filtering, so the only way of avoiding this problem is not to produce them in the first place. On the other hand, it is possible to use foldover to produce frequency shifting if this effect is desired.

8. Basic Programming Concepts for Computer Music

At the center of the method of sound generation by means of a digital computer is a program that produces the samples that are later converted to sound. Many different kinds of programs have already been written by different people for different purposes, and there is a very wide range of variation that encompasses the purposes and viewpoints of the people that have been drawn to this medium. It will be our purpose in this section to explore some of the basic points that programs of this nature have in common, and the musical problems that must be dealt with by the programs.

Most computer sound-generating programs consist of a large package of routines that incorporate basic procedures for almost any of the normal problems that are encountered in dealing with music, to which the individual user adds items that are appropriate for his own purposes. The user generally adds two quite distinct components: an "orchestra," consisting of "instruments" of his own specifications; and a "score," consisting of "notes" that play the instruments at the appropriate times and with the appropriate data. The orchestra is usually a subprogram written in a suitable programming language for the computer and for the other routines in the program, and the score is in the form of data. Sometimes the user also adds additional subprograms for various purposes. Sometimes the orchestra itself is in the form of data, as the score.

Usually it is unnecessary for the user to have more than a vague notion of the internal workings of the program, but it is essential that he understand a few points about its broad outlines. The input that the user prepares in his score is normally expressed numerically in terms more meaningful to a musician than to a computer. Before the data can be used by the instruments various conversions must take place: time values must be converted from beats to seconds, notes must be arranged chronologically, etc. These conversions are accomplished by making various "passes" over the score. Each pass processes all of the data and transmits its results to the next pass by means of a scratch file. (A *scratch file* is a dataset used during the execution of the program but not saved afterward.)

The actual operation of a computer sound-generating program is discussed in detail in Chapter 8. All of these programs must provide some way of dealing with the same basic problems, however. One problem concerns the form in which the user is required to express his input. Most programs allow the user to provide his input in several ways that are meaningful and intuitive as a description of the music to be generated. Before the sound is actually generated, however, the input must be translated into the form required by the computer. One pass of the program, therefore, may be devoted to reading the input, and another to preparing it for the computer. A third pass will then be used to generate the music, and a fourth or fifth pass to process the music after it has been generated. This processing may include features such as rescaling the output or displaying the samples generated in graphic or numerical form.

The user's orchestra is the subprogram that actually generates the samples that represent the music. The instruments in the orchestra are assembled from *unit generators,* which are subprograms or procedures that simulate electronic signal-generating and -processing devices like those found in an electronic music studio. The unit generators incorporate a wide variety of mathematical algorithms for sample generation that free the user from worrying about the messy details of defining his music in this fashion. They enable the user to specify music roughly in terms of the perceptible characteristics he would like the sound to contain. Each unit generator controls a separate aspect of the sound generated by the instrument. For most purposes, the user does not need to know or understand the mathematical algorithms that the unit generators employ. Rather, he needs to have some concrete idea about the relationship between his specifications and the sounds themselves; in other words, he must know what his specifications "sound like."

In general, there are no restrictions as to the number of unit generators available in a particular orchestra. Exceptions to this principle include unit generators that require a significant amount of storage. In practice it is common to have hundreds or even thousands of unit generators in an orchestra, all operating independently and with complete precision. There are also no restrictions on the rhythm in which the instruments can be played. This means that complete compositions of any rhythmic complexity can be generated at one time, without any additional mixing or rerecording.

The note concept and the unit-generator concept require the user to be absolutely precise with respect to all of the details of the sound qualities in his music. While this is not so unusual for composers who have had some experience with electronic music, it is generally more difficult for composers whose prior experience was restricted to instrumental composition. Many details must be specified that these composers have come to take for granted in instrumental composition, and the terms in which the sounds themselves are described involve new concepts. This is one of the sacrifices made in order to achieve the advantage of complete control over all aspects of the music. Computer sound synthesis is a medium for obtaining what you specify; you get all and only that. At least, one is always in the position of knowing what one has, whether or not that was what one wanted.

9. Sampling of Stored Functions

In computer music there may often be many functions, used frequently in the course of a composition, that are periodic in nature. Often the computation of these functions would be extremely time-consuming if they had to be recomputed on each cycle. In order to avoid this circumstance, one cycle of such a function is computed only once and stored in a table of values for subsequent reference. It is then called a *stored function,* and is used in the manner described below.

A stored function is a table of numbers with values between −1.0 and +1.0 that are stored in successive locations in the computer. For historical reasons, 512 locations have been used for stored functions, a convienient number for many purposes. (Note that 512 is a power of 2.) The fact that the values in the function range between −1.0 and +1.0 insures that when they are all multiplied by a constant their absolute values will range from 0 to the constant.

For example, suppose that the values in the function represent a sampling of one cycle of a sine wave. If an instrument plays each successive value of this function on successive samples, the result will be one cycle of a certain frequency. Since there will be 512 samples per cycle, the frequency will be $\frac{SR}{512}$, or approximately 19.5 cps at a sampling rate of 10,000 samples per second. If we return to the first location in the function after the last, we can obtain a periodic wave form, or a steady tone, in this manner.

Let us suppose that we want to obtain some frequency other than 19.5 cps by using the same function. We could obtain a frequency of approximately 39 cps (at a sampling rate of 10,000 samples per second) by taking every second location in the function. But in order to obtain a frequency between 19.5 and 39 cps, we would have to take values between two successive locations in the function.

Let us introduce some terminology to describe the process of sampling a stored function: the *phase* (abbreviated PHS) is the location in the function that is taken on a given sample. The *sampling increment* (SI) is a value that, when added to the phase, tells which location to take next. In addition, there is an *amplitude* (AMP) by which the value in the function is multiplied after it has been selected. For continuous sampling, the phase is determined by adding the sampling increment *modulo 512*. (*Modulo 512* means that when the phase exceeds 512, it is reduced by subtracting 512 until the result is within the range 0 to 511.) In this manner, each of the 512 locations in the function is referred to by an integer between 0 and 511 inclusive.

Let us assume that we want to obtain a frequency of approximately 29 cps (halfway between 19 and 39 cps) at a sampling rate of 10,000 samples per second. The sampling increment for this frequency is 1.5 (halfway between 1 and 2). If we begin sampling the function at its first location (location 0), the next location is supposed to be 1.5. Confronted with this circumstance, there are three alternatives: we can *truncate* the fractional part of the phase; we can *round off* the phase to the nearest location; or we can make a linear *interpolation* between the two adjacent locations in the function. In all of these cases we nevertheless preserve the correct fractional value of the phase so that the next time the sampling increment is added to it the result will be 3.0. In practical situations, the amount of error produced when generating a frequency by sampling a stored function is nearly the same for both truncation and rounding off. Interpolating is much more accurate, but it is more costly in computer time.

When we adopt one of the above alternatives, we can generate any frequency up to ½SR by sampling a stored function. In order to compute the sampling increment for a particular frequency, the formula

$$SI = \frac{cps * 512}{SR}$$

may be used.

It is important to recognize that the process of sampling a stored function employs the same principle of sampling that was described above when considering the way in which an analog signal is represented in digital form. (See section 5.) The difference between these situations is that the stored function is already in digital form, whereas when we sample an analog signal the signal is in analog form. Therefore, the fewer locations used to represent the frequency produced by sampling the stored function, the more inaccurate the result.

Stored functions may be used to represent any periodic function, and they may be applied to any characteristic of a sound. For example, a straight-line function can be used to control amplitude and produce a crescendo or diminuendo. In this situation the sampling increment used to determine subsequent locations in the function represents *duration* instead of frequency in order that the crescendo be applied once over the course of a note. The relationship between duration and frequency is shown by the formula

$$DUR = \frac{1}{FREQ}$$

so that, for example, the duration of one cycle of a frequency of 500 cps is $\frac{1}{500}$ second. Thus, a sampling increment representing duration is given by the formula

$$SI = \frac{512/SR}{DUR}.$$

Since stored functions are tables of numbers, they can also be used to contain nonperiodic functions, or simply any abstract tables used for a variety of purposes. Many of the unit generators described in Chapter 8 make use of stored functions in a number of different ways.

For some purposes, the standard function length of 512 locations is inconvenient. Nevertheless, it is complicated to establish programming conventions for stored functions of variable sizes. Since this may be a feature that some users would desire, it is important to understand all of the items in the MUSIC4BF program (see Chapter 8) that must be altered to accommodate it. Not only must all the unit generators be changed to locate the function they use in some other manner; all of the GEN subroutines that store the functions must be similarly revised, and the format of F cards must be changed. All units that compute sampling increments must be changed to take the function length into account.

10. Samples out of Range; Rescaling

With a digital-to-analog converter of n bits, the highest absolute amplitude level that may be specified is $2^{n-1} - 1$. If n equals 16, the highest level is $2^{15} - 1$, or 32,767. The reason there is apparently one less bit available than the converter contains is that one bit functions as a *sign* bit, and the amplitudes vary from $-32,767$ to $+32,767$.

Some sound-synthesizing programs convert samples to integer form as soon as they are computed and write them on the digital tape. When this occurs, any samples greater than the highest permissable amplitude level are *out of range*, and only the lower n significant bits are retained on the tape. Samples out of range produce discontinuities on the analog tape, as illustrated on Figure 7–10.1,[6] and they may ruin an otherwise perfect synthesis of a composition.

In order to obtain the maximum possible signal-to-noise ratio for a sound,

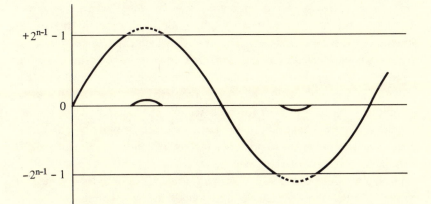

Figure 7–10.1: A sample out of range retains only the lower n significant bits (where n is the number of bits in the converter), producing a discontinuity in the analog signal.

[6]Not all converters produce the discontinuities shown in Figure 7–10.1 when samples are out of range. Sometimes the out-of-range portion appears at the opposite extreme rather than at 0.

it is necessary to make the maximum amplitude come *as close as possible* to the maximum permitted with the converter, but *not greater* than this maximum. The maximum amplitude level of a musical composition quite naturally occurs at the loudest point in the piece, but note that the statement above refers not to the *signal level* of the sounds but to the *signal-to-noise ratio;* the signal level is determined by the volume setting on the preamplifier of the tape recorder which records the sounds as they are converted and later, of course, by the speaker amplifiers and playback conditions. Using the greatest possible number of values within the setting of a given signal level insures the greatest resolution within this level.

One can never be exactly certain what the maximum amplitude of a musical composition will be until the entire composition has been computed. This value depends on all the complex interferences between the components of the sounds as they vary with time, and often the result will be different if only the sampling rate is changed.

The samples computed by a sound-synthesizing program are almost always calculated with greater precision than they are ultimately written out with. It is indeed shortsighted to lose this extra precision before it is clear whether or not this is significant in the present context.

The solution to these problems is to *store all the samples* of the sound wave, as they are computed, on an *intermediate tape* and to *rescale* the contents of this tape to the correct amplitude level, once the maximum achieved on this tape is known. The tape on which the rescaled output is written is now referred to as the *final tape*. In case a composition is computed in several separate runs, each of the intermediate tapes must be saved until the entire composition has been completed in order that the same maximum amplitude is used for each section of the piece. Since storing samples on intermediate tapes takes twice as much or more space as final tapes, it is often necessary to provide a method of continuing the intermediate tape on a second or third reel.

When a rescaling process such as this is used, all amplitudes specified by the user during the synthesis of the sounds are simply relative to one another and have no absolute significance except in relation to the maximum achieved. The input amplitude levels can therefore be of any magnitude with no loss of significance in the output.

Rescaling the output thus solves two problems simultaneously: it eliminates any samples out of range, and it insures the maximum signal-to-noise ratio for a musical composition.

CHAPTER EIGHT

Detailed Description of a Computer Sound-Generating Program: MUSIC4BF

1. INTRODUCTION

In this chapter, we are going to consider a sound-synthesizing program, MUSIC4BF, in detail. Our main reason for choosing this program is that it is written entirely in Fortran, which is not only a very simple language to learn, but also is capable of being run on nearly any large general-purpose computer that the reader is likely to have available. Most of our discussion will be written in such a way that it will not require any previous knowledge of computer programming other than materials presented in this book. Parts of our discussion will assume a working knowledge of Fortran, which can be learned from any of a number of manuals or books available, or from a basic-level course in computer science. When a knowledge of Fortran is assumed, this fact will be indicated in the text by the symbol [*].

It hardly needs to be pointed out that neither this chapter nor this book will discuss all aspects of a program such as MUSIC4BF. This chapter specifically omits details more appropriate for a publication such as a reference manual. However, by covering MUSIC4BF in the manner that we do, we can gain much insight and understanding of the operation of any sound-synthesizing program. We will review the objectives and operating principles of all of the more important aspects of the program. Users will learn how to employ these characteristics to suit their own purposes. Computer programming is, after all, a method of adapting the computer's resources to satisfy individual needs.

One point must be made about the operation of MUSIC4BF and other sound-synthesizing programs that are generally run on large computers rather than on minicomputers and hybrid systems: these programs synthesize the entire content of a sound wave and produce a digital tape that is then converted to sound through a digital-to-analog conversion system such as that described in Chapter 7. (See Figure 7–6.2.) No other special-purpose analog or digital equipment is employed. The computer is not used to control analog or digital equipment in any of the manners described as "Hybrid Systems" in Chapter 9.

The MUSIC4BF program is an outgrowth of several other programs that have had a long history of use by many different composers employing a wide variety of compositional styles and approaches. This development is still continuing today, and there are presently many different programs that have been written subsequently to MUSIC4BF and that have expanded its resources in a number of ways. This type of development will always continue, and years from now we may have a totally different view of these programs.

MUSIC4BF is a direct descendant of MUSIC4, a program written for the IBM 7094 by Max V. Mathews and Joan E. Miller of Bell Telephone Laboratories. MUSIC4 was itself a descendant of three other MUSIC programs that changed and evolved over several years and with many different computers.[1]

MUSIC4 was expanded into a new program called MUSIC4B by Godfrey Winham and myself during 1964 and 1965. While this program also employed the same computer and basic structure of MUSIC4, its resources were greatly expanded, and the program was simplified and made more intelligible and intuitive for musicians.

At this point in history, the IBM Corporation introduced what has been called the "third generation" of computers with its System/360 series of computers. MUSIC4 and MUSIC4B had been machine dependent on the IBM 7094, and could not easily be adapted to the new computers. In order not to be upset by any subsequent generation of computers as well as to be able to run the program on the System/360, MUSIC4B was translated entirely into Fortran.[2] The first version of MUSIC4BF was written by me

[1] In James Tenney's article, "Sound Generation by Means of a Digital Computer," *Journal of Music Theory,* VII/1 (1963), 24–70, reference is made to MUSIC3, the predecessor of MUSIC4.

[2] The first all-Fortran computer music program was MUSIC4F, written by Arthur Roberts. (Arthur Roberts, "MUSIC4F, an All-Fortran Music-Generating Computer Program," paper presented at the seventeenth annual meeting of the Audio Engineering Society, October 11–15, 1965, preprint no. 397.)

in 1966 and 1967, but this program has been altered and expanded further by Godfrey Winham and myself into the form in which it is presented in this book. Since that time, other people have introduced more modifications, and this work continues today.

At the present time, many different programs have been written and are available at many installations across the country. MUSIC4 has been replaced by MUSIC5 at Bell Telephone Laboratories.[3] Several new machine-dependent programs have been written, which are, in many ways, simpler to use and certainly more efficient in execution than programs in Fortran or any symbolic computer language. The most well known of these programs are MUSIC7,[4] a program for the XDS Sigma-7 computer by me, and MUSIC360,[5] for the IBM System/360 computer by Barry L. Vercoe.

MUSIC4BF is designed to be run on a large general-purpose computer under a batch-processing operating system. It normally requires a moderately large amount of computer memory during execution and it may require a great amount of computer time. The amount of time required is completely dependent on the complexity of the music generated, and it is, therefore, meaningless to talk about the ratio of the duration of music generated to the length of time required.

At the present time, MUSIC4BF has been adapted to the following computers: the IBM System/360, models 30,[6] 40, 44, 50, 65, or 91; the CDC 6400, 6500, or 6600; and the XDS Sigma-7 or Sigma-5. Other computer manufacturers certainly make computers on which MUSIC4BF could be run, but the programming has not yet been done.

MUSIC4BF consists of a large number of subprograms to which the user must add two distinct parts: an *orchestra* consisting of *instruments* of his own specifications; and a *score* consisting of *notes* that play the instruments at the appropriate times and with the appropriate data. A very basic decision about the structure of the program was made (in MUSIC4) concerning this organization. Other programs may require the user to enter his notes in the form of a program, or to enter his instruments in the form of data.

---

[3]This program is described by Max Mathews in his book *The Technology of Computer Music* (Cambridge, Mass., 1969).

[4]MUSIC7 and MUSIC4BF are available from me.

[5]MUSIC360 is available from Barry L. Vercoe, Department of Music, Massachusetts Institute of Technology, Cambridge, Mass.

[6]The version for the 360/30 is a much-abbreviated and very restricted program, and is not the same as those for the other models.

The instruments in the user's orchestra are analogous to "instruments" assembled with an electronic music synthesizer: they are made up of distinct components called *unit generators* or *units,* which perform the same function as the signal and control generating and processing equipment of an electronic music synthesizer. One of the advantages of allowing the user to enter his instruments in the form of a program is that, with a few exceptions, the "equipment" is virtually unlimited with respect to the number of units available and the manner in which they may be assembled. Most units may be used interchangeably to generate or process what would be regarded as audio signals or control voltages on analog equipment. Notes in the score provide timing information and other data, and thereby produce what is analogous to timing pulses or triggers on analog systems. The user's orchestra program defines the unit generators used in the instruments, how they are assembled or "patched" together, and the correspondence between the instruments and the variable data in the score. Instruments normally have some characteristics that are fixed or the same for each note, and some characteristics that are variable, that must be entered into the instrument from each "note card" in the score.

The user's score consists primarily of two kinds of input statements: *notes* and *functions.* The notes, of course, are analogous to what we would regard as the notes in a musical score written out in conventional musical notation. In fact, the way in which MUSIC4BF separates the functions of the orchestra and the score is by analogy with live music, in which a series of instructions is presented to performers, whose instruments possess capabilities more or less well defined, at least by orchestration textbooks. The notes that make up the computer composer's score may be organized in many different ways from the notes in a conventional score, however. For one thing, we may distinguish between the "micronote level" and the "macronote level" as described in Chapter 4 (see page 70). More importantly, the sonic characteristics produced by the computer instruments are not restricted by the same limitations that live instruments have, so that the materials in the user's score may denote musical qualities for which there are no standard symbols in musical notation. For this reason, all data in the user's score are presented in numerical form. Several problems that may arise when translating a musical score into computer input are discussed in detail below.

Functions are tables of numbers used by the instruments in calculating the music the composer specifies. Functions usually are *sampled* according to the processes described in Chapter 7 (see section 7.9), although in other cases functions may be used simply as tables. The function statements in the score are used to define the characteristics of the functions needed by the orchestra, and they must be generated or *stored* before any actual reference to them is made by an instrument. Functions control many different musical characteristics, especially waveshapes and amplitude variation specifications, and functions may actually be used to control *any* musical characteristic.

Several other statements are included in the score to simplify the organization of the notes and functions. The score may be divided into several contiguous sections that reduce the amount of material in each portion. The tempo may be set so that all times may be transcribed in beats rather than in seconds. The notes may be stored so that they can be modified or extended by optional subprograms.

Most large batch-processing computer installations employ punched cards for input, and for this reason the individual statements on both the orchestra and score are referred to as *cards,* sometimes with further qualifications—e.g., "note cards" or "function cards." Over the next several years, this situation may change so that the input to computers will be prepared at individual teletype consoles or terminals. Nevertheless, the single statements produced at these devices have the same functions as the single cards produced at keypunches, so that the same terminology can be used.

The MUSIC4BF program makes three *passes* over the score. Pass 1 reads and prints the score, providing a record of the input data. The user may actually generate or modify his score by means of optional subprograms during this pass; in other words, he may use the computer to "compose" his music during this pass. In this case the Pass-1 score will contain only functions and a few cards that direct the subprograms to compose the music. The actual notes that the computer determines will be printed out in full during Pass 2, the next pass.

Pass 2 takes the score in the form that Pass 1 has left it and prepares it for the synthesis of the music, which takes place during Pass 3. First, all of the notes and functions are sorted into chronological order. This means that the Pass-1 input may appear in any order. Pass 2 may also convert time values from *beats* into *seconds,* or *rescale* a series of input values to an indicated maximum level. Pass 2 may also call additional optional subprograms to perform further modifications upon the score. These modifications normally occur at this point only when they must be performed upon the sorted score; easier modifications may be made during Pass 1. Finally, the revised score is *printed,* showing all modifications made by Pass 2.

Pass 3 now reads the score and calls the user's orchestra to generate the music specified. Pass 3 prints a record of the performance, showing the maximum amplitude reached during each time segment of the music and other features. Only Pass 3 requires a significant amount of computer time.

2. THE SCORE

When the computer is ready to begin to generate the samples that represent a piece of electronic music (i.e., ready for Pass 3), the score must be organized in only one manner: all elements in the score must be represented as numbers (actually single-precision floating-point numbers); the notes and functions must be arranged in chronological order; and there must be special indications for the ends of sections and the end of the entire score. Notes are different from functions in that they have durations as well as starting times, and in the final score separate entries are made for the beginning time and the ending time of the notes. (The ending-time indications are not printed in the Pass-2 listing of the score.) It would be possible for the composer to prepare the score in this form himself, and in certain simple cases it may actually not be difficult. All Pass-1 and Pass-2 processing is concerned with simplifying the preparation of the score by the composer. As we discuss these features, it is important to keep this ultimate form of the score in mind, in order that we perceive the purpose of each individual feature.

Input Format

Almost all input to large batch-processing computers today is in the form of eighty-column punched cards. It is customary to use only columns 1 through 72 for data and columns 73 through 80 for identification or sequence numbering. These seventy-two columns are organized as follows for MUSIC4BF score cards:

Column 1 is the *operation field* or *OP field* and contains an *OP symbol*, which is one of the letters I, F, S, E, T, R, B, A, N, or C. A card with I in column 1 is called an I card, and similarly for the other letters.

Columns 2 and 3 constitute the *first parameter field* or *P(1) field*.

Columns 4 through 6 constitute the *NUM field* and may contain a *storage number*.

Columns 7 through 12, 13 through 18, . . . 67 through 72 constitute the

P(2), P(3), . . . P(12) fields respectively; thus, except for P(1), each *P field* P(*n*) occupies six columns ending with column (6 $\times$ *n*).

Columns 73 through 80 are ignored, except that they are printed along with the rest of the card.

Each card may thus contain one operation and up to twelve parameters. When more than twelve parameters associated with a given card are desired, a *continuation card* may be placed after a card with an OP symbol in column 1, which is now called the *header card* of a *block.* The format of continuation cards is the same as that for header cards, except that columns 1 through 6 are now treated as a single six-column field as P(2) through P(12) on the header card. This field is referred to as P(13), and the next as P(14), . . . P(24). Most score cards may be followed by several continuation cards (up to forty), and the "P field" designations increase with each successive card: the third card contains P(25) through P(36), the fourth P(37) through P(48), etc. The entire group of cards beginning with an I card and followed by its continuations is called an *I block,* and similar names are used for the other OP symbols.

The format in which individual P fields are read is referred to as "F6.0" format in Fortran, except for P(1) and the NUM field, which are, respectively, "F2.0" and "I3." This means that each field may be entirely blank or contain numbers, with or without signs; plus signs are permitted, but unnecessary. Since all P fields contain floating-point numbers, decimal points are supplied following the last column of the field, unless they appear within it. Blanks within the field are treated as zeros. This means that, when there is no decimal point, the numbers should be *right aligned* within the field. For example, if the punches representing the number 123 are contained in columns 10, 11, and 12 of a score card, the program will interpret this value as 123.0 in P(2) of the card. If the same punches occur in columns 11, 12, and 13, however, then P(2) will be interpreted as 12.0 and P(3) as 300,000.

The NUM field is read as a three-digit integer, which means that it must either be blank or contain a positive number with no decimal point. Right-alignment is necessary for the same reason as in P fields. (The number must be positive because it is used to refer to a storage location.)

In order to simplify the process of preparing note cards, *blank fields* occuring in the first five cards of an *I block* (i.e., note card) are given a special meaning. When a blank field occurs on a card in this situation, it *"carries"* from (i.e., is given the same value as) the corresponding P field in the previous I block, provided that P(1), which designates the instrument number, is the same as the previous P(1) (or blank, in which case it carries in the same way as other P fields), and that no card with a different OP symbol intervenes between the present block and the one from which it carries. Thus, when all of the notes for an individual instrument are placed together in the score, values on these cards need to be indicated only on the *first card* or when they *change* from the previous value. Note that the *order of cards* determines the manner in which the values carry, but that this order has no particular relation to the *chronological order* of notes in the score. (See Figure 8–2.1.)

The Pass-1 printing of the score shows the effect of the carry feature, so that it is not identical to a listing of the cards. Also, note that the carry feature affects only the first five cards, P(1) through P(60), and that it affects only I cards.

[*] When a *storage number* is placed in the NUM field of a score card, the card is not "executed" or written on the scratch file for Pass 2, but it is stored in a series of locations referred to by NUM. A code designating the OP symbol is stored in STOP (NUM), and the P fields P(1) to P(12) are stored in STP(1,NUM) to STP(12,NUM) respectively. Continuation cards following the header card are automatically stored at locations designated by NUM + 1, NUM + 2, etc. Cards are stored in order to be modified by optional subprograms, and it is the user's responsibility to "execute" them after all the appropriate modifications have been made.

Since P(1) and NUM are only two and three columns in length respectively, the highest decimal number that they can contain is 99 and 999. These limitations are used directly to determine the maximum numbers of various quantities in the program. P(1) on I cards determines the instru-

I	1	50	2.6	14	8.09	7	.025
I		0	1.1		7.06	2	
I		15	9		10.01		.005
I	1	50	2.6	14	8.09	7	.025
I	1	0	1.1	14	7.06	2	.025
I	1	15	9	14	10.01	2	.005

Figure 8–2.1: The carry feature. When notes for the same instrument are placed together in the score, values "carry" from the previous card into blank fields on subsequent cards. The three cards above indicate the form in which the user has prepared them; the following listing indicates the form in which the program interprets them according to the carry feature.

ment number; therefore, a maximum of 99 instruments may be used in an orchestra. NUM determines the storage number; therefore, a maximum of 999 notes may be used in an individual section. (In the "short" version of MUSIC4BF, this limitation is reduced to 500 notes.)

Note Cards

Score cards with I in column 1 are called *note cards* or *I cards*. Each I card contains the values of certain parameters used by the instrument that plays this note in Pass 3. The first three P fields have a standard interpretation that cannot be altered:

P(1): instrument number.

P(2): starting time, in arbitrary units called *beats*.

P(3): duration, also in *beats* (the same units as for the starting time).

All of the fields above P(3) are optional, and the manner in which these are interpreted depends on the instrument design. The following additional points must be noted about I cards:

Only the first five cards in an I block are affected by the carry feature.

Beats are evaluated as *seconds* unless there is a T card (see below).

Starting times are relative to the beginning of a *section*, which is assigned time 0. This means that, when transcribing a passage of music that has four beats per measure, the first measure starts at time 0, the second at time 4, the third at time 8, etc. Starting times are *not* relative to the beginning of a measure.

The starting time P(2) of a note may be the same as the ending time P(2) + P(3) of another note on the same instrument; but the notes must not actually *overlap*.

Note cards within a section need not be entered in the order of their starting times; they are sorted on this basis in Pass 2.

No special score card is needed to indicate a *rest* on an instrument; a rest is indicated by the fact that an instrument is simply not used during a certain period of time.

In the simplest application of note cards, each note indicates a separate pitch starting at a certain time with a certain duration, etc. All properties of the note except for the starting time and duration could be determined by the instrument itself, as constants or as random values.

S and E Cards

S and E cards are used to mark the end of a *section* (S card) or the end of the entire score (E card). They have no other function. They are significant in that all sorting and other Pass-2 processing is done section by section. At the beginning of a section, the time to which all starting times are relative is set to 0.

The E card is sometimes used to convey certain values to the orchestra program that remain *constant* for the entire performance. These include such properties as the number of instruments in the orchestra, the sampling rate, the number of output channels (mono, stereo, or quad), and the number of output tapes used by the job. Alternative ways of specifying these quantities are usually available to the user. (See "Orchestra Program Sections.")

Tempo Cards

A *tempo card* or *T card* sets the *tempo* and specifies the accelerations or retardations to occur within the section, by converting *beats* into *seconds*. The following fields have a standard interpretation on T cards:

P(2) indicates the number of seconds to be taken as the period referred to by the *tempos* given in the T block. *Normally 60*, since this causes the tempos to be interpreted as *beats per minute*.

P(3), P(5), P(7), . . . : referenced *times*.

P(4), P(6), P(8), . . . : *tempos* for the referenced times $P(n - 1)$.

Events preceding the time P(3) are all in the tempo given by P(4). Similarly, events later than the last referenced time $P(z)$ will all be in the tempo given by $P(z + 1)$. The last referenced time is recognized as such by 0 or a blank in an odd-numbered P field (other than P(3)), so that T-block parameters must be placed in consecutive P fields.

In the simplest application of a tempo card, then, a "metronome mark" is placed in P(4), and the entire section is interpreted in that tempo.

Between referenced times, the duration between each pair of events is determined by *proportional interpolation* between the tempos indicated. The segment that *ends* at time $P(n)$ will have the duration indicated by the tempo $P(n + 1)$.

In order to specify accelerations or retardations, then, it is necessary to specify the starting and ending time of the change in tempo at each of these times. Halfway between these two times, the tempo will be at a speed equidistant between the two tempos indicated.

A tempo card applies only to the section in which it appears; it may appear anywhere in the section. If there is no T card in a section, the beats are simply understood as seconds.

The Pass-2 printing of the score shows the effect of the T card. All starting times and durations are printed there in seconds.

R Cards

An R card causes the contents of some set of corresponding P fields in all I blocks in a section to be *rescaled* to a given maximum of the *sum* for all instruments playing at any one time.

An R block can contain only five cards (four continuation cards), affecting the first sixty P fields of the I blocks. In all P fields, the number given is the *desired maximum* of the sum for the corresponding P fields in the I blocks, unless the maximum is 0, in which case no rescaling is done on that P field.

R cards were designed for the purpose of causing the output amplitudes of all instruments to come as close to the maximum amplitude allowed on the digital-to-analog converter as possible, in order to maximize the signal-to-noise ratio. In practice, usually this kind of rescaling cannot be accomplished by means of an R card. The R card rescales the *input amplitudes* before these levels are processed by unit generators that follow the signal generator in the instrument. The *output* level may be quite different from the input, and the output maximum usually does not equal the sum of its inputs because of phase cancellations of the signal components or destructive interference. Furthermore, an R card affects only one P field in each I block; it is not possible to rescale the maximum level when amplitudes are specified in two or more P fields, which may happen when variations such as crescendo or diminuendo occur. Because of these disadvantages, the R card is rarely used. *Output* rescaling, described in Chapter 7 (see section 7–10), is an integral part of MUSIC4BF, however.

Comment Cards

Comment cards are score cards with C in column 1. They are entirely ignored by the program, except that their contents are *printed* along with the other cards in the Pass-1 listing. Columns 2 through 80 may contain any information; there are no field distinctions.

Comment cards are useful simply as indications or reminders to the user of things that he may forget, or as titles to sections of the score. The plentiful use of comment cards is encouraged.

Comment cards are noteworthy in the following respects: when inserted between I blocks they do not turn off the carry feature; they may be inserted between the header or continuation cards of any block without affecting the block in any way; and they cannot be numbered, since columns 4 through 6 are simply treated as part of the comment.

How to Encode a Musical Score as Computer Input

Let us consider the *first six measures* of Anton Webern's *Fünf Sätze* for string quartet, Op. 5, as an example of a musical score which we wish to translate into note cards for input to MUSIC4BF. This excerpt is reproduced in Figure 8–2.2. (This example has many more complications than the reader is likely to encounter in a typical score, and it is intended to help the reader confront new problems of this sort.)

A glance at the score reveals several characteristics that we will have to represent in our computer score, but that we will not discuss here in respect to the way that the computer instruments will produce them: the notations indicating the use of the mute *(mit Dämpfer),* which is present throughout the excerpt; the pizzicato and arco indications; and the direction to play certain tones at the bridge *(am Steg).* We must also indicate the pitch of each tone, including certain "double-stops" or simultaneous pitches on a single instrument. We must indicate dynamic levels, including a provision for a change of dynamics in the form of a crescendo or diminuendo. Slurs are present in the score, and so we will also include an indication of whether a note is the first or last note or in the middle of a slurred passage, or whether it is not part of a slur at all. We must find a way of expressing the tremolos[7] at the beginning of the first- and second-violin parts. We must

---

[7]Though the same term is used, this kind of "tremolo" does not indicate amplitude modulation.

express the differences in timbre among the instruments, two of which are identical. Finally, there are several tempo markings that must be expressed in our score. For the purpose of this illustration, we choose to ignore the indications *äusserst zart* and *äusserst ruhig*.

In deciding how to encode the notes in any score, we must make certain decisions about the correspondences between the events in the musical score and the P fields in the computer score. The instrument will then make its interpretations of the numbers in the P fields and assign these values to various inputs in the unit generators in the instrument. The following discussion is intended to elucidate various aspects of the process by which the composer decides these correspondences.

Let us begin by assuming that we do not want to design a computer instrument that plays both tremolos and single- and double-stops all at the same time. We will actually design only two kinds of instruments: one that plays single tones with all of the characteristics necessary; and another that plays the tremolos. In order to obtain double-stops, we will employ two of the single-tone instruments simultaneously. Furthermore, the tremolo instrument does not have to be as complicated as the single-tone instrument because the tremolos occur only on notes with a limited range of the characteristics of the other notes.

Considering the single-tone instrument first, we must now decide how we will represent these various characteristics. Let us agree that we will represent the pitch of each note in octave-point pitch-class or 8VE.PC form (see PITCH below, page 216) and punch this number in P(4) of the note card.

Let us choose to represent the dynamic level *ppp* by the number 2 and *pp* by the number 3. Choosing 2 for *ppp* gives us a method of specifying a level *below ppp* when a diminuendo begins from this level. We can divide these numbers into fractions to indicate partial changes of level, as when, for example, a diminuendo of one level occurs over several notes, as in the first-violin part in measure 3. We do not mean to assign any absolute meaning to the numbers 1, 2, or 3, which we have used to denote amplitude levels. Rather, we are assuming that our instrument will use these numbers as references to whatever actual amplitude values are needed to produce the loudnesses denoted by *pp*, *ppp*, and the softer level. While there may be a complicated translation process implied here, we do not need to express these complications themselves in the score, nor are they specified in Webern's score.

Since our instrument must be capable of making changes in amplitude, we will give two levels for each tone: a beginning level, which we will punch in P(5), and an amount of change, which we will punch in P(6). When a tone remains at one level throughout, we will simply indicate 0 as an amount of change. Let us assume that a negative change represents a diminuendo.

At this point we must consider a complication in the score concerning dynamic levels. There are some crescendo and diminuendo markings in the score, such as the cello part in measure 5, in which the crescendo and diminuendo apply to a single tone. This type of change implies a different *shape* from a single crescendo or diminuendo. A crescendo or diminuendo can both be specified by an ascending straight line, since a negative amplitude will produce a decrease along the line; but a crescendo and diminuendo on the same note require a line that ascends and then descends. Either shape can conveniently be represented in a stored function. Therefore, we require a third P field, P(7), to indicate the function that represents the shape of change of amplitude. Let us use 1 for a simple crescendo or diminuendo and 2 for the rise-and-fall function. When P(6) is 0, there is no change in amplitude, and it does not matter which shape is indicated.

Now let us consider the slurs. We can establish a simple code for this purpose: 1 means first note of a slur, 3 means last note of a slur, and 2 means middle note of a slur; 0 means that the note is not connected by a slur. We will punch this number in P(8). Our instrument must be capable of decoding these indications and applying characteristics to the sounds that are appropriate for these purposes. Note that we have not discussed the notes in the first two measures of the cello part, which have slurs leading to nowhere. If we want to represent this characteristic, the appropriate manner would probably be to increase the duration of the tones. Furthermore, notes that are tied across the bar line are not considered slurred even though the same symbol is used in musical notation, and we will represent these notes as single tones with durations including both components.

In representing the use of the mute, the pizzicato and arco indications, and the direction to play certain tones at the bridge, we may decide upon a *binary code* to indicate the presence (1) or absence (0) of each of these characteristics. Since the mute is employed throughout, we can simply ignore it and include it as a constant characteristic of the instrument. (If we do this, we cannot use the same instruments to play the other movements, which are not muted.) Let us indicate pizzicato as 1 in P(9) and arco as 0 in P(9), and the *am Steg* indication as 1 and the absence of it as 0 in

P(10). Here our task is to represent these characteristics in our score. The task of decoding this information and producing these characteristics as faithfully as live string instruments is left to the computer instrument.

While the timbral differences of the notes in Webern's score are indicated by the fact that they are played on different physical instruments, it is not necessary that we employ different computer instruments to achieve these differentiations; all we need is an indication in one P field that specifies the "timbre," and we can assume that the instrument is capable of producing the correct qualities. Let us adopt a code of 1 in P(11) to indicate violin, 2 for viola, and 3 for cello. Now we must observe that we need two instruments in the orchestra to play each of the violin parts, because our instrument can play only one tone at a time, and we need one instrument for the viola part and two for the cello part. Since any one of these instruments can play a tone of any timbre, actually we need only a total of six instruments, because there are no more than six tones present simultaneously (at the end of measure 2).

In order to take full advantage of the carry feature in Pass 1, let us indicate our instrument numbers in the score in terms of *groups* of instruments of the same structure. This will enable us to call for simultaneous notes on the same instrument in Pass 1, but the notes will be renumbered in Pass 2. We have only two groups of instruments: the single-tone instruments and the tremolo instruments. We will number the former 1 and the latter 2. We must also include a B1 card in the score, which calls the instrument-numbering subroutine. (See "Optional Subprograms.") Note that the carry feature allows values to carry even across comment cards.

The tremolo instruments do not involve many of the complexities of the single-tone instruments. Since they occur only on a few notes, many of the characteristics that we had to indicate in the score above can be handled as constants within the instruments. The constant characteristics include the dynamic level, *ppp* (never changing), the *am Steg* indication, the absence of slurs, the use of only arco bowing, and the lack of any timbral differentiation. Even the speed of the tremolo is not indicated in the score itself. The only characteristics we need to indicate are the pitches involved in the tremolo. Let us indicate the first pitch in P(4) and the second in P(5) (both 8VE.PC form). We need two instruments in this group, which we will number 2 but which will be renumbered 7 and 8 by subroutine B1.

The tempo indications in the score will be handled by a T card, which must indicate the ritardando beginning in measure 5 in terms of the tempo that we arrive at by the end of the ritardando. Let us (arbitrarily) assume that the tempo slows to a metronome mark of 52 at this point.

Finally, we must choose a time value to represent the beat. The tempo in the score is given in terms of an eighth-note beat, but it is not necessary that we use this unit in our transcription. If we continue to transcribe the passage beginning in measure 7, where eighth-note triplets are used, with the same unit as beat, we will have to indicate the durations of those tones as two thirds of a beat, which produces a repeating decimal value. Further complications are encountered in measure 6, where sixteenth notes occur, and in the last measure, where sixteenth-note quintuplets occur. We can avoid these problems by using the lowest common denominator of 2, 3, 4, and 5, which is 60, as the beat, and then every starting time and duration can be indicated as an integer. While this leads to large numbers to represent small durations (every measure lasts 180 beats, and the duration of an eighth note is 30 beats), we avoid any problem of using repeating decimal values, which always lose a fraction of accuracy. (For example, 3 times 0.333 equals 0.999, not 1.0). We must adjust our tempo to agree with this new value by multiplying it by 30. However, since our six-measure excerpt has no problem with repeating decimal values, let us use the eighth note as the beat unit, and indicate sixteenth notes as 0.5 beats. (Note that we have used fractions rounding off one third of a level for amplitude specifications, however.)

Figure 8–2.3 illustrates a complete transcription of the first six measures of this composition according to the assumptions that we have made. Note that we have taken advantage of the carry feature to avoid repeating values on subsequent cards, and that we indicate all tones on the first violin first, the second violin second, the viola third, and the cello fourth. At the end of our score we have placed an S card to mark the end of a section (arbitrarily).

This transcription has provided an illustration of some of the programming problems that must be dealt with in transcribing a musical score into computer input. Of course, it has presented several unusual complications that are not encountered in all cases, particularly when we are not concerned with translating instrumental music into computer input. Normally the composer has a more concrete idea of his intentions, which he can represent directly in terms appropriate for the computer rather than in the awkward generalizations used in instrumental scores. Note that the means we chose to represent these characteristics are not at all unique, and we could have found several alternative ways of transcribing all of them. Furthermore, the computer instruments that perform these notes can also interpret the numbers in a variety of ways. It is only when the correspondences between the numbers and the musical objects they denote are known that these numbers have any particular meaning for us, or for the computer.

Let us summarize the procedure for transcribing a musical score into computer input in the following steps:

1. Decide which characteristics of the music are to be represented in the note cards, and work out the range of values in which these characteristics appear. In transcribing the notes, it is usually a good idea to represent all characteristics on the note cards, whether or not these are actually interpreted by the instruments in the performance. By this practice the user will probably avoid having to retranscribe the notes in case the first synthesis of the music is deemed unsatisfactory because it lacks the characteristics omitted.

2. If there are great differences between the characteristics of different groups of notes, the notes may be played by different computer instruments. Alternatively, a single computer instrument may be designed that has the capacity to play any of the characteristics optionally. The latter solution is generally more difficult to program than the former.

If more than one instrument of each type is needed, the instruments may be numbered according to groups, and a B1 card may be included to renumber the instruments in Pass 2.

3. Choose a time value to represent the beat. This value should be large enough to avoid repeating decimal values for starting times and durations. Include a T card to translate these values into seconds.

4. If there are more than 999 notes in the transcription, or if there are any natural places of division in the music, divide the piece into contiguous sections.

Finally, it is, of course, obvious that the transcription of the score cannot ultimately be separated from the design of the instruments and the realization of the music. We have described this as a separate procedure because, first, it is a simple task that can be learned before instrument design is studied, and, more importantly, since the same score can be used with a number of different instruments, it is best to get the transcription out of the way early in order to concentrate on the more important aspects of the synthesis that will crop up in designing the instruments.

Figure 8–2.2: Anton Webern, *Fünf Sätze* for string quartet, Op. 5, fourth movement.

C	WEBERN, FUNF SATZE IV, MEAS. 1–6										
T	0	60	27	58	36	52					
B	1										
C	FIRST VIOLIN, TREMOLOS										
I	2	2	2	10.04	10.00						
I		6		10.06	9.11						
C	SECOND VIOLIN, TREMOLOS										
I		2		9.05	8.11						
I		6			9.00						
C	FIRST VIOLIN, SINGLE TONES										
I	1	11	1	10.00	2	0	1	0	1	0	1
I				10.04							
I		13		10.06	3	−.33	1	0	1		
I		14		9.11	2.67		2				
I		15		9.05	2.34	−.34	3				
I		16	3	9.00	2	0	0				
I		23	1	8.00	2	.5	1				
I		24		8.05	2.5		2				
I		25		8.01	3	−.5					
I		26		8.00	2.5		3				
I		27	2	8.02	2		1				
I		29		8.01	1.5		3				
C	SECOND VIOLIN, SINGLE TONES										
I		11	1	9.05	2	0		0	1	0	
I				8.11							
I		18		9.11	3	−.25	1	0			
I		19		9.04	2.75		2				
I		20		8.10	2.5						
I		21		8.05	2.25		3				
I		32.5	.5	8.00	2	0	1				
I		33		8.04			2				
I		33.5		8.06							
I		34		8.11							
I		34.5		9.01		−.33					
I		35		9.07	1.67						
I		35.5		9.10	1.34	−.34	3				
C	VIOLA										
I		9	1	8.04	2	0	1				2
I		10	2	8.06		1	2	3			
I		15		8.04		1	1				
I		17		8.06	3	−1	3				
I		23	3	7.06	2	1	1		1		

Continued on page 194.

I	26	2	7.07	3	0		2		
I	28	3	7.06		−1		3		
C	CELLO								
I	4	2	7.03	2	0		0	0	3
I	8	4							
I	17	2	8.01	2	−1		1		
I	18	1	7.07	1	0		3		
I	21	1	7.06	3	−.33		1	1	
I	22		6.11	2.67			2		
I	23		6.05	2.34	−.34		3		
I	24		6.00	2	.33		1		
I	25		6.05	2.33	.34		2		
I	26	2	6.01	2.67		2			
I	28		6.00		−.67	1	3		
I	30		6.02	2	−.5		1		
I	32		6.01	1.5			3		
S									

Figure 8–2.3: Transcription of the first six measures of the fourth movement of Anton Webern's *Fünf Sätze,* for string quartet, Op. 5. This transcription shows the form in which the user's data is prepared, not how it is affected by the carry feature in Pass 1 or the T card, B 1 card, or sorting of Pass 2.

Function Cards

Score cards with F in column 1 are called *function cards* or *F cards*. An F card causes a *GEN subroutine* to be called in Pass 3 in order to generate a *stored function* that may be used by the instruments. The first three P fields have a standard interpretation for F cards:

P (1): function number.

P (2): time at which the function is to be generated, in *beats*.

P (3): number of GEN subroutine to be called (1 to 20).

The format of all other P fields is determined by the GEN subroutines individually.

The number of stored functions available to a particular orchestra depends entirely upon the amount of computer memory available to the program. Each function is stored in 512 locations (single words).

When a function is stored, it is *erased* only by the generation of another function with the same number (not, for example, by a section ending).

A stored function may be used by any number of unit generators in any number of instruments simultaneously. There is hardly ever any reason to generate the same function twice within a particular run.

P (2) is affected by the tempo card, so that it is converted from beats into seconds in Pass 2.

All *amplitude values* that are indicated in the P fields for nearly all GEN subroutines are *relative to one another.* The values stored in the function itself are all between -1.0 and $+1.0$. In all of the standard GEN subroutines, this is assured by *rescaling* the function to a maximum absolute value of 1.0. However, if P (3) is *negative,* the function is not rescaled.

The GEN subroutine to be called actually depends only on the absolute value of the integer part of P (3), so that the sign and fractional part are available as parameters of the subroutine. With most GEN subroutines it is possible to obtain a printed *picture* of the stored function by including a positive fractional part in P (3) (e.g., 9.1 instead of 9).

Types of Stored Functions

Stored functions are used to control a wide variety of musical parameters in MUSIC4BF, and, therefore, a number of GEN subroutines are necessary to generate functions appropriate to different characteristics. For example, routines that store sums of sine-wave components are necessary to generate musical timbres. Routines are available that store straight lines and exponential curves, in order to control changes in amplitude. In this section we will describe a number of different GEN subroutines with respect to the types of functions they produce and the manner in which the user specifies their components.

GEN08, GEN09, and GEN10[8] store functions which consist of *one cycle* of a *sum of sine waves* of different frequencies. When these functions are sampled repeatedly by unit generators such as OSCIL (*q.v.*), the frequencies must all consist of *harmonic partials* of a fundamental; nonharmonic partials would cause phase discontinuities. Functions consisting of nonharmonic partials may be used for other purposes, however. These three GEN subroutines differ in the manner in which the information in the P fields is specified by the user.

---

[8]The names of GEN subroutines consist of the letters *G,E,N,* followed by two digits indicating the number of the subroutine, which is punched in P (3) of the F card. The preceding zeros in 08 and 09 do not have to be indicated on the F card, although they are part of the name.

GEN10 requires only that the amplitude of each partial of a harmonic series (up to the 477th) be specified in successive P fields beginning with P (4). An initial phase of 0 is assumed for all partials; a negative amplitude value indicates a phase of 180 degrees. Unwanted harmonics may be indicated by leaving the relevant P fields blank. For example, the following indications

P (4)	P (6)	P (12)
3	1	−.3333

call for the fundamental, third, and ninth partials in the relative amplitude proportions that they would have in a square wave; but the ninth partial is "upside down."

GEN08 and GEN09 require that the user specify, in consecutive groups of three P fields, the *partial number, relative amplitude,* and *initial phase* in degrees. In GEN09 the amplitude value specified by the user is taken directly, whereas in GEN08 the *reciprocal* of the amplitude value is taken. The advantage of GEN08 and GEN09 over GEN10 is that the user can specify the partial number and initial phase directly; the advantage of GEN10 is that a specific series of harmonic partials can be specified in fewer P fields. For example, using GEN09, the following P-field indications

P (4)	P (5)	P (6)	P (7)	P (8)	P (9)	P (10)	P (11)	P (12)
1	3	0	3	1	0	9	.3333	180

call for the same stored function as the GEN10 example above. Using GEN08, the following data

P (4)	P (5)	P (6)	P (7)	P (8)	P (9)	P (10)	P (11)	P (12)
1	1	0	3	9	180	5	25	0

call for the first three partials of a triangle wave.

GEN18, GEN19, and GEN20 are identical in terms of input format to GEN08, GEN09, and GEN10, except that they store the function in a different form, which is the form required for the waveform input (NF2) to the unit generator FORMNT (*q.v.*). GEN02 also generates stored functions for the waveform input to FORMNT, but the F-card format is the same as for GEN05, GEN06, and GEN07. It is described below.

GEN05, GEN06, and GEN07 store functions consisting of interpolations between values at specified points. The points are the 512 locations in the functions, and the values are the amplitudes of the function at these points. In GEN07, the interpolation is *linear,* and the function, therefore, consists of straight-line segments. The user specifies the amplitude at the first location in the function in P (4); each subsequent odd-numbered P field indicates the *number of locations* to the next point (not, for example, the location number of the next point). The amplitude value at the next point is indicated in the next even-numbered P field. For example, the following card

P (4)	P (5)	P (6)
0	512	1

calls for a simple linear rise from 0 to 1 over 512 locations.

The first value in each segment will always be the value given for the beginning of the segment. When the value for the next segment is different, the last value of the segment will be close but not equal to this. For the last segment, interpolation proceeds as if toward an $(n + 1)$th value where n values are called for. In the preceding example, the final value of the function would be $\frac{511}{512}$, but since this is the maximum, it becomes 1.0 upon rescaling.

As another example, the following card

P (4)	P (5)	P (6)	P (7)	P (8)	P (9)	P (10)
1	255	1	1	−1	256	−1

calls for a square-wave cycle. (Note that if this function is sampled by OSCIL or OSCILI it will produce foldover frequencies, since a pure square-wave contains an infinite series of harmonic partials.)

In GEN05, the interpolation is *exponential* instead of linear. This means that the increase or decrease along a segment is by equal proportions between pairs of adjacent values instead of by equal differences. It follows that no value on a segment can be 0, and that all even-numbered P fields must have values with the same *sign*. For example, the following card

P (4)	P (5)	P (6)
1	512	100

calls for an exponential rise over the function. Thus, before rescaling, the 257th value of the function would be 10, the geometric mean between 1 and 100.

In GEN06, the interpolation is also exponential, except that the increase or decrease along a segment is proportional to the *ratios* of the arguments instead of to the difference between them; the arguments are the integers 1 to 512. Imagine, for example, that the arguments corepresent the frequencies of a harmonic series. By setting any mth argument to have the value $(\frac{1}{m})^2$ where the first argument was given the value 1, the value $(\frac{1}{n})^2$ would be specified for *each* argument n such that n was less than or equal to m. The following card

P (4)   P (5)   P (6)

1   9   .01

calls for nine values along the curve mentioned above, since interpolation proceeds as if toward a tenth value of $(\frac{1}{10})^2$.

GEN02 provides a convenient way of specifying combinations of up to 170 partials for the waveform input of the unit generator FORMNT. The F-card format is the same as for GEN05, GEN06, and GEN07. The frequencies of the partials are determined by the *sign* and *fractional part* of P (3) as follows:

If P (3) = 2.0, the frequencies form a harmonic series, with as many partials as are specified in odd-numbered P fields from P (5) on.

If P (3) = − 2.0, the same partials are requested, but all *even-numbered* partials are eliminated. In this case the numbers in the odd-numbered P fields from P (5) on represent not the number of partials desired, but the number of partials to be calculated before eliminating the even-numbered ones. For example, the following card

P (3)   P (4)   P (5)   P (6)

−2   1   9   .1

calls for the first *five* odd-numbered partials (1, 3, 5, 7, and 9) in the amplitude relationship they would have in a square wave.

If P (3) > 2.0, the frequencies are to be the same *interval* apart, the interval being given by the fractional part of P (3) in 8VE.PC form (actually just the ".PC" in this case; see PITCH, page 216). The lowest frequency is assigned the value 1. For example, the following card

P (3)   P (4)   P (5)   P (6)

2.015   1   12   4

calls for twelve partials at intervals of 1.5 semitones apart, with amplitudes increasing exponentially. The seventh partial will have an amplitude of 2 before rescaling.

Since the fractional value of P (3) is used for a special purpose with GEN02, no printed picture of the function can be obtained.

In GEN05, GEN06, and GEN07, the points and values on the interpolation curves are specified directly as relative amplitudes and distances to the next point. In GEN03 and GEN04, the 512 locations are spread uniformly over the frequency continuum (from 0 to $\frac{511}{512}$ of ½ SR cps), and the points on this curve are expressed as *pitches* in 8VE.PC form. The stored function thus represents a fixed frequency formant function and is intended to be used in the NF3 or NF4 input of the unit generator FORMNT *(q.v.)*

GEN03 is identical to GEN05, and GEN04 to GEN06, in the manner in which interpolation proceeds from point to point. Zero values must not be used as amplitudes for the same reason as with GEN05 and GEN06. The user specifies the relative amplitude at frequency 0 in P (4). Beginning with P (5) the user specifies the pitch in odd-numbered P fields, and the relative amplitude of the formant at that pitch in the next even-numbered P field. The following card

P (4)	P (5)	P (6)	P (7)	P (8)	P (9)	P (10)	P (11)	P (12)
1	8.09	20	9.09	5	10.09	20	11.00	1

calls for a formant function with peaks at A (440 cps) and at the A two octaves higher, with a trough at the intervening octave and a steep cutoff after the second peak. The same data values could be used for either GEN03 or GEN04, but for GEN03 the increase or decrease from one harmonic partial within a segment to the next is by equal proportions over equal differences in frequency; for GEN04 the increase or decrease along a segment is by equal proportions over equal musical *intervals* instead of over equal cps differences.

GEN05, GEN06, and GEN07 allow straight lines and exponential curves to be obtained with ease. GEN01 and GEN13 produce shapes between these two patterns.

GEN01 simply stores 512 values along a monotonic curve. The first value (before rescaling) is P (4) and the last is P (6). The shape of the curve is determined by P (5), which is the *middle* value, according to the formula

$$x^{y^z} \qquad 0 \le y \le 1$$

where f (0) = P (4), f (.5) = P (5), and f (1) = P (6). From this information GEN01 determines the values of x and z. Thus the curve may be a nearly straight line, an exponential, or any desired compromise between these.

GEN01 also allows the alternative of specifying the exponent z in the above formula directly. If P (5) is 0, $z =$ P (7) and f (.5) is calculated accordingly.

One principal use of GEN01 is to control produced amplitude as a function of intended loudness. Neither a straight line nor an exponential curve is a very good approximation of this relationship, and GEN01 can conveniently provide a plausible intermediate shape. Nevertheless, GEN13 is explicitly intended for this purpose.

GEN13 stores 512 values along a monotonic curve, like GEN01; but in this case only the first and last values are specified and interpolation is made according to the *sone* scale of amplitude relationship.[9]

P (4) and P (5) specify the initial and terminal values, and all further P fields are ignored. For precise results, P (4) and P (5) should be set to the lowest and highest amplitude levels actually used, and intermediate values should be determined by proportional interpolation along the curve.

GEN11 merely transfers the P array into the function array. If P (4) is greater than 0, the contents of the function from location 1 to the location specified in P (4) are initially erased. Otherwise, the function is left as it was found and only those locations specified in the rest of the P fields are replaced.

Each P field beginning with P (5) is processed in groups of two fields. The odd-numbered fields specify the function *location* (1 to 512), and the even-numbered fields specify the *value*. As soon as a 0 or negative odd-numbered field is encountered, scanning of the remaining P fields is terminated. A single function may be constructed by means of several GEN11 cards using the optional erasing feature in P (4).

GEN12 allows functions or parts of functions that have previously been stored by other F cards to be combined. In this case P (1) indicates one of the functions involved in the combination and the function in which the result is stored.

In groups of three P fields beginning with P (4), P (*i*) indicates the first location in the two functions involved in the combination, P (*i* + 1) the last location, and P (*i* + 2) both the second function and the operation. If P (*i* + 2) is *positive* with no fractional part, it indicates that the two functions are to be *added;* if P (*i* + 2) is *negative* with no fractional part, it indicates that the second function is to be *subtracted* from the first; if P (*i* + 2) is *positive with a fractional part,* it indicates that the two functions are to be *multiplied;* and if P (*i* + 2) is *negative with a fractional part,* it indicates that the first function is to be *divided* by the second function.

GEN12 terminates upon encountering a 0 in P *(i),* and the function is then rescaled to 1.0 (unless P (3) is negative).

In addition to these standard GEN subroutines, GEN numbers 14 through 17 are unassigned so that the user may add his own subroutines

[9]S. S. Stevens, "The Measurement of Loudness," *Journal of the Acoustical Society of America,* XXVII/5 (Sept., 1955), 815–829.

[*] Optional Subprograms

It is by no means the case that the user of MUSIC4BF must always prepare all of his data on punched cards in advance of a MUSIC4BF run. The computer may be employed to assist the user in this task during either Pass 1 or Pass 2, through *optional subprograms. A subroutines* are called during Pass 1, and *B subroutines* during Pass 2.

There are several different levels at which optional subprograms may be employed. At one extreme, these programs may be used actually to compose the music itself, by going through a series of decision-making processes analogous to what the composer himself would perform in making the choices of events in his music. At the other extreme, the programs may make minor corrections or additions to a score already prepared in most respects. Most applications of optional subprograms fall somewhere between these two extremes, but more toward the latter than the former. At the former extreme, there exist complete computer programs that carry out musical composition in various ways, but these are usually written as entirely separate programs rather than as MUSIC4BF subprograms.

Blank COMMON storage in Pass 1 is ordered and dimensioned as OP, P (12), STOP (999), STP (12,999), NST (480). In the "short" version of MUSIC4BF, STOP and STP are dimensioned at (500) and (12,500) respectively. This version is used on computers that do not have sufficient memory for the regular version. The STOP (store OP code) and STP (store parameters) arrays are reserved for notes or functions that are to be written on the scratch file for Pass 2. If the user desires to deal with one note card at a time, the OP and P arrays may be used.

When a numbered card is encountered in Pass 1, its contents are automatically *stored* in STOP (NUM), which contains the OP code, and STP (1 to 12, NUM), which contain the parameters. When this card image has been modified in all desired respects and is ready to be written on the scratch file for Pass 2, SUBROUTINE WRITER may be called. WRITER has two integer arguments, M and N. The Fortran statement CALL WRITER (M, N), where M is less than N, causes WRITER to write the contents of STOP (M to N) and STP (1 to 12, M to N). If M and N are both 0, the contents of OP and P (1 to 12) are written. Once these card images have been written on the scratch file for Pass 2, they will be treated in exactly the same way as if they had originated in unnumbered cards.

In order to simplify the process of numbering score cards, the *N card* may be used. An N card controls *automatic numbering* of score cards. It has only two relevant parameter fields:

P (1): subscript for NST array.

P (2): if *positive,* turns on automatic numbering, beginning with the number indicated; if 0 (or blank), turns off numbering; if *negative,* continues numbering from NST *(n),* where $n = $ ABS (P(2)).

When P (2) is positive or negative, the *first* number used is stored in NST (P(1)). When P (2) is 0, the *last* number used is stored in NST (P(1)). In this manner, automatic numbering can later be continued from this number by setting P (2) on the N card which continues numbering to $-$ P (1) of the N card which stops numbering. The NST array can be used to find the first and last note numbers to process in an A subroutine. The note numbers that are determined by the N card are displayed in the NUM field of the Pass 1 printing of the score.

Subroutine A10 is a standard A subroutine used to write the card images that have been stored in STOP and STP on the scratch file for Pass 2, and thus avoid having to call WRITER from other user-written A subroutines. A10 has four parameters:

P (2): number of first card to be written.

P (3): number of last card to be written.

P (4): increment between cards to be written.

P (5): maximum number of cards in each I block to be written.

A10 processes cards from P (2) to P (3) with increment P (4). If P (2) or P (3) is negative, the limits are taken from NST *(n),* where *n* equals ABS(P(2) or P (3)). P (5) is used to cause continuation cards beyond a specified limit to be deleted in case the information on these cards was of only transient value and is not needed by the instruments.

Blank COMMON storage in Pass 2 is increased from Pass 1, and is ordered and dimensioned as follows: OP, P (12), STOP (999), STP (12,999), T (480), R (12,5), B (12,5,5), INORD (1998), ITOT, NUM. *B subroutines* are called after the sorting and other processing of a *section* in Pass 2, in the order in which the B cards were encountered in the section. When a B subroutine is called, STOP (1) to STOP (NUM) and STP (1 to 12,1) to STP

(1 to 12,NUM) contain the I and F blocks for this section in the order that these card images were written on the scratch file for Pass 2; these card images have been modified as was required by any T or R card. INORD (1) to INORD (ITOT) indicate the sorted order in which the I and F blocks are to be written on the scratch file for Pass 3, in the following manner: if INORD (J) contains K, this means that STOP (K) and STP (1 to 12, K), together with its continuations, are to be written Jth on the file; but if INORD (J) is negative (− K), this means that a note-termination indication is to be written Jth. ITOT, therefore, contains the number of card images other than continuations to be written on the scratch file for Pass 3. T (1 to 480) and R (1 to 12, 1 to 5) contain the T-block and R-block parameters. B(1 to 12, 1 to 5,n) contain the B-block parameters for each subroutine Bn.

B subroutines are preferable to A subroutines only in the unusual case that the modifications they perform must be done after the other Pass-2 processing of each section. The one standard B subroutine, B1, is a good illustration of the kind of problem appropriate for B-subroutine processing.

Subroutine B1 is a standard B subroutine that is used to compute *instrument numbers* when the starting times and durations of notes overlap in such a way that it is difficult to determine them manually. In Pass 3, if a note is called for on an instrument that is already playing another note, the second note is automatically deleted.

When subroutine B1 is used, the numbers in P (1) of I cards do not refer to individual instruments but instead to *groups* of consecutively numbered instruments of the *same structure.* Hence, the carry feature may be used in Pass 1 to avoid repeating values on note cards when they do not change.

Subroutine B1 processes all notes with the same reference numbers and assigns instrument numbers as they are required. The maximum number of instruments needed in each group will be the greatest number of notes playing simultaneously in that group. Instruments in the next group will be renumbered with the first number following the last instrument in this group. For example, suppose that there are two groups of instruments required for a particular orchestra and that group 1 has twelve instruments playing simultaneously at one point in a section and that group 2 has sixteen instruments playing simultaneously at some point. Subroutine B1 will determine instrument numbers for all notes in such a way that no two notes ever overlap on the same instrument and that notes in instrument group 1 have numbers from 1 to 12 and notes in group 2 have numbers from 13 to 28.

P (2) on the B1 card indicates a number of instruments to be *skipped* at the beginning of the numbering process. The first instrument number assigned is P (2) + 1. For example, if P (2) equals 20, I cards in the first instrument group will be numbered from 21.

Parameters beginning in P (3) of the B1 block indicate a *minimum* number for group $n - 2$; if P (n) is less than the number of instruments actually found to be playing simultaneously, the number in P (n) is overridden. This feature is necessary to cause the instrument numbering for several sections to correspond. For example, if seven instruments are needed for group 1 in one section but none is needed in another, placing 7 in P (3) of the B1 card will insure that instruments in group 2 will be numbered beginning with P (2) + 8.

Subroutine B1 will continue to compute instrument numbers even when the total number of instruments it finds exceeds 99, and these numbers will be printed in the Pass-2 score. The orchestra program cannot contain more than ninety-nine instruments, however.

I cards with 0 in P (1) are *not* processed by subroutine B1.

[*] 3. THE ORCHESTRA

When the Pass-2 processing of the score is complete, it consists of the following elements, each of which has its own event time: indications to generate functions together with the data defining the function; indications to turn on instruments in order to play a note together with the data defining the note; and indications to turn off instruments. There are also indications marking the end of sections and of the entire performance. It is the job of the orchestra program to take the input data describing the note in whatever form these data are presented and cause the samples defining the sound to be generated and written on the digital tape. This is a very complicated task, requiring extensive programming, but most of it has already been completed in the various subprograms of the MUSIC4BF program. All that the user must really do is organize the structure of his orchestra in terms of how these subprograms are called in order to achieve his desired results. Most of the sample generation is carried out in the *unit generator* functions, which are described in detail below. Other operations, such as packing the samples in a form suitable for the digital-to-analog converter and writing them on the output tape, are performed automatically by other subroutines called by Pass 3. Let us describe the precise manner in which Pass 3 works before describing the internal structure of the orchestra.

The Operation of Pass 3 in Detail

The function of Pass 3 is to read the output file of Pass 2, which contains the sorted notes and functions, and to call the orchestra program to generate the music described. Pass 3 contains two internal time indicators named T and TT: T contains the current time of the piece within the current section being processed, and TT contains the current time starting from the very beginning of the piece (in section 1). Time is processed in *segments* that are defined by the event times of notes (starting and ending times) and functions (generation time of the function). At the beginning of each section T is set at 0; TT is set at 0 only at the very beginning. Pass 3 reads the next card image (including continuations) off of the output file from Pass 2. If the event time specified by that card image is *the same* as the current time T, Pass 3 calls the appropriate subroutine to carry out the action specified: either to generate a function or to turn on or off an instrument. Since Pass 2 gives precedence in the sorting process to functions when notes and functions are called for at the same time, all functions preceding the current note will be available at the time that that note is initialized. If the event time specified by the card image read off of the output file from Pass 2 is *later* than the current time T, Pass 3 then generates the time segment of music from the current value of T to the new time, which becomes the next value of T. After this time segment is generated, a message is printed showing the beginning and ending values of T, the ending value of TT, and the absolute value of the maximum amplitude achieved in each output channel during this time segment. Pass 3 also displays the number of samples out of range and any error messages pertaining to the time segment, if appropriate.

Orchestra Program Sections

The user's orchestra subroutine contains three distinct program sections, each of which performs a separate logical function. These sections may be organized as separate subroutines or usually more conveniently as separate entry points within one subroutine.

Relevant Pass-3 COMMON storage is ordered and dimensioned as follows: P(480), SR, INSNO, INSTRS, NCHNLS, ON(99), JUNK(529), F(512,n). TAPE, NFILES, and SPLICE are other important COMMON variables.

P contains the parameters for the current note or function during its initialization.

SR contains the sampling rate.

INSNO contains the number of the instrument currently playing. (IN-SNO will be abbreviated N in our examples at the end of this chapter, in order to avoid unnecessary keypunching.)

INSTRS contains the total number of instruments in the orchestra.

NCHNLS contains the number of output channels (one, two, or four).

ON(INSNO) contains zero if instrument number INSNO is off, is greater than zero if it is on, and is less than zero if it is being called for note initialization.

JUNK contains all additional Pass-3 common variables, which the user does not have to know about individually, and which are skipped by including them in one array like this.

F contains the stored functions needed for the current job. F and JUNK must be indicated in this manner only when more than twenty-eight stored functions are needed for the regular version or fourteen stored functions for the short version of MUSIC4BF, because the Pass-2 blank COMMON contains much extra room that had been occupied by the STP array.

TAPE is negative if no output tape is to be written for the current job (i.e., it is a test job), is 0 if only a final tape is to be written (i.e., there is no output rescaling), and is greater than 0 if both intermediate and final tapes are to be written (i.e., there is output rescaling). If TAPE is greater than or equal to 2.0, only an intermediate tape is written.

NFILES indicates a number of files to skip on the output tape before writing the current job. This allows several jobs to be written consecutively on the same digital tape.[10]

If SPLICE is greater than 0, it indicates a *duration* of music that is *skipped* on the final tape, thus "splicing" the current job onto the end of another tape.

Note that INSNO, INSTRS, NCHNLS, and NFILES are integer variables, while P, SR, ON, TAPE, and SPLICE are floating-point variables.

—————

[10]In the version for the IBM System/360, file skipping is accomplished by the LABEL parameter on the DD card for the output tape, and is not indicated in P (5) on the E card; SPLICE is indicated in P (5), and P (6) is not used.

This is not the complete list of Pass-3 COMMON storage, which is extensive, but it is all that one needs to know for most purposes.

Entry INITL is called only *once* at the very beginning of the performance (i.e., when TT is set to 0). Its function is *orchestra initialization.* Orchestra initialization consists of defining any variables that remain *constant* throughout the *entire performance* and setting the initial values for all other variable data used by the instruments, where this action is necessary. The variables that remain constant throughout the entire performance always include the following items, and, therefore, a convenient method of setting them has been established by associating them with various P fields on the *E card (q.v.)*: INSTRS is determined by P (1), SR by P (2), NCHNLS by P (3), TAPE by P (4), NFILES by P (5), and SPLICE by P (6).[11] These values on the E card are always stored in the relevant COMMON storage locations, but they may be overridden by the orchestra program in entry INITL.

The initial values for other variable data used by the instruments include all items for which a previous value is assumed in calculations. These include items such as phase inputs in OSCIL and other units, which can usually simply be set at 0. The reason this is necessary is that most Fortran compilers assume that the user will provide initial values for all variable data, and if this is not done the initial value may be totally out of range of any expected value, such as a floating-point number with an exponent of seventy-five digits after the decimal point.

Entry SETUP is called *once* at the beginning of *each note* for each instrument in the orchestra; its function is *note initialization.* Note initialization includes the following items, each of which will be explained in detail:

(1) Any parameters contained in the P array that are used by the instrument in calculating the note must be *saved* in a special data area reserved for this instrument. When SETUP is called, all of the parameters defining the note are contained in the P array; but while ORCH is called and the note is being generated, P will contain other data. Therefore, these values must be transferred to data space that will not be destroyed while the note is generated.

(2) Many unit generators have *inputs that must be defined at note-initiali-*

[11]See note 9.

zation time. These inputs are indicated in the unit-generator descriptions below by the appendage of the subscript 1 to the name of the input. In addition to these note-initialization inputs, many unit generators also require that various *initialization subroutines* be called at note-initialization time. Initialization subroutines have arguments that consist of the note-initialization inputs together with a *data area* or *A array* that contains values used in the performance of the note. Whenever the name "A" is used in the unit-generator descriptions, it denotes a variable used for this purpose. If A is followed by a number *n* in parentheses, it indicates that A itself is the *first location* of an array of *n* locations.

In writing the Fortran code for an instrument, it is usually convenient to use only one variable name—e.g., "Z"—dimensioned at a sufficient size, for all unit-generator inputs and data areas used by that instrument. In this case, it is necessary to keep careful track of subscripts used to denote data areas of more than one location. If Z is a singly subscripted variable, and the unit-generator description indicates that the data area must contain five successive locations in the array, it is necessary to indicate only one location within Z, for example Z(10), and then skip the next *four* locations, so that Z(10) through Z(14) are used by that one unit generator. If Z is a doubly subscripted variable, the *first subscript* should point to the first location of the data area, for most Fortran compilers follow the convention that adjacent locations are denoted when the first subscript varies and all other subscripts are the same. In this case, Z(10,1) through Z(14,1) could be denoted by using only the first subscripts and skipping Z(11,1) through Z(14,1). In the examples of orchestra programs given below, we will always follow these conventions when indicating data areas.

(3) Any *unit generators* that need to be executed only *once for each note* should be executed at note-initialization time. These unit generators normally control characteristics that may be different for each successive note, but that remain constant during the note. Because these unit generators need to be executed only once, it is advantageous to use them whenever possible, for they result in a saving of execution time. In our discussion of instrument flowcharting below, we will follow the convention that these unit generators will *not* receive a graphic symbol in the flowchart. Instead, they will be indicated at the input of the note-performance unit generator that they affect.

(4) Any *function inputs* used by unit generators requiring stored functions must be defined at note-initialization time. Function inputs are different from all other unit-generator inputs (and outputs) in that they are

integers rather than floating-point numbers. Function inputs may thus be indicated as integer constants or variables, and if a function number is to be computed from a value in a P field or in some other manner, it should be converted to integer form during the note-initialization section of the instrument. Function numbers thus cannot be contained in the data area used for floating-point variables, but can be stored in a separate array that is declared as integer or begins with one of the letters I through N. When integer constants are included in the argument list of a unit-generator function, care must be taken not to indicate a decimal point; on the other hand, when floating-point constants are included in the argument list, a decimal point must be indicated even if there is no fraction.

Entry ORCH is called once for *each sample* of output for *each instrument* that is playing during a current time segment; its function is *note performance*. By far the bulk of computer time that is needed to calculate a piece of music is used in this subroutine. Execution-time efficiency is, therefore, a primary consideration in this section.

Each instrument in entry ORCH contains a number of calculations that employ *unit generators* and terminates after one sample of output has been computed. Unit generators are Fortran Function subprograms, whose arguments consist of the inputs to the unit together with its data areas, which determine one sample of output. Most instruments terminate by adding the sample of output that has been computed to the total output of the orchestra, which is achieved by calling one of the output subroutines (MONO, STEREO, or OUTPUT); but instruments may also terminate in other ways.

The note-performance section of an instrument usually contains one statement for each of the symbols in the instrument flowchart, but sometimes two or more symbols may be combined into one Fortran statement.

When an orchestra consists of several instruments of different structure, there must be a transfer to the appropriate instrument at the beginning of both entries SETUP and ORCH. The number of the instrument currently being called is indicated by INSNO, the third variable in the Pass-3 blank common area, which is also named N (for brevity) in some of our examples. This transfer may conveniently be accomplished by means of a computed GO TO statement or an IF statement. If the orchestra contains many different types of instruments, it may be more convenient to organize each of them as a separate subroutine with entries for both note initialization and note performance. Other factors necessary or helpful in orchestra programming are indicated below.

Unit Generators

In this section we describe all the MUSIC4BF unit generators together with their inputs, initialization subroutines, flowchart symbols, and instructions for their use. The following conventions will be employed in the description of arguments:

1. All inputs except function inputs are single-precision floating-point variables.

2. The subscript 1 to an argument in the note-performance calling sequence denotes an input that is normally defined only during the initialization section of the instrument. These inputs denote data areas unique for each call to the unit generator. All other arguments in the note-performance calling sequence may be varied either during the initialization or performance section of the instrument.

3. All arguments in the note-initialization calling sequence denote inputs that must be defined during the note-initialization section of the instrument.

4. When the variable A followed by a parenthesized integer n occurs in the calling sequence for either the note performance or both the note-performance and note-initialization sections of a unit generator, it denotes a data area consisting of a subscripted variable of n locations. The variable specified in both the initialization and performance sections must be the same.

5. Function inputs are integer constants or variables, and are indicated in the argument lists beginning with the letters NF. Function inputs may be changed only during the initialization section of an instrument.

It is possible that all or part of the initialization code for an instrument may be executed during the course of the performance of a note. Such "reinitialization" may be used to reset any properties of a note on the "micronote level."

Performance: CALL MONO(OUTPUT)
Initialization: none
Flowchart symbol:

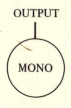

OUTPUT

MONO

Description: This unit adds the value of a given sample OUTPUT to the output of the entire orchestra. It is called only for monaural orchestras (i.e., when NCHNLS equals 1).

Performance: CALL STEREO (OUTPUT, PROP)
Initialization: none
Flowchart symbol:

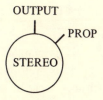

OUTPUT

PROP

STEREO

Description: OUTPUT*PROP is added to the output of channel 1 of the entire orchestra; OUTPUT*(1.-PROP) is added to the output of channel 2. PROP, which should be between 0. and 1. inclusive, thus determines the spatial location of the sound.

Performance: CALL OUTPUT (A, B, C, D)
Initialization: none
Flowchart symbol:

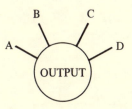

B   C

A   D

OUTPUT

Description: For each channel up to a maximum indicated by NCHNLS, A is added to the total output of channel 1 of the entire orchestra, B to channel 2, C to channel 3, and D to channel 4. If NCHNLS is less than 4, it is still necessary to indicate arguments (such as 0) in the calling sequence to OUTPUT, even though they are not processed; but in this case excess inputs may be dropped from the flowchart symbol. No location processing is performed.

Performance: OSCIL (AMP, SI, NF, PHS₁)
Initialization: PHS = X, where 0. ≤ X < 512. (optional)
Flowchart symbol:

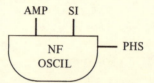

Description: Function number NF is sampled modulo 512 with increment SI and the value thus determined is multiplied by AMP.

PHS is the *phase,* to which increment SI is added modulo 512 on each sample. Only the integer portion of PHS (+1) is used to determine the location within the function, although the fractional part is saved for subsequent incrementing. For continuous sampling of the function (continuous from the last value of PHS on the previous note), PHS is not altered during the initialization section of the instrument.

SI may be negative, for reverse sampling.
Notes: PHS may be left off the flowchart symbol if it is never altered or reset. The shape of the function, if it is simple in design, is drawn inside the flowchart symbol.

Performance: OSCILI (AMP, SI, NF, PHS₁)
Initialization: PHS = X, where 0. ≤ X < 512. (optional)
Flowchart symbol:

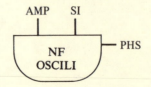

Description: This unit is identical to OSCIL *(q.v.)* except that it produces a linear interpolation between adjacent locations in the function to correct for the fractional value of PHS. The integer portion of PHS is used to determine the first location in the function, and the fractional part is multiplied by the difference between the next location (modulo 512) and the first location.

All other comments about PHS and SI of OSCIL also apply to OSCILI.

When used as a signal generator, OSCILI will produce significantly less harmonic distortion than OSCIL. For most other purposes, interpolation is not necessary.

Performance: OSCIL1 (AMP, SI, NF, PHS$_i$)
Initialization: PHS $=$ X, where X may have any positive or negative value (optional)
Flowchart symbol:

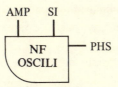

Description: The inputs to OSCIL1 have the same meaning as in OSCIL and OSCILI; however, OSCIL1 samples the function only *once,* holding the value of the beginning and end. SI thus normally indicates a *duration.*

While PHS is *less than or equal to 0,* OSCIL1 holds the value of F(1,NF), the first location in the function. While PHS is *greater than 0 but less than 511.,* OSCIL1 outputs the value of F(PHS $+$ 1, NF), where only the integer portion of PHS is used. While PHS is *greater than 511.,* OSCIL1 holds the value of F(512,NF). In all cases the value obtained from the function is multiplied by AMP, and SI is added to PHS.

To hold the value of the first location in the function for a specific duration DUR (in seconds), PHS should originally be set to SI $-$ DUR*SI*SR. After the initial delay, the function is sampled once with increment SI, and then the value of the last location is held for the remainder of the note.

If SI is negative, the function will be sampled *backward.* In this case, PHS should initially be set to 511. or to SI $+$ DUR*SI*SR $+$ 511. in order to hold the value of the last location for an initial duration DUR.

If PHS is not reset during the initialization of a note, the function will be sampled starting at the point where the previous note left off.

Performance: FORMNT (RMS, SI, NF1, NF2, NF3, NF4, A(3))
Initialization: A(1) = X, where 0. $\leq$ X < 512. (optional)
Flowchart symbol:

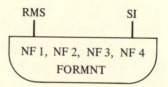

Description: NF1, a sine-wave cycle, is simultaneously sampled at various frequencies according to a set of parameters stored in NF2. These parameters specify only relative frequency, the controlling absolute frequency being given by SI as a sampling increment. They also specify relative amplitude and phase, the overall phase being determined continuously. Thus, NF2 may specify harmonic or nonharmonic partials of the basic frequency determined by SI. Nonharmonic partials are represented in NF2 only to an accuracy of $\frac{1}{128}$ of a partial.

The amplitudes of the various partials are also affected by NF3, which is a relative-amplitude function of the fixed frequencies from 0 to $\frac{511}{512}$ of ½ SR—i.e., a "formant." The scale of the total output is set by RMS, which gives not the peak amplitude, but the root-mean-square value.

NF4 is an *optional* function of the same fixed frequencies as NF3; but instead of affecting the relative amplitudes of the partials, it affects the total amplitude of the output. Thus, it may be used to compensate for the different response of the ear to different frequencies, or simply to rescale the total output uniformly. (*N.B.* NF4 must not have the value 0 for any frequency less than ½ SR.) If NF4 is *equal to 0,* no change is made in the output following the modification by NF3.

SI must be positive. If the frequency of any partial for which NF2 specifies a non-0 amplitude, for some given value of SI, equals or exceeds ½ SR, the unit ignores this and all subsequent NF2 specifications. NF2 thus does not have to be changed to avoid calling for partials higher than ½ SR on high notes.

A (1) is the phase of the unit, which has the same meaning as PHS in OSCIL, OSCILI, and other units.

Notes: NF1 (a sine wave) is generated by GEN08, GEN09, or GEN10. NF2 (the input waveform) is generated by GEN02, GEN18, GEN19, or GEN20.

NF3 (the formant) and NF4 (the frequency-response curve) are generated by GEN03 or GEN04.

Performance: BUZZ (AMP, SI, HN, NF1, PHS$_1$)
Initialization: PHS = X, where 0. $\leq$ X $<$ 1024. (optional)
Flowchart symbol:

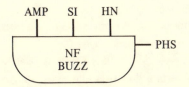

Description: NF1 is the first half of a sine-wave cycle stored over two consecutively numbered functions. HN indicates a number of harmonic partials. The output of BUZZ is a signal with amplitude AMP and *fundamental* frequency determined by SI, a sampling increment, containing a series of *harmonic* partials up to and including HN at *equal* amplitudes. PHS is the phase of the unit, except that unlike OSCIL and other units it is determined modulo 1024, which is the length of two stored functions.

BUZZ is normally used to provide a source signal to a series of filters (RESONs or VRESONs). In order to avoid foldover frequencies, HN must not specify harmonic partials higher than ½ SR. If all harmonic partials up to ½ SR are desired, HN should be set to AINT ((SR/2.)/CPSPCH(PCH)), where PCH is expressed in 8VE.PC form. Note that HN must be a floating-point number containing *no fractional part.*

BUZZ is more accurate for large values of HN than for smaller values. For fewer than five harmonics some excessive sample values may occur.
Notes: A single sine-wave cycle may be stored over two consecutive functions by calling for partial number .5 for each function, and a phase of 0 for the first and 180 degrees for the second.

Performance or initialization:

PERIOD (DUR)
CYCLE (CPS)
PITCH (PCH)
OCTAVE(OCT)

Flowchart symbol:

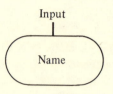

Input

Name

Description: These units convert an input representing either a *frequency* or a *duration* into a *sampling increment.*

PERIOD outputs $\frac{512./SR}{DUR}$, unless DUR is 0, in which case it outputs 511.999. It thus converts a duration expressed in *seconds* into a sampling increment. Specifying a duration of 0 is interpreted as calling for the maximum possible sampling increment, the effective duration then being actually one sample.

CYCLE outputs $\frac{CPS * 512.}{SR}$, thus converting a frequency expressed in *cycles per second* or *Hertz* (Hz) to a sampling increment.

PITCH converts frequency expressed in the *octave-point pitch-class* (i.e., *8VE.PC) form* to a sampling increment. In this form the integer part of the number (PCH) represents the *octave* in which the pitch lies, with 8.0 as middle C. (The frequency of middle C is roughly 2^8 cps.) The first two digits after the decimal point indicate the *pitch class,* i.e., the number of *semitones* above C. Subsequent digits represent additional tenths, hundredths, etc., of semitones. For example, in 8VE.PC form the numbers 8.09 and 7.21 both indicate the same pitch, namely A 440. Similarly, 8.015 and 7.135 both indicate the pitch halfway between C# and D above middle C. This form is thus useful for indicating pitches in twelve-tone equal temperament.

OCTAVE converts a frequency expressed in *octave form* to a sampling increment. In this form the entire number represents the "octave" in which the pitch occurs, with 8.0 as middle C. The number 8.5 indicates a pitch halfway between middle C and an octave above middle C, or 8.06 in 8VE.PC form. Octave form is useful for representing pitch on a purely linear scale.

Notes: If these units are used only in the initialization section of an instrument, they are not given symbols in the flowchart but are simply written out at the input where they are used.

Performance or initialization:

OCTPCH (PCH)
OCTCPS (CPS)

CPSOCT (OCT)
CPSPCH (PCH)
PCHCPS (CPS)
PCHOCT (OCT)

Flowchart symbol:

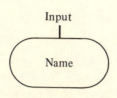

Description: These units convert frequency expressed in one form to another form. The first three letters of the name of the unit indicate the form of the *output,* and the last three the form of the *input.* These relationships are summarized in Figure 8–3.1.

OCTPCH converts frequency expressed in 8VE.PC form to octave form.

OCTCPS converts frequency expressed in cycles per second to octave form.

CPSOCT converts frequency expressed in octave form to cycles per second.

CPSPCH converts frequency expressed in 8VE.PC form to cycles per second.

PCHCPS converts frequency expressed in cycles per second to 8VE.PC form.

PCHOCT converts frequency expressed in octave form to 8VE.PC form.

Notes: If these units are used only in the initialization section of an instrument, they are not given symbols in the flowchart but are simply written out at the input where they are used.

Form of Output	Duration	CPS	Octaves	8VE.PC
Sampling increment	PERIOD	CYCLE	OCTAVE	PITCH
CPS			CPSOCT	CPSPCH
Octaves		OCTCPS		OCTPCH
8VE.PC		PCHCPS	PCHOCT	

Figure 8–3.1: Table of frequency-conversion functions.

Performance: **VOCTAVE(OCT,XINT,SI,NF,A(3))**
Initialization: A(1) = X, where 0. $\leq$ X < 512. (optional)
Flowchart symbol:

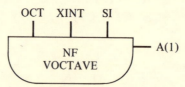

Description: This unit converts to a sampling increment a pitch that results from the variation of an initial pitch OCT by an interval XINT, both expressed in octave form, the variation being done by sampling function number NF with increment SI.

The variation is done by an OSCIL internal to the unit; hence it may be *cyclic for vibrato* or *linear for glissando.* A negative XINT normally indicates a *downward* glissando—i.e., it causes the value in the function to be multiplied by a negative number. Pitch is converted according to a linear scale, so that a linear change of equal amounts produces equal musical intervals.

A(1) is the phase of the internal OSCIL, which may be reset during the initialization.

Notes: To express the inputs for VOCTAVE in 8VE.PC form or in cycles per second, the OCTPCH or OCTCPS functions may be used.

Certain Fortran compilers, such as the Fortran IV/G compiler for the IBM System/360 computers, require that all variable names be six characters or less in length. In these cases the name of this unit is spelled V8VE or VOCTAV.

While the 8VE.PC form is a very convenient notation for pitches, it is not convenient for computations on pitches. For example, 8.00 − .01 = 7.99, or 15.03, but *not* 7.11 in 8VE.PC form, which is the next lower pitch. These problems are solved by converting pitches into octave form before carrying out any further operations.

Performance or initialization: **VFMULT(AMP,SL,NF)**
Flowchart symbol:

Description: This unit outputs AMP*F(I,NF), where I is the residue modulo 512 of the absolute value of SL. No sampling is involved.

Performance: SLOPE(A_1,B_1)
                       EXPON(A_1,B_1)
Initialization: CALL SLPSET(A,B,DUR)
                       CALL EXPSET(A,B,DUR)

Flowchart symbols:

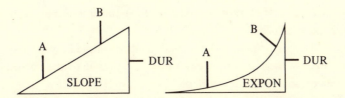

Description: These units calculate interpolations between values specified over a duration (in seconds). For SLOPE the interpolation is *linear,* and for EXPON it is *exponential* such that the geometric mean value is reached at one half of the duration. All inputs must be determined entirely during the initialization.

If DUR is less than P(3), the interpolation continues beyond B; whereas if DUR is greater than P(3), the value B is never reached.

For SLOPE, A and B may be any positive or negative values. For EXPON, neither A nor B may be 0 and both must have the same *sign.* For both SLOPE and EXPON, A and B may be the *same* value.

Notes: The value of DUR is not used during the performance and is not affected by the initialization subroutines SLPSET and EXPSET.

Performance: LINENS(AMP,A(8))
Initialization: CALL LINSET(RISE,DUR,DECAY,A(8))
Flowchart symbol:

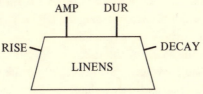

Description: This unit produces a linear envelope with rise time RISE, decay time DECAY, and duration DUR. All times are expressed in seconds and must be determined entirely during the initialization of each note. AMP is the maximum steady-state amplitude reached during the course of the note and may be varied during the performance. The shape of the rise and decay is linear.

RISE and DECAY may be 0 to obtain tied notes. DUR may *not* be 0. If RISE is longer than P(3), the maximum amplitude is never reached. Similarly, if the sum of RISE and DECAY is longer than P(3), the unit never decays to 0. If DUR is shorter than P(3), the unit outputs 0 after DUR seconds have elapsed.

Notes: AMP is indicated in the second position on the flowchart symbol in order to allow the rise and decay times to be input to the corresponding locations on the flowchart symbol.

The use of LINENS requires the statement "REAL LINENS" in the orchestra program.

Performance: ENVLP(AMP,NF1,NF2,A(5))
Initialization: CALL EVPSET(DELAY,RISE,DUR,DECAY,NF1,
                                NF2,A(5))

Flowchart symbol:

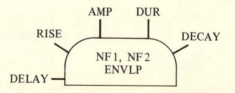

Description: This unit is a general envelope-control generator, allowing the shape of the rise and decay to be determined by stored functions.

DELAY is an initial delay time, which occurs before the rise time begins. RISE is the length of the rise time, and DECAY is the length of the decay time. DUR is the duration, encompassing the DELAY, RISE, and DECAY times. All times are expressed in seconds.

NF1 determines the shape of the rise, and NF2 the shape of the decay. NF2, however, is sampled *backward* in order that the same function may be used for both the rise and decay shapes.

At the beginning of the note, F(1,NF1) is held for DELAY seconds, and at the end of the note, if DUR is shorter than P(3), F(1,NF2) is held. If RISE is longer than P(3), the maximum amplitude is never reached, whereas if the sum of DELAY, RISE, and DECAY is longer than P(3), the unit never decays to 0.

AMP is the steady-state amplitude. If the final value of NF1 or NF2 is less than 1.0, the maximum amplitude reached during the rise or decay time may exceed the value specified by AMP.

Performance: TONE (X,A(3))

                             RESON (X,A(5))

Initialization: CALL TONSET (HP,XINIT,A(3))

                             CALL RSNSET (CF,BW,SCL,XINIT,A(5))

Flowchart symbols:

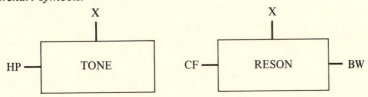

Description: These units are digital filters with a signal input X and fixed frequency-response characteristics.

TONE is analogous to the effect of the "tone" control on an amplifier. It is only a low-pass or high-pass filter, and the formulas for calculating its half-power point are exact. HP indicates the half-power point (in cycles per second). Since power is proportional to the square of amplitude, the amplitude is reduced by a factor of the square root of 2 at the half-power point. TONE is assumed to be a low-pass filter, unless HP is negative, in which case it specifies a high-pass filter with half-power point at $\frac{SR}{2}$ − ABS (HP).

RESON simulates a two-pole band-pass filter with center frequency CF and bandwidth BW, both expressed in cycles per second. *Bandwidth* is the difference of frequency between the half-power points on either side of the center. RESON becomes a low-pass filter if the center frequency is set to 0, and it becomes a high-pass filter if the center frequency is ½SR.

SCL is the *scaling factor* of the filter. If SCL is 1., the gain of the filter is set at 1 at its center frequency—i.e., no frequency is ever boosted and the amplitude of the output is less as the signal's component frequencies deviate farther from the center frequency. This type of scaling is automatic for TONE. If SCL is 2., the gain of the filter is set at 1 on a random input; hence this should be used for filtering noise. If SCL is 0., it indicates no scaling; in this case the user must provide his own method of scaling the output.

XINIT is the *initialization factor* of the filter. Filtering involves a feedback network in which the two previous samples are used. If XINIT equals 0, the "previous samples" are set to 0. XINIT should be set to 0 the first time the unit is used, and it should be set to anything other than 0 on tied notes.

Notes: RESON can be "reinitialized" during the course of a note to provide a kind of variable control over the center frequency and bandwidth.

Performance: VRESON (X,CF,BW,FL$_1$,NF,A(5))
Initialization: CALL VRSSET (PK,XINIT,A(5))
Flowchart symbol:

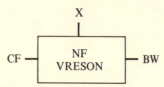

Description: This unit simulates a two-pole band-pass filter with signal input X and with variable center frequency CF and bandwidth BW. Both CF and BW are expressed in cycles per second.

Setting the gain of the filter requires computing a cosine function. (A cosine function is identical to a sine function at a phase of 90 degrees.) Since this would be very time consuming for the computer to recalculate on each sample, a cosine function is instead stored in function NF. However, since the entire function is not usually needed, it is necessary to store only part of a cycle in the function. FL indicates what portion of the cycle is stored in NF; the number given in FL is the number of locations that would be needed to contain a complete cycle. For example, if FL equals 512., the entire cycle is stored in one function; if FL equals 1,024., half a cycle is stored in the function; etc. The relation between FL and the partial number specified on the F card that generates the cosine function is

$$FL = \frac{512.}{PTL}.$$

The size of the cosine function needed depends on the highest value of the center frequency expected during the note. The formula for computing FL is

$$FL = 512. * \frac{SR}{CF}.$$

For the filter to be able to respond to the highest frequency available for a given SR, which is ½SR, $FL = 512. * \frac{SR}{SR/2.} = 1024.$, and one half of a cosine function is stored in NF.

Since there are 512 locations in the function, the difference in frequency between each location is $\frac{1}{512}$ of the highest frequency. If the above function, which represents half a cosine cycle, were used, there would be a great difference in pitch between successive locations at the lower end of the function. If this creates a problem on certain notes, a smaller portion of the cosine cycle can be stored in NF, with FL being correspondingly increased. For example, one twentieth or 0.05 of a cosine cycle could be stored in NF, with FL set to 10,240. This would allow very accurate frequency quantization, but would only go as high as $\frac{1}{20}$ SR, or 1,000 cps at a sampling rate of 20,000 samples per second.

A compromise between these extremes that is often satisfactory is to let FL equal 2,560. and to store one fifth or 0.2 of a cosine function in NF. This function allows frequencies up to 4,000 cps at a sampling rate of 20,000 samples per second with gaps of approximately 8 cps between successive locations.

PK is the anticipated maximum input amplitude which will be achieved during a given note.

XINIT is the initialization factor (identical to XINIT in TONE and RESON); it should be set at 0 except on tied noted.

Even when these suggestions are followed, the amplitude output of VRESON can vary greatly. If this causes a problem, the amplitude can be corrected by BALNCE (*q.v.*) or rescaled in some other way.

Performance: BALNCE (Y,X,A(6))
Initialization: CALL BLNSET (BW,XINIT,A(6))

Flowchart symbol:

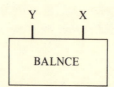

Description: y is a signal that has been passed through a series of filters (TONEs, RESONs, or VRESONs), and X is another signal, such as the same signal before passing through the filters. BALNCE rescales the amplitude of Y so that it is in the same range as X (i.e., it "balances" the signals).

BW is the bandwidth of two TONEs internal to the BALNCE. It is usually set at approximately 10 cps or at some other value appropriate for the internal averaging filters.

XINIT is the initialization factor (identical to XINIT in TONE, RESON, and VRESON); it should be set at 0 except on tied notes.

When the frequency of the input signal X changes suddenly, such as at the beginning of a new note, BALNCE may jump out of range while it adjusts to the new value. For this reason, it is best to turn on the instrument for a very short duration (such as 500 samples) before the note begins, and delay the attack during this time.

Notes: With all digital filters, the envelope and other amplitude modifications should be placed *after* the filter processing in the instrument design.

Performance: RANDOM(X)
Initialization: none
Flowchart symbol:

Description: This unit outputs a random number X in the range $0. \leq X \leq 1$. For a given input value X, the output will always be the same. When X is set to the *previous* random-number output, the unit will produce white noise over successive samples. The unit can be thought of as producing a random series beginning at the first number specified.

Performance: RAND(X,A)
Initialization: A = previous value, where $0. \leq A \leq 1.$
Flowchart symbol:

X

RAND

Description: This unit outputs white noise with an R.M.S. amplitude of X.
Notes: A is a data value used internally by the unit. A does not need to be reset, but a separate data value is required for each unit.

Performance: RANDH(AMP,SI,A(2))
Initialization: A(1) = 512.
Flowchart symbol:

AMP   SI

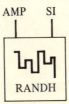

RANDH

Description: RANDH outputs AMP multiplied by a random number in the range 0. to 1.0. Each random number is *held* for $\frac{512}{SI}$ samples; thus SI can be expressed as a sampling increment.

When A(1) equals 512., it causes the unit to generate a new random number. This should be done the first time the unit is used.

Performance: RANDI(AMP,SI,A(4))
Initialization: A(1) = 1.
               A(3) = previous random number, where $0. \leq A(3) \leq 1.$

Flowchart symbol:

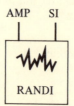

Description: This unit produces a linear interpolation between random numbers in the range -1.0 to $+1.0$ and multiplies the result by **AMP**. New random numbers are generated every $\frac{512}{SI}$ samples; thus SI can be expressed as a sampling increment.

When A(1) equals 1., it causes the unit to generate a new random number. This should be done the first time the unit is used.

Performance: COMB(XIN,RVT,An))
ALPASS(XIN,RVT,An))
REVERB(XIN,RVT,Am))

Initialization:

for COMB and ALPASS: CALL CMBSET (XLOOPT, XINIT,A(n))
for REVERB: CALL RVBSET (XINIT,A(m))

$$n = (XLOOPT*SR) + 5$$

$$m = \frac{1{,}583*SR}{10{,}000} + 30$$

Flowchart symbol:

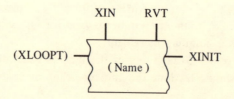

Description: **COMB** stores an input signal **XIN** for a duration **XLOOPT** (in seconds) and then feeds back the signal continuously so that the amplitude is reduced by a factor of .001 over RVT seconds. COMB thus produces *echoes* each time the signal passes through the feedback loop. Since this process is equivalent to a filter with resonance peaks at every multiple of the reciprocal of the loop time, it is called a *comb filter*.

ALPASS is equivalent to COMB except that it has a feature that cancels the frequency-response characteristics of COMB, thus passing all frequencies at the same amplitude.

REVERB reverberates a signal input XIN with reverberation time RVT seconds. REVERB is equivalent to four COMBs with feedback loop-times of .0297, .0371, .0411, and .0437 seconds, which are added together and passed through two ALPASSes with loop times of .0050 and .0017. (The theory behind this procedure for generating reverberation was originally suggested by M. R. Schroeder.) These loop-time constants are all prime to one another, so that the feedback loops do not reinforce one another very often.

XINIT is the initialization factor of each unit. When XINIT is set at 0, the unit is "erased" during the initialization. Otherwise, whatever has been left in the loop remains.

Notes: A is a data area in which the samples used by the feedback process are stored. The formulas for calculating the amount of storage necessary are shown above. These dimension specifications denote the *maximum* amount of storage needed for the greatest value of XLOOPT. Thus, XLOOPT can be changed to different values during the initialization of different notes, as long as there is sufficient storage for the loop in the data area.

Since REVERB requires so much storage, it is often necessary to mix the output of all instruments using reverberation into one or two separate instruments and thus avoid duplicating the unit several times. This procedure also gives independent control over the durations of the reverberated signals and the input signals.

Arithmetic Operations

Naturally, Fortran arithmetic statements and library functions may be used in instruments. When arithmetic expressions are written out, it is important to remember the hierarchy in which Fortran executes unparenthesized elements, which is as follows:

1. exponentiation (**)
2. multiplication (*) and division (/)

3. addition (+) and subtraction (−). According to these conventions, the formula

$$A + B*C**D$$

would be executed as

$$A + (B*(C**D)).$$

When these operations are executed during the performance section of instruments, the following flowchart symbols may be used:

Exponentiation:

Multiplication or division:

Addition or subtraction:

Instrument Flowcharting

In a sense, the design of a computer instrument must be worked out in two different ways: first, the *logical structure* of the instrument is planned, in which the user makes various decisions about the kinds of musical characteristics the instrument is supposed to control and the unit generators necessary to produce them. Second, this logical structure is *coded* in a suitable programming language and run on the computer.

A *flowchart* is a diagram of the logical structure of an instrument, show-ing all of the units it contains and their interconnections and inputs. A flowchart is completely analogous to a *patch chart* of interconnections of an analog electronic music synthesizer. The advantage of a flowchart is both that it graphically depicts the logical structure of the instrument and that it is independent of the programming language in which the instrument is coded. It is a good habit to work out the flowchart for an instrument before writing the code, and we will follow this practice in the examples later in this chapter. In order to be as accurate as possible, there are several impor-tant conventions we will observe when writing flowcharts:

(1) Only unit generators that produce characteristics that vary over the course of the duration of a tone are represented in the flowchart. In MUSIC4BF terminology, this means that unit generators computed during note-performance time are indicated in the flowchart.

(2) Unit generators and calculations computed at note-initialization time are indicated at the input of the units that use them, but are not given symbols in the flowchart.

(3) Inputs to the flowchart symbol are distinguished by the *location* at which they enter the diagram. In OSCIL, for example, the amplitude input is always indicated feeding into the left side of the top of the symbol and the sampling-increment input feeding into the right side. Generally the order of inputs feeding into the symbol is the same as the arguments are indicated in the Fortran calling sequence, but sometimes this order is vi-olated in favor of one of the following conditions: all note-performance inputs are indicated first in the calling sequence, and sometimes an input is indicated at a certain location because it is intuitive for the shape of the flowchart symbol.

(4) The unit generators in the flowchart are often numbered with small numbers outside of the symbol. These numbers are used when referring to the units in a discussion of the flowchart in order to distinguish two or more units with the same name.

Flowcharts can also be written for analog patch-chart diagrams, and if similar conventions are adopted the resulting diagram both will show the logical structure of the patch and will be independent of an individual electronic music system. Flowcharting is an excellent form of notation for electronic musical instruments.

Figure 8-3.2: Table of unit generators.

CALL MONO(OUTPUT)	none	monaural output routine
CALL STEREO(OUTPUT,PROP)	none	stereophonic output routine
CALL OUTPUT(A,B,C,D)	none	direct output routine
OSCIL(AMP,SI,NF,PHS$_1$)	PHS=X, where $0. \leq X < 512.$	periodic function sampler
OSCILI(AMP,SI,NF,PHS$_1$)	PHS=X, where $0. \leq X < 512.$	interpolating oscillator
OSCIL1(AMP,SI,NF,PHS$_1$)	PHS=X	sample-and-hold "oscillator"
FORMNT(RMS,SI,NF1,NF2,NF3,NF4,A(3))	A(1)=phase	formant generator
BUZZ(AMP,SI,HN,NF1,PHS(1))	PHS=X, where $0. \leq X < 1024.$	buzz generator
VFMULT(AMP,SL,NF)	none	AMP*F(SL,NF)
PERIOD(DUR)	none	DUR to SI
CYCLE(CPS)	none	CPS to SI
PITCH(PCH)	none	PCH to SI
OCTAVE(OCT)	none	OCT to SI
OCTPCH(PCH)	none	PCH to OCT
OCTCPS(CPS)	none	CPS to OCT
CPSOCT(OCT)	none	OCT to CPS
CPSPCH(PCH)	none	PCH to CPS
PCHCPS(CPS)	none	CPS to PCH
PCHOCT(OCT)	none	OCT to PCH
VOCTAVE(OCT,XINT,SI,NF,A(3))	A(1)=phase	variable pitch generator

SLOPE(A,,B,)	SLPSET(A,B,DUR)	linear interpolation from A to B
EXPON(A,,B,)	EXPSET(A,B,DUR)	exponential interpolation from A to B
LINENS(AMP,A(8))	LINSET(RISE,DUR,DECAY,A(8))	linear envelope generator
ENVLP(AMP,NF1,NF2,A(5))	EVPSET(DELAY,RISE,DUR,DECAY, NF1,NF2,A(5))	function envelope generator
TONE(X,A(3))	TONSET(HP,XINIT,A(3))	simple filter
RESON(X,CF,BW,FL,NF,A(5))	RSNSET(CF,BW,SCL,XINIT,A(5))	fixed filter
VRESON(X,CF,BW,FL,,NF,A(5))	VRSSET(PK,XINIT,A(5))	variable filter
BALNCE(Y,X,A(6))	BLNSET(BW,XINIT,A(6))	filter balancer
RANDOM(A)	A = previous random number	random number generator
RAND(X,A)	A = previous random number	noise generator
RANDH(AMP,SI,A(2))	A(1) = 512.	random hold
RANDI(AMP,SI,A(4))	A(1) = 1.,A(3) = previous random number	random interpolate
COMB(XIN,RVT,A(n)) *	CMBSET(XLOOPT,XINIT,A(n))	comb filter
ALPASS(XIN,RVT,A(n)) *	CMBSET(XLOOPT,XINIT,A(n))	"all-pass' filter
REVERB(XIN,RVT,A(m)) **	RVBSET(XINIT,A(m))	reverberator

* n equals XLOOPT*SR + 5   ** m equals 1583*SR/10000 + 30

Instrument Programming

Instrument programming is analogous to the patching together of analog devices that one carries out when working with an electronic music synthesizer. The analog devices of the synthesizer are replaced by the unit generators of the computer program, but while they serve analogous functions, their precise operation is quite different in many cases. A thorough understanding of the operation of the unit generators is essential to instrument programming, of course. This information is summarized in the unit-generator descriptions above. In practice it is not necessary to memorize all of this information, but simply to keep this book handy in order to look up any points about which you are not sure. Here we will trace through several examples of instruments, illustrating their structure by means of flowcharts and the actual Fortran code for the orchestra program, and explain the reasons for many of the statements in the program. A knowledge of the unit generators used in each instrument will be assumed when it is discussed, so the reader is advised to look back to the appropriate descriptions if he or she is unsure of the explanations. A knowledge of all the unit generators would enable the reader to decide alternative methods of solving the musical problems presented in the examples. Of course, it is also assumed that the reader has an understanding of the syntax and language elements of the Fortran programming language.

EXAMPLE 1

In this example we would like to have an orchestra consisting of six instruments that play single tones with the following characteristics:

(1) An exponential decay from an indicated maximum starting amplitude level to one tenth of this level over a duration of 1.5 seconds, which we choose because we imagine that this may be analogous to the way in which tones decay on the piano. (Such an assumption is subject to experimental verification, but actually here we are not as much attempting to imitate the piano as we are simply choosing an arbitrary characteristic.)

(2) An envelope consisting of an attack and decay of .01 seconds, each of which is linear in shape.

(3) A pitch that remains constant over the duration of each note but that may be different for each successive note.

(4) A timbre, consisting of harmonic partials of various amplitudes and

phases (the specific values of which we will not enumerate here), that remains constant over the duration of each note, but that may be different for each successive note.

(5) A location that may be situated at any of five equidistant points which include the two speakers and three points between them.

Figure 8–3.3 illustrates the flowchart for an instrument that produces these characteristics. The exponential decay is controlled by an EXPON, which begins at the level indicated in P(4) of the note card and decays to 10 per cent of that level over 1.5 seconds. The envelope is controlled by a LINENS. Note that the inputs for the attack and decay times and the duration of the LINENS are indicated going into the analogous positions on the shape of the flowchart symbol, which is meant to show a linear envelope. These inputs are not indicated in this order in the Fortran calling sequence. The pitch is given in P(5) of the note card and converted into a sampling increment, as required by OSCILI, by the PITCH unit generator. Since this statement can be ex-

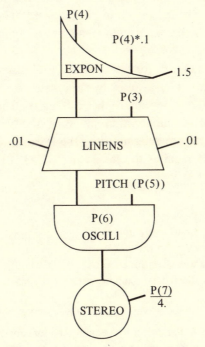

Figure 8–3.3: Flowchart for Example 1.

ecuted during the initialization of the note, it does not receive a flow-chart symbol, but is indicated at the input of the OSCILI. The tone is generated by OSCILI, which samples a function that is specified in P(6) of the note card. The precise characteristics of the timbre are given on the F card that generates the function, which is not shown here. P(6) simply indicates the number of this function. The location of the sound is controlled by the STEREO subroutine, which outputs the signal gene-rated by the OSCILI at a location determined by P(7) divided by 4. P(7) is thus an integer between 0. and 4. inclusive. If it is 0., the sound is distributed entirely in channel B; if it is 2., the sound is divided evenly between channels A and B; etc. The function and parameter in-puts to this instrument are summarized in Figure 8–3.4.

In Example 1 there is only one variable amplitude that is processed by each successive unit generator. The EXPON produces a steady am-plitude which decays in the manner described above. When this is pro-cessed by the LINENS, only the first and last .01 seconds of the note are affected. When it is processed by the OSCILI, an oscillating varia-tion is produced that generates the pitch desired. These steps in which the final sound is processed are illustrated in a simplified form in Figure 8–3.5.

Acceptable Fortran code for this orchestra is illustrated in Figure 8–3.6. Note that all of the data areas used by the instruments are given an initial value of 0 in a DATA statement, so that nothing at all needs to be executed during the orchestra initialization in entry INITL. (SR, NCHNLS, INSTRS, and TAPE are determined by the E card.) The use of the unit generator LINENS requires the statement "REAL LINENS" in the or-

P(1):   instrument number
P(2):   starting time
P(3):   duration
P(4):   amplitude, in arbitrary units
P(5):   pitch, in 8VE.PC form
P(6):   number or waveform function used by OSCILI
P(7):   location, indicated as a number between 0. and 4.

Functions are waveforms generated by GEN08, GEN09, or GEN10.

Figure 8–3.4: Parameter inputs and functions for Example 1.

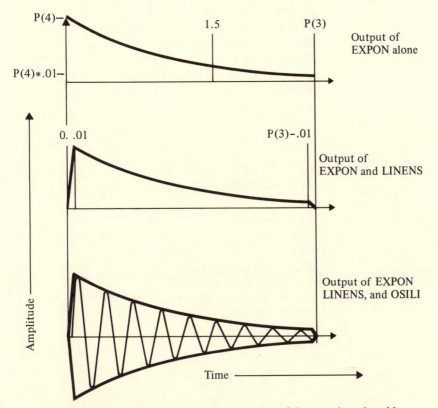

Figure 8–3.5: Intermediate steps in the generation of the sound produced by the instrument in Example 1.

chestra. No branching is required at the beginning of entries SETUP and ORCH since all instruments in this orchestra are of the same structure. A RETURN statement is required at the end of each orchestra program section. Note that I is a singly-subscripted variable because it consists of only one element for each instrument. A(4,N) through A(10,N) are skipped because LINENS requires a data area of eight successive locations, beginning with A(3,N).

```
SUBROUTINE INITL
COMMON P(480), SR,N
DIMENSION A(13,6),I(6)
DATA A/78*0./
REAL LINENS
RETURN
ENTRY SETUP
A(1,N)=P(4)
A(2,N)=P(4)*.1
CALL EXPSET(A(1,N),A(2,N),1.5)
CALL LINSET(.01,P(3),.01,A(3,N))
A(11,N)=PITCH(P(5))
I(N)=P(6)
A(13,N)=P(7)/4.
RETURN
ENTRY ORCH
X=EXPON(A(1,N),A(2,N))
X=LINENS(X,A(3,N))
X=OSCILI(X,A(11,N),I(N),A(12,N))
CALL STEREO(X,A(13,N))
RETURN
END
```

Figure 8–3.6: Fortran code for the orchestra of Example 1.

EXAMPLE 2

In this example we require an orchestra consisting of two different kinds of instruments. For the first instrument, of which we need three numbered 1 to 3, we desire the following characteristics:

(1) A tone that begins at an indicated pitch and makes a glissando of a specified interval over the course of its duration. The glissando will be linear with respect to pitch—i.e., it will cover equal musical intervals over equal durations.

(2) The amplitude of the sound will be adjusted by a frequency-response curve that compensates for the uneven response of the ear to different frequencies in order to produce equal subjective loudness. The adjustment will be only with respect to the fundamental frequency of the tone, however.

(3) The timbre of the tone will be constant during the course of its duration, but may be changed for each new tone.

(4) The envelope of the sound will consist of a linear attack of .05 seconds and a linear decay of .2 seconds.

(5) The sound will be located entirely in channel 1 of a two-channel tape.

For the second instrument in this orchestra, which will be instrument number 4, we desire the following characteristics:

(1) Each tone will consist of a cluster of nonharmonic partials transposed to an indicated pitch level. The specific group of partials may be changed for each new tone. The amplitudes of each of the partials will be adjusted in the same way as the tones in the instrument above in order to compensate for the uneven response of the ear to different frequencies.

(2) The sound will be amplitude modulated above and below an indicated level by a specified amount. The shape and speed of modulation will be indicated for each tone. The speed will remain constant over the course of the tone.

(3) The sound will receive a linear envelope with an attack time of .05 seconds and a steady-state time of .2 seconds, with the decay time occupying the rest of the duration of the tone.

(4) The sound will be located entirely in channel 2 of a two-channel tape.

Figure 8–3.7 indicates flowcharts for instruments that meet these specifications. The glissando in instruments 1 through 3 is controlled by a VOCTAVE unit generator, although the inputs, specified in P(4) and P(5), are in 8VE.PC form. These inputs are converted to octave form for VOCTAVE by OCTPCH. The function inside the VOCTAVE is a straight line rising from 0 to 1 over 512 locations. PERIOD (P(3)) produces a sampling increment that samples this function exactly once over the duration of the note. Nevertheless, the phase of the VOCTAVE must be set at 0 at note-initialization time to insure that each note begins exactly at the beginning of the function. VFMULT performs the adjustment of the amplitude by the frequency-response curve, the details of which are specified in function 2. VOCTAVE produces a sampling-increment output representing the fundamental frequency of the tone. Since a sampling increment represents frequencies from 0 to ½ SR as numbers from 0 to 256, multiplying the sampling increment by 2 represents these frequencies on a scale from 0 to 512, which is appropriate for the function used by VFMULT. The tone is generated by OSCILI, and the envelope is controlled by LINENS. Calling OUTPUT with the signal input only in the left argument and all other arguments 0 plays the sound entirely in channel 1.

The flowchart for instrument 4 is shown beside that for instruments 1 through 3 in Figure 8–3.7. The amplitude modulation is controlled by an OSCIL and an addition instruction. The maximum amplitude output of the OSCIL will be the sum of the values in P(5) and P(6), but this result will then be processed by the frequency-response curve in FORMNT. The speed of modulation is expressed in P(7) in cycles per second, and the shape is controlled by the function whose number is indicated in P(8).

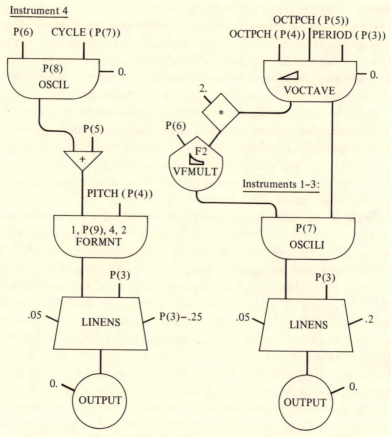

Figure 8–3.7: Flowcharts for Example 2.

FORMNT generates the entire cluster of nonharmonic partials and adjusts their amplitudes by the frequency-response curve. The way in which this happens is controlled by the four functions specified in the inputs. The first function, F(1), is a sine-wave cycle, which is sampled repeatedly to produce each of the frequencies specified in the second function. The second function, then, must indicate all of the nonharmonic partials and their relative amplitudes and phases. The number of this function is specified in P(9) in this instrument. The third function, F(4) in this instrument, designates a fixed-frequency "formant," or a curve indicating the way in which the amplitudes of partials over the frequency continuum are to be increased or decreased. In this instance, however, the entire manner in which the amplitudes and partials are structured is given by the second function. Therefore, F(4) specifies an "all-frequency formant curve," which passes all frequencies uniformly and does not change the specifications of the second function. An "all-frequency formant curve" is simply a straight line from 1 to 1 over the entire function. Finally, the fourth function input is the frequency-response curve that compensates for the response of the ear to different frequencies. This function is F(2), the same used by the VFMULT in instrument 1; this feature is an automatic optional feature of FORMNT.

The remaining characteristics of the instrument are self-explanatory from the flowchart diagram. Note that the decay time is P(3) — .25 seconds; the .25 seconds covers both the .05-second attack time and the .2-second steady-state time. This kind of arithmetic operation can be indicated directly in the input to LINSET. Finally, the OUTPUT instruction places the entire output in channel 2, instead of channel 1, which is used by instruments 1 through 3.

The parameter and function inputs to these instruments are summarized in Figure 8–3.8.

Instruments 1 through 3:

P(4):   pitch from which glissando begins, in 8VE.PC form
P(5):   interval of glissando, in 8VE.PC form
P(6):   amplitude
P(7):   number of timbre function

Instrument 4:

P(4):   pitch level of cluster of nonharmonic partials
P(5):   amplitude
P(6):   amount of amplitude modulation
P(7):   speed of amplitude modulation, in cycles per second
P(8):   number of function specifying shape of amplitude modulation
P(9):   number of function indicating cluster of partials

Functions:

1:   sine wave, generated by GEN08, GEN09, or GEN10
2:   frequency-response curve
3:   straight line rising from 0 to 1
4:   straight line from 1 to 1

Other functions indicated by P(7) of instruments 1 through 3 and P(8) and P(9) of instrument 4.

Figure 8–3.8: Parameter inputs and functions for Example 2.

```
        SUBROUTINE INITL
        COMMON P(480),SR,N
        DIMENSION A(16,3),I(3),B(17),J(2)
        DATA A/48*0./,B/17*0./
        REAL LINENS
        RETURN
        ENTRY SETUP
        IF (N.GE.4) GO TO 40
C       INITIALIZATION FOR INSTRUMENTS 1-3
        A(1,N)=OCTPCH(P(4))
        A(2,N)=OCTPCH(P(5))
        A(3,N)=PERIOD(P(3))
        A(4,N)=0.
        A(7,N)=P(6)
        CALL LINSET(.05,P(3),.2,A(9,N))
        I(N)=P(7)
        RETURN
C       INITIALIZATION FOR INSTRUMENT 4
     40 B(1)=P(6)
        B(2)=CYCLE(P(7))
        J(1)=P(8)
        B(3)=0.
        B(4)=P(5)
        B(6)=PITCH(P(4))
        J(2)=P(9)
        CALL LINSET(.05,P(3),P(3)-.25,B(10))
        RETURN
        ENTRY ORCH
        GO TO (1,1,1,4), N
C       PERFORMANCE FOR INSTRUMENTS 1-3
      1 Y=VOCTAVE(A(1,N),A(2,N),A(3,N),3,A(4,N))
        X=VFMULT(A(7,N),Y*2.,2)
        X=OSCILI(X,Y,I(N),A(8,N))
        X=LINENS(X,A(9,N))
        CALL OUTPUT(X,0.,0.,0.)
        RETURN
C       PERFORMANCE FOR INSTRUMENT 4
      4 X=OSCIL(B(1),B(2),J(1),B(3)) + B(4)
        X=FORMNT(X,B(6),1,J(2),4,2,B(7))
        X=LINENS(X,B(10))
        CALL OUTPUT(0.,X,0.,0.)
        RETURN
        END
```

Figure 8–3.9: Fortran code for Example 2.

EXAMPLE 3

In this example we desire five instruments with the following characteristics:

(1) A tone consisting of all harmonic partials up to 5,000 cps at equal amplitudes, which is passed first through a low-pass filter with a cutoff frequency of approximately 2,500 cps and then through a variable band-pass filter that begins at an indicated center frequency and sweeps up to another center frequency and back over the course of each note. The bandwidth of the variable band-pass filter is 10 per cent of the center frequency. The highest center frequency ever used will be less than 4,000 cps at a sampling rate of 20,000 samples per second.

(2) Each tone will have an envelope consisting of an initial delay of .025 seconds and an exponentially shaped attack with a time of .02 seconds and a steady-state time of approximately .1 seconds. The decay time will also be exponentially shaped and will occupy the rest of the note.

(3) Each tone will be reverberated with a reverberation time of 2 seconds.

Figure 8–3.10 shows a flowchart for these instruments. We note first that we have mixed the outputs of the five instruments into a sixth instrument containing the reverberator. The reverberator requires 3,196 storage locations, and it would be prohibitive to have a separate unit of this size in each instrument. This process also provides independent control over the duration of each input tone and the reverberated tones, which are extended in duration.

The tones are generated by BUZZ, which uses both functions 1 and 2, although only function 1 is indicated since these two functions are stored consecutively. The pitch of each tone is indicated in P(4) in 8VE.PC form.

The output of the BUZZ is passed through a RESON for the low-pass filter and through a VRESON for the variable band-pass filter. The variation of the center frequency of the band-pass filter is produced by an OSCIL1 followed by an addition. Note that the input to the OSCIL1 must be the difference between the maximum and minimum center frequencies. Function 3 provides the shape of variation and function 4 is used by the VRESON. The information about the maximum center frequency being less than 4,000 cps was necessary to compute the length of the cosine cycle stored in function 4. The VRESON is followed by a BALNCE, which brings the amplitude output of the VRESON into the same range as the output of the BUZZ.

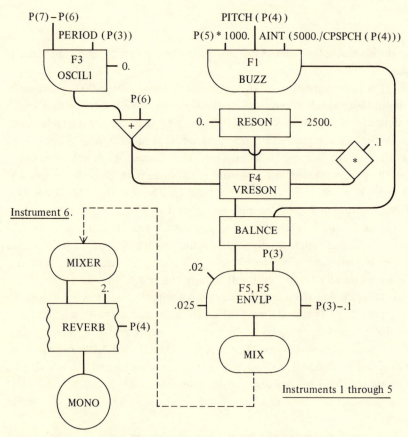

Figure 8–3.10: Flowchart for Example 3.

The envelope is generated by ENVLP, and the exponential shape of the attack and decay times is controlled by function number 5. The functions and parameter inputs are summarized in Figure 8–3.11, and the Fortran code is shown in Figure 8–3.12.

EXAMPLE 4

At the end of Chapter 1, we explained how complex spectra may be obtained by frequency modulating a sine wave by another sine wave. The instrument described below uses this principle to produce dynamically varying spectra in a remarkably simple manner.[11] The flowchart for the

———

[11]This instrument is adapted from John Chowning, "The Synthesis of Complex Audio

Instruments 1 through 5:

P(4): pitch, in 8VE.PC form
P(5): amplitude, in arbitrary units
P(6): initial center frequency of variable band-pass filter
P(7): final center frequency of variable band-pass filter

Instrument 6:

P(4): initialization factor of reverberator

Functions:

1: first half of sine-wave cycle (0 degrees)
2: second half of sine-wave cycle (180 degrees)
3: shape of variation of center frequency of variable band-pass filter
4: first fifth of the cycle of a cosine function
5: exponential attack shape

Figure 8–3.11: Parameter inputs and functions for Example 3.

instrument is illustrated in Figure 8–3.13, and the following points describe the salient features of the instrument:

(1) The carrier and modulating frequencies are indicated in P(5) and P(6) respectively, in cycles per second. These frequencies will determine the resulting frequencies in the sidebands, but are not necessarily harmonic partials of the spectrum. Figure 1–10.1 should be consulted to determine the resulting spectrum for given values of P(5) and P(6).

(2) The dynamic variation of the spectrum is controlled by the amplitude of the OSCIL 4, which controls the frequency deviation. This amplitude is the sum of the OSCIL1 2 and the adder 3. These units are related in such a way that P(7) is the lowest value and P(8) the highest value of the function F(3) in the case where F(3) contains only positive values. F(3) is a function of time describing the manner in which the frequency deviation varies over the course of the duration of a note. If P(7) is less than P(8), the frequency deviation will follow the pattern described by F(3), with P(7)*P(6) as its lowest value and P(8)*P(6) as its highest value; but if P(7) is greater than P(8), the "mirror image" of the function will be produced. P(7) and P(8)

Spectra by Means of Frequency Modulation," *Journal of the Audio Engineering Society,* XXI/7 (Sept., 1973), 526–534.

```
      SUBROUTINE INITL
      COMMON P(480),SR,N
      DIMENSION A(29,5),B(3196)
      DATA A/145*0./,XMIX/0./
      RETURN
      ENTRY SETUP
      IF (N.EQ.6) GO TO 20
      A(1,N)=P(5)*1000.
      A(2,N)=PITCH(P(4))
      A(3,N)=AINT(5000./CPSPCH(P(4)))
      CALL RSNSET(0.,2500.,1.,0.,A(5,N))
      A(10,N)=P(7)-P(6)
      A(11,N)=PERIOD(P(3))
      A(12,N)=0.
      A(13,N)=P(6)
      CALL VRSSET(A(1,N),0.,A(14,N))
      CALL BLNSET(10.,0.,A(19,N))
      CALL EVPSET(.025,.02,P(3),P(3)-.1,5,5,A(25,N))
      RETURN
   20 CALL RVBSET(P(4),B)
      RETURN
      ENTRY ORCH
      IF (N.EQ.6) GO TO 2
      X=BUZZ(A(1,N),A(2,N),A(3,N),1,A(4,N))
      X=RESON(X,A(5,N))
      Y=OSCIL1(A(10,N),A(11,N),3,A(12,N)) + A(13,N)
      Z=VRESON(X,Y,Y*.1,2560.,4,A(14,N))
      X=BALNCE(Z,X,A(19,N))
      XMIX=XMIX+ENVLP(X,5,5,A(25,N))
      RETURN
    2 X=REVERB(XMIX,2.,B)
      CALL MONO(X)
      XMIX=0.
      RETURN
      END
```

Figure 8–3.12: Fortran code for Example 3.

thus allow the lowest and highest values of the *modulation index* to be specified directly.

(3) Function F(2) describes the temporal envelope of each note, and the amplitude is specified in P(4).

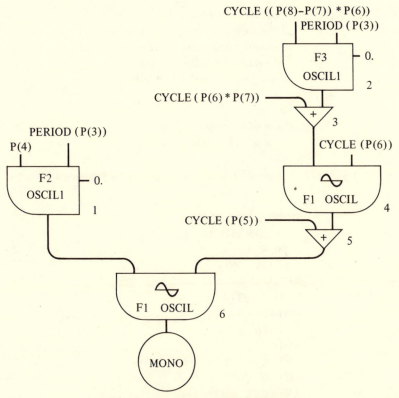

Figure 8–3.13: Flowchart for Example 4.

(4) The left input to the OSCIL1 2 and the adders 3 and 5 are converted to sampling increments by CYCLE during the initialization section of the instrument, because the result of these calculations, which is the output of the adder 5, is used for the frequency input of the OSCIL 6, which requires a sampling increment.

(5) When the frequency deviation is greater than the carrier frequency, or when P(6)*P(7) or P(6)*P(8) is greater than P(5), the output of the adder 5 will sometimes be a negative value. For this reason, the Fortran code for the OSCIL 6 must be modified to accept a negative sampling increment. (This change has already been made standard for OSCIL and OSCILI of the current version of MUSIC4BF, but may not have been made for earlier versions.)

Figure 8–3.14 summarizes the parameter inputs and functions for this instrument, and the Fortran code is illustrated in Figure 8–3.15.

A great variety of sounds containing both harmonic and inharmonic

P(4):   amplitude, in arbitrary units
P(5):   carrier frequency, in cycles per second
P(6):   modulating frequency, in cycles per second
P(7):   first value of modulation index
P(8):   second value of modulation index

F(1):   sine wave
F(2):   temporal envelope
F(3):   envelope of frequency deviation

Figure 8–3.14: Parameter inputs and functions for Example 4.

```
SUBROUTINE INITL
COMMON P(480),SR,N
DIMENSION A(10)
DATA A/10*0./
RETURN
ENTRY SETUP
A(1)=PERIOD(P(3))
A(2)=P(4)
A(3)=0.
A(4)=CYCLE((P(8)−P(7))*P(6))
A(5)=0.
A(6)=CYCLE(P(7)*P(6))
A(7)=CYCLE(P(6))
A(9)=CYCLE(P(5))
RETURN
ENTRY ORCH
X=OSCIL1(A(2),A(1),2,A(3))
Y=OSCIL1(A(4),A(1),3,A(5)) + A(6)
Y=OSCIL(Y,A(7),1,A(8)) + A(9)
X=OSCIL(X,Y,1,A(10))
CALL MONO(X)
RETURN
END
```

Figure 8–3.15: Fortran code for Example 4:

spectra may be obtained from this instrument, and users are encouraged to experiment with different data to see what kinds of musical differentiations result. Chowning has even attempted to duplicate the qualities of live instruments by employing special data that he has developed.

One problem that will be encountered frequently is foldover, which will be produced whenever the amplitudes of extremely high partials become significant. Foldover can be eliminated by employing appropriate values of the modulation index. The highest value should not exceed a value slightly less than $\frac{SR/2 - c}{m}$, where SR is the sampling rate and c and m are the carrier and modulating frequencies respectively. (The exact value depends on the smoothing filters of the digital-to-analog converter.)

The input required by this instrument—carrier and modulating frequencies in cycles per second, and numerical values for the modulation index—are not very intuitive as a description of the output obtained. In this situation, it would be practical for the user to prepare his input in some other form and use an A subroutine to translate it into the form required by the instrument. Figure 8–3.16 illustrates an A subroutine for this purpose.

The input is prepared as follows: P(4) is the amplitude, and is unaffected by the subroutine. In P(5) the user indicates the desired fundamental frequency in 8VE.PC form. P(6) specifies a code describing the desired spectrum. For simplicity, we will assume that the ratio between the carrier and modulating frequency is $1/m$, and that P(6) specifies m. If P(6) is set to 2, then the spectrum would contain odd harmonic partials. (See Chapter 1, Figures 1–10.1 and 1–10.2.) P(7) and P(8) indicate the values of the modulation index; but if either value is greater than $\frac{SR/2 - c}{m}$, it will be reduced

```
          SUBROUTINE A1
C         A-SUBROUTINE TO PROCESS DATA FOR EXAMPLE 4
          COMMON OP,P(12),STOP(999),STP(12,999),NST(480)
          J=NST(1)
          K=NST(2)
          DO 1 I=J,K
          STP(5,I)=CPSPCH(STP(5,I))
          STP(6,I)=STP(6,I)*STP(5,I)
C         P(2) OF A1 CARD INDICATES 1/2 SR IN CPS
          X=(P(2)-STP(5,I))/STP(6,I)
          IF (STP(7,I).GT.X) STP(7,I)=X
          IF (STP(8,I).GT.X) STP(8,I)=X
    1     CONTINUE
          CALL WRITER(J,K)
          RETURN
          END
```

Figure 8–3.16: A subroutine to process input data for Example 4.

to this amount, in order to avoid foldover frequencies. The value of ½SR is passed to the A subroutine in P(2) of the A card. Figure 8–3.17 illustrates some sample data for the instrument, together with the appropriate numbering cards and A card.

N 1	1						
I 1	1	3	1000	6.08	2	0	20
I	4			8.07	1	15	0
N 2	0						
A 1	5000						

Figure 8–3.17: Sample data for subroutine A1 in Figure 8–3.16.

The most important aspect of this instrument is its inherent simplicity, which allows sounds of great complexity to be produced without corresponding complexity of computation. On many computers, this instrument can generate music faster than in real time.

CHAPTER NINE

Systems of the Future

It is always hazardous to try to predict the future, especially in a field like electronic music, where we would like to believe that today's problems will all be solved and fantastic new systems of sound synthesis will be available. To be sure, almost any imaginable development is within the grasp of contemporary technology, but the financial and social support necessary for the investments that would be needed to underwrite this research and development are not likely to be made available. The most obvious reason for this is that there is not much money to be made in electronic music, and it would require many years of steady sales to make back the initial investments if such developments were attempted on a private commercial basis. The more important underlying reason for this state of affairs is simply that society does not place very much value on music at all.

Still, it is likely that some of these predictions will actually come true, as, indeed, all of the systems described previously in this book have already come into being when almost nobody would have predicted so until they were there. At this time, there is no way of knowing which of these developments, if any, will occur, nor do we know how their presence will change the shape of the field and hence its future direction. Thus, we will be very optimistic and try to present as complete a picture of future possibilities as we can. It seems most useful to divide future systems into three categories: analog systems, computer systems, and combined computer-analog or hybrid systems. It will be seen that as we reach the final stage of development above, the whole distinction between digital and analog systems becomes very fuzzy indeed.

1. NEW ANALOG SYSTEMS

Analog electronic music synthesizers have already improved in many ways over the last few years. Today one does not have to worry much about unstable oscillators and such problems, and operational methods have become refined as people have developed skills with their equipment.

The one serious disadvantage of these newer, improved analog synthesizers is their cost. While the components and production methods may often be less expensive than in previous years, the cost of the research and development that led to the designs that use these components and methods has been passed on to the consumer in the form of higher prices. If people who are planning to purchase a synthesizer are aware of the current market prices, they will be better able to plan their budgets in order to meet their requirements. They must also be aware of the great discrepancies in price and performance between large, modular systems and small, prepackaged systems.

These small systems are one of the blights of the recent period of refinement and growth. While some of them are well designed and suited to the purposes for which they are advertised, almost all of them have been designed in such a way as to oversimplify the needs and problems of electronic music. Some of these machines ought to be called "toys," not at all in a disparaging way, but to indicate that they are intended to allow people to "play" with electronic sounds. This is a completely legitimate activity, but it ought not to be confused with musical composition, even if "playing" is an important aspect of composition. These systems are intended for school children as opposed to college students, and people should be aware of their limitations before they purchase one of them.

The most important technological development that is directly relevant to analog systems is the present boom in integrated circuits (ICs), which are currently replacing the technology of transistors. This development is occurring so rapidly that it is impossible to predict just where it will end and how it will affect the field of electronic music. It is already the case that many complete circuits such as oscillators and amplifiers can be obtained in a single IC or "chip." In the near future, it is possible that one will be able to assemble an entire electronic music synthesizer out of a dozen or so ICs. Digital ICs are being developed even more rapidly than analog ICs, so that the same predictions apply to computer systems.

2. NEW COMPUTER SYSTEMS

"Pure" computer systems, where the only hardware consists of the computer and its digital-to-analog converters, have already achieved a very advanced stage of development, at least with regard to the music that can be produced by these systems. There are nevertheless several areas in which we can look for improvements in the next few years.

The most important improvement will come with the more widespread availability of these systems. This seems more related to the availability of digital-to-analog converters of sufficient quality than to the availability of computers themselves. Computers are available today on almost all college campuses, although most musicians have not made use of them.

Innumerable developments are presently occurring in the area of computer technology, as they have been ever since computers were invented, and it is important to know which of these are likely to be of most benefit to computer musicians. These developments can be categorized according to hardware improvements and software improvements.

The most important hardware improvement that is currently being introduced consists of faster and faster computer logic, which is the direct result of miniaturized components. The faster a computer works, the more it can accomplish in a given time, and the less it will cost to perform the same calculations. Another improvement that is important for computer music includes data-storage devices that hold more information and have faster data-transfer rates. Of less importance are faster and fancier printers and plotters, although these may be of interest for aesthetic reasons.

Software includes not only the programs that the user provides, such as the MUSIC4BF program, but also the operating system under which the computer runs. In this regard it is important to know that computer music programs are best suited for multiprogramming batch-processing systems rather than time-sharing systems. The advantages of time sharing are almost completely irrelevant to the application of computer music, with the one exception that if digital-to-analog conversion could be implemented from a terminal so that the feedback the user obtained was in the form of sounds rather than printed output, then time sharing would be preferred. Computer music synthesis tends to consume greater amounts of CPU execution time than one can reasonably expect to obtain from a time-shared terminal, and for this reason it is more practical to implement the programs on fast, scientifically oriented computers that use batch-processing operating systems.

Improvements in the programs used for computer music synthesis such as the MUSIC4BF program will also continue to occur. Here it is important to state that machine-dependent programs such as Music4B, MUSIC360 and MUSIC7[1] are more likely to be easier to use and to run faster than the MUSIC4BF program. These other programs have already proved their superiority at most institutions that use them, and they are, furthermore, completely compatible in all possible respects. The main advantages of MUSIC4BF are that it can be implemented on any large general-purpose computer, and special machine-dependent programs have not been written for every such machine; furthermore, since it is in the Fortran language, the operation of the MUSIC4BF program is more accessible to users with a minimum knowledge of programming. In fact, a user does not require more than a minimum knowledge of programming to be a very competent user of MUSIC4BF.

One of the most exciting developments currently occurring in the field of computer technology is the development of special-purpose minicomputers. These machines can often be as fast or faster than many large general-purpose maxicomputers, and when assembled for some specific application they can be unmatched. A computer music synthesis program written for a minicomputer specially assembled for this application could well be the most versatile and attractive system yet produced. Such a system could offer the mutual advantages of immediate feedback, so that a user could hear his music as soon as it was computed; fast execution, since the hardware would be well suited for this application; and all of the advantages of the programmability of the music that are available with programs such as MUSIC4BF.

Since such a system could well become a reality in the near future, it would be helpful to comment on some of its likely characteristics, since these would be slightly different from those associated with systems designed for large general-purpose computers.

The main difference between a minicomputer and a maxicomputer as far as computer music is concerned is likely to be the amount of memory or storage available. While it is advantageous to purchase as much memory

[1]Details of these programs are given at the beginning of Chapter 8.

as possible, this is still not likely to be anywhere near as much on a minicomputer as would be available on a large computer. Here it should be mentioned that the memory of a small computer can be expanded tremendously
by the use of the "virtual memory" technique if a disk is available. Briefly,
this technique operates by storing portions of memory on the disk and
swapping these in and out of the actual memory as they are addressed by
the program. Since this technique offers such a great expansion of the
memory usable to the program, a disk is an almost indispensable require-
ment of a special-purpose minicomputer music system.

Minicomputers also have many applications with regard to hybrid systems (discussed below), and it is possible—and even likely—that the same
computer could be used both for the type of system discussed here and for
a hybrid system. Even at today's prices, such a system could probably be
assembled for less than $100,000.

3. *HYBRID SYSTEMS*

Hybrid systems of the future offer the most variety with respect to the
possible components and configurations in which they may be assembled,
and since there are really several separate avenues of approach to this area,
we will discuss them one at a time.

Digital Control

Digital control refers to the use of a computer, usually a minicomputer,
to control electronic signal generating and processing equipment. The computer is like a supercontroller of an analog electronic music synthesizer,
which allows many advantages over present controllers: very precise control of variable parameters; preprogramming capability that may extend to
an entire composition and upon which ancillary computations, such as
Passes 1 and 2 of MUSIC4BF, may be made; the ability to control many
different variables simultaneously; real-time intervention and modification
of control settings or preprogrammed characteristics; and many other features. The type of equipment controlled by the computer may include the
analog devices of present synthesizers or any of the newer equipment discussed below in this chapter.

Pioneering work has been done in the area of digital control by Peter

Zinovieff in England,[2] who built the first such system of this kind, and by Max Mathews, whose "GROOVE" program[3] has already been used by many composers. Through the work of these men and others, such systems have become a reality and have progressed through many stages of development.

One thing that must be borne in mind about digital-control systems is the great expense of the hardware. There is no way in which "any number" of devices can be simulated through programming. If one needs to control ten oscillators, ten physical oscillators must exist in some form. The amount of equipment available is one of the most obvious limitations of these systems. Furthermore, only one person may work on the system at a time, so that it is necessarily restricted to a small number of users. By contrast, a larger number of users can be accommodated with a computer sound-synthesizing system oriented to a program like MUSIC4BF, since most of their work is spent away from the computer, either programming or keypunching input for their runs. A similar situation may be created for a digital-control system if a group of "remote terminals" can be established to allow users to prepare input for the system without tying up the central facility.

The prospect of a digital-control system immediately suggests a number of special devices that are needed for the new modes of operation that it requires. These are covered separately below.

The software for a digital-control system must be different from that appropriate for other methods. Nevertheless, there is no reason why the program cannot accept input similar to that for the MUSIC4BF program, and allow special processing options such as those found in Passes 1 and 2. One of the most useful features of the phase of operation in which the music is actually generated is to have special controls allowing the user to manipulate "time" on the spur of the moment. For example, he should not only be able to change tempo but also to "stop" time at a given point to hear the steady-state features of a particular sound. An even fancier option would allow a new item to be "edited" into or deleted from the middle of a musical passage as it is being generated.

[2]Peter Zinovieff, "A Computer Controlled Electronic Music Studio," *DECUS Fourth European Seminar* (Maynard, Mass., 1968), pp. 139–145.

[3]M. V. Mathews and F. R. Moore, "GROOVE, a Program for Real Time Control of a Sound Synthesizer by a Computer," *Proceedings of the American Society of University Composers, 1969,* IV (New York, 1969), 27–31.

Digital Equipment

Programs like MUSIC4BF use computer subprograms to simulate analog signal generating and processing equipment, and recently people have begun to experiment with constructing special devices that perform the same functions. There are innumerable ways in which such devices may be designed, and only some of them will be indicated here.

A digital oscillator that acted exactly like an analog device would contain an internal digital circuit that produced the oscillation, but would have digital inputs and a digital-to-analog converter on its output. Alternatively, it could accept analog inputs if it had analog-to-digital converters that translated them into digital form. Thus, for all external purposes it would be an analog device, but internally it would be a digital device. This is an example of an area in which the distinction between analog and digital systems becomes blurred and seems almost irrelevant. A device of this design would most likely be constructed only if its components costed less than comparable analog components, but another advantage of a digital oscillator is that it could be completely free of drift in pitch, since its internal representation of the pitch would be in digital form.

A digital oscillator could be built as a special-purpose device interfaced to a computer that ran a program like MUSIC4BF. When an oscillator was needed, instead of executing the code associated with the unit generator OSCIL, the computer would simply call this device, which would return the appropriate value. The advantage of such a device would be that it could save considerable execution time if the computer were spending much time on oscillations. Furthermore, if the device could return the appropriate value in a few nanoseconds, then a single device could actually produce several polyphonic voices and play and even alter these lines in real time.

Instead of performing the function of just a simple oscillator, a special-purpose device could actually contain several unit generators that were frequently used in series, such as a combination oscillator–filter–envelope-generator–reverberator, any component of which could be deactivated for a given tone. If all this required just a few nanoseconds to compute, then one superdevice of this nature could also generate several tones simultaneously in real time.

One possibility of digital equipment is that it can be programmed in as many ways as the unit generators in the MUSIC4BF program. A waveshape needs to be stored inside a digital oscillator, and if this can be altered then the same oscillator could perform tones of different timbres. Sometimes, however, as with devices that are digital internally but analog externally, this type of programmability is not practical, and so the waveshape has to be made permanent.

Sometimes it is practical to design digital equipment in such a way that a very large number of devices can be included within a single package at a very small cost per device. The reason for this is that they can all share some components of the circuit, and those they do not share require only a small additional expense. In this way "oscillator banks" or "filter banks" of, say, 256 separate devices could be constructed for a few thousand dollars, or at a cost of perhaps $10 per device.

It may seem incredible to conceive of a device that could perform several complex, special-purpose calculations in a few nanoseconds, but circuits of this type have been appearing more and more recently. Newer computer logic is not only faster, it is also considerably cheaper than previous equipment. This is just one of the many ways in which new advances in computer technology are happening so fast that they make existing equipment seem obsolete.

Ancillary Equipment

A hybrid system provides a whole new relationship between the user and the equipment, and it is one with which few people have had any real experience, and for which new modes of operation are certainly going to be needed. This is a problem to be solved by human engineering, and people have already begun to foresee some of the types of devices that will be required.

A *switching matrix* or *patching matrix* is a device that allows automatic or instantaneous changes in patchings and control settings of signal-generating and -processing equipment. This type of device is particularly useful for systems that employ analog equipment, where the number of units available is always likely to be inhibited by cost factors. A switching matrix would be useful whether or not the system had a digital-control mechanism, since it would be useful to change patchings instantaneously for any kind of live performance. Setting up patchings and control settings can occupy a great amount of time, and if this information can be preserved and reset instantaneously it insures a more efficient use of the system.

Similar to a switching matrix is a _hard-wire patch_. This is a device that may be plugged into a specially constructed synthesizer that defines an entire patching configuration of the equipment, sometimes including control settings as well. Switching from one patch to another is not instantaneous, but a new patch may be inserted only in a matter of seconds. Several new products of this kind have appeared recently, including the "prestopatch" for the Synthi AKS and the "program board" for the Buchla Music Easel.

Many people believe that work on a hybrid electronic music system would be facilitated by various kinds of active displays, particularly in graphic form. These would allow parametric information sent to or monitored from devices to be displayed to the user, who could thereby make performance decisions with greater ease. Such devices are certainly attractive, but it must be added that they would increase the operating complexity of the system. The operator could not keep track of very many displays, particularly if he were busy with other aspects during the performance. However, such a display mechanism could enable him to find errors or uncover other problems much more easily than he could without them.

Just as graphic displays are useful for output, many people believe that input devices that allow information to be represented in graphic form would also be useful. Such a device has already been used experimentally at Bell Telephone Laboratories,[4] but whether graphic input is really needed for musical characteristics has not yet been shown.

When the precise operating characteristics of an individual device on a hybrid system are determined by a combination of live and preprogrammed information, it is useful to have some method whereby these operating characteristics could be preserved so that a particular event that came about fortuitously could be repeated. The information required is not the analog data or the sounds themselves, which could be recorded on magnetic tape, but the parametric information that produced the sounds. Hence, what is required is a simple digital-recording mechanism. Happily, several such devices are already available as laboratory test equipment.

The future of electronic music depends on the development of systems such as those described here if the field is ever going to progress beyond the problems of today's methods. It will be difficult to raise the resources to finance these developments, however. In retrospect, the generosity of the

[4]M. V. Mathews and L. Rosler, "Graphical Language for the Scores of Computer-Generated Sounds," _Perspectives of New Music,_ VI/2 (spring-summer, 1968), 92–118.

RCA corporation when it built the first electronic sound synthesizer in the mid-1950s[5] seems to have triggered an entire generation of electronic music synthesizers that might never have been invented were it not for that original stimulus. The similar role of Bell Telephone Laboratories, as exemplified in the work of Max Mathews, has been prominent in spawning an entire generation of computer music; and this research is continuing today.

The future of electronic music is bright, expecially if some of today's problems can be overcome. Whereas the history of electronic music has been characterized by the acceptance of great limitations in compositional methods, and even the institutionalization of some of these limitations in various "schools" of composition, it is likely that fewer and fewer restrictions will be imposed upon future composers, so that the electronic music of the future can be guided by musical considerations alone, rather than by the limitations of the methods of sound synthesis.

[5]Milton Babbitt, "The Revolution in Sound: Electronic Music," *University,* 4 (spring, 1960), 4–8.

Appendix A

FREQUENCY EQUIVALENTS FOR PITCHES ON THE PIANO

Pitch	CPS	Pitch	CPS	Pitch	CPS
4.09	27.5000	7.03	155.5635	9.08	830.6094
4.10	29.1352	7.04	164.8138	9.09	880.0000
4.11	30.8677	7.05	174.6141	9.10	932.3275
5.00	32.7032	7.06	184.9972	9.11	987.7666
5.01	34.6478	7.07	195.9977	10.00	1046.5023
5.02	36.7081	7.08	207.6523	10.01	1108.7305
5.03	38.8909	7.09	220.0000	10.02	1174.6591
5.04	41.2034	7.10	233.0819	10.03	1244.5079
5.05	43.6535	7.11	246.9417	10.04	1318.5102
5.06	46.2493	8.00	261.6256	10.05	1396.9129
5.07	48.9994	8.01	277.1826	10.06	1479.9777
5.08	51.9131	8.02	293.6648	10.07	1567.9817
5.09	55.0000	8.03	311.1270	10.08	1661.2188
5.10	58.2705	8.04	329.6276	10.09	1760.0000
5.11	61.7354	8.05	349.2282	10.10	1864.6550
6.00	65.4064	8.06	369.9944	10.11	1975.5332
6.01	69.2957	8.07	391.9954	11.00	2093.0045
6.02	73.4162	8.08	415.3047	11.01	2217.4610
6.03	77.7817	8.09	440.0000	11.02	2349.3181
6.04	82.4069	8.10	466.1638	11.03	2489.0159
6.05	87.3071	8.11	493.8833	11.04	2637.0205
6.06	92.4986	9.00	523.2511	11.05	2793.8259
6.07	97.9989	9.01	554.3653	11.06	2959.9554
6.08	103.8262	9.02	587.3295	11.07	3135.9635
6.09	110.0000	9.03	622.2540	11.08	3322.4376
6.10	116.5409	9.04	659.2551	11.09	3520.0000
6.11	123.4708	9.05	698.4565	11.10	3729.3101
7.00	130.8128	9.06	739.9888	11.11	3951.0664
7.01	138.5913	9.07	783.9909	12.00	4186.0090
7.02	146.8324				

Appendix B

ELECTRONIC MUSIC EQUIPMENT MANUFACTURERS

1. Moog Music, Inc.
   Academy Street
   Williamsville, New York 14221

   Moog Music Inc. is the successor to the R. A. Moog Co., one of the first companies to produce electronic musical instruments. They manufacture small, medium, and large synthesizers in both portable and studio models, several small and compact performance synthesizers, accessories and a variety of miscellaneous instruments. Their products are distributed by the Chicago Musical Instrument Company, 7373 N. Cicero Avenue, Lincolnwood, Illinois 60646, and are widely available in music stores throughout the world.

2. Buchla & Associates
   Box 5051
   Berkeley, California 94705

   Founded by Donald Buchla in 1964, Buchla & Associates is one of the most experienced electronic music equipment manufacturers in the field. The company makes a variety of products ranging from small portable performance synthesizers to large studio systems. The equipment is not distributed in music stores and must be ordered directly from the manufacturer.

3. ARP Instruments, Inc.
   320 Needham Street
   Newton, Massachusetts 02164

   ARP Instruments, Inc., a division of Tonus, Inc., manufactures both large and small electronic music systems as well as other musical instruments. The synthesizers are not sold from the factory and must be purchased from a local music dealer.

4. Electronic Music Studios (London), Ltd.
   49 Deodar Road
   London SW15, England

EMS, the largest independent manufacturer of electronic music systems in Europe, makes many products ranging from small performance-oriented synthesizers to large studio-type systems to custom-built computerized electronic music systems and accessories. Although many of their products are sold in music stores in the United States and throughout the world, their large custom systems must be ordered in consultation with the manufacturer in England.

Bibliography

This bibliography is not intended to be comprehensive, but to offer the reader a list of references in which he may pursue the materials covered in the book in more detail. References dealing with the subject matter of each major part of the book are listed in separate groups, and where a book is particularly recommended a brief description is given. Only books that have been read and inspected personally by the author are included; no references are taken from the bibliographies of other books. (These books have extensive bibliographies can be used to find further materials.)

Articles in professional journals dealing with relevant subject matter are not listed in the bibliography, although several are cited in the footnotes within individual chapters. Important journals themselves are listed, together with information about how to get them. It is recommended that the reader look through many of the recent issues of these journals as well as new issues when they appear, for these are the pages where new ideas and developments are revealed first.

PART I: ACOUSTICS AND PSYCHOACOUSTICS

Backus, John. *The Acoustical Foundations of Music.* New York: Norton, 1969. 312 pp.

> The only book recommended for musicians with no previous background in physics. It has a very good presentation of the physics of sound, room acoustics, and an introduction to the structure of musical instruments, but is weaker on psychoacoustics.

Licklider, J. C. R. "Basic Correlates of the Auditory Stimulus." In S. S. Stevens, ed., *Handbook of Experimental Psychology.* New York: Wiley, 1951. 985–1035.

> A good introduction to psychoacoustics, now somewhat out of date.

Roederer, Juan G. *Introduction to the Physics and Psychophysics of Music.* New York, Heidelberg, Berlin: Springer-Verlag, 1973. 161 pp.

> A new book, which is more sophisticated from a musical viewpoint than other books.

Also recommended:

Olson, Harry F. *Music, Physics, and Engineering.* New York: Dover, 1967. 460 pp.

Stevens, S. S., and Halowell Davis. *Hearing.* New York: Wiley, 1938. 489 pp.

Taylor, C. A. *The Physics of Musical Sounds.* New York: American Elsevier, 1965. 190 pp.

Winckel, Fritz. *Music, Sound and Sensation: A Modern Exposition.* Tran. from the German by Thomas Binkley. New York: Dover, 1967. 189 pp.

PART II: ELECTRONIC MUSIC EQUIPMENT

Allison, Roy F. *High Fidelity Systems: A User's Guide.* Cambridge, Mass.: Acoustic Research, 1962. 70 pp.

    All the details that a hi-fi buff needs to cope with his equipment. This book is especially recommended for people who have no previous experience with tape recorders and hi-fi equipment.

The ARP Synthesizer Series 2600 Owner's Manual. Newton Highlands, Mass.: Tonus, 1971. 116 pp.

    While obviously oriented toward the APR 2600 synthesizer, this is an excellent instructional manual.

Electronic Music: Systems, Techniques, and Controls. Dubuque: Wm. C. Brown, 1972. 160 pp.

    Although not always offering clear explanations and even containing some errors, this book is nevertheless recommended for its discussion of electronic music synthesizers and tape recorders.

Villchur, Edgar. *Reproduction of Sound.* Cambridge, Mass.: Acoustic Research, 1962. 93 pp.

    More detailed than Allision's *High Fidelity Systems,* this book explains some of the theoretical basis for the way in which equipment works. Strange, Allen.

Also recommended:

Trythall, Gilbert. *Principles and Practice of Electronic Music.* New York: Grosset & Dunlap, 1973. 214 pp.

PART III: COMPUTERS AND ELECTRONIC MUSIC

IBM System/360 and System/370 Fortran IV Language. IBM Systems Reference Library File No. 5360–25, Order No. GC28–6515–8. IBM Corp., 1133 Westchester Avenue, White Plains, New York 10604. 159 pp.

This manual, or another published by a computer manufacturer, is recommended over any commercially available textbook on Fortran programming, because the examples in textbooks are rarely instructive for someone interested in music applications.

Mathews, M. V., et al. *The Technology of Computer Music.* Cambridge, Mass., and London: MIT Press, 1969. 188 pp.

The first part of the book presents comprehensive information, including mathematics, on basic aspects of computer sound generation. The remaining parts of the book are oriented toward Music V, a specific sound-synthesizing program.

Risset, Jean-Claude. *Computer Study of Trumpet Tones.* Murray Hill, N.J.: Bell Telephone Laboratories, 1968. 40 pp. plus appendix, figures, and accompanying recording. Abstract published in *Journal of the Acoustical Society of America,* XXXVIII/912 (November, 1965).

Presenting a detailed explanation of objectives, methods, and results, this study concludes with a demonstration tape revealing the high degree of accuracy of the analysis.

_____ *An Introductory Catalog of Computer Synthesized Sounds.* Murray Hill, N.J.: Bell Telephone Laboratories, 1970. 105 pp. plus accompanying recording.

Detailed technical descriptions of various sounds used by the author in two compositions together with an attempt to classify them in a manner suggesting comparison to live instruments.

von Foerster, Heinz, and James Beauchamp, eds. *Music by Computers.* New York: Wiley, 1969. 139 pp.

Papers from a session on "Computers and Music" at the 1966 Fall Joint Computer Conference in San Francisco.

OTHER BOOKS RECOMMENDED

Flanagan, J. L. *Speech Analysis, Synthesis and Perception.* 2nd edition. New York, Heidelberg, Berlin: Springer-Verlag, 1972. 444 pp.

The *vade mecum* for speech research.

Fowler, Charles B., ed. *Music Educators Journal.* November, 1968. Available from
NEA Publication Sales, 1201 Sixteenth Street N.W., Washington, D.C. 20036.
    Special issue on electronic music.

Schwartz, Elliott. *Electronic Music: A Listener's Guide.* New York, Washington:
Praeger, 1973. 306 pp.
    The best introduction to electronic music literature currently available.

PROFESSIONAL JOURNALS

There have been two journals devoted to electronic music exclusively, but both
have become defunct only shortly after starting publication. Many copies of these
journals are still around, and they are highly recommended. They were:
Electronic Music Review. Published from January, 1967, till July, 1968, by the
Independent Electronic Music Center, Inc., Trumansburg, New York 14886.
Synthesis. Published from 1970 to 1971 (two issues only) by Scully-Cutter Publish-
ing, Inc., 1315 Fourth Street S.E., Minneapolis, Minnesota 55414.

The following are professional musical journals, which frequently contain articles on electronic music:

Journal of Music Theory. Published biannually by Yale School of Music, New
Haven, Connecticut 06520.

Perspectives of New Music. Subscriptions available from P.O. Box 271, Yardley,
Pennsylvania 19067. Biannually.

Proceedings of the American Society of University Composers. Published by the
American Society of University Composers, c/o American Music Center, New
York, New York. Published annually.

The following are professional scientific and technical journals which frequently contain articles relevant to electronic music:

Journal of the Acoustical Society of America. Published by the American Institute
of Physics, 335 East Forty-fifth Street, New York, New York 10017.

Journal of the Audio Engineering Society. Published by the Audio Engineering
Society, 60 East Forty-second Street, New York, New York 10017.

Index

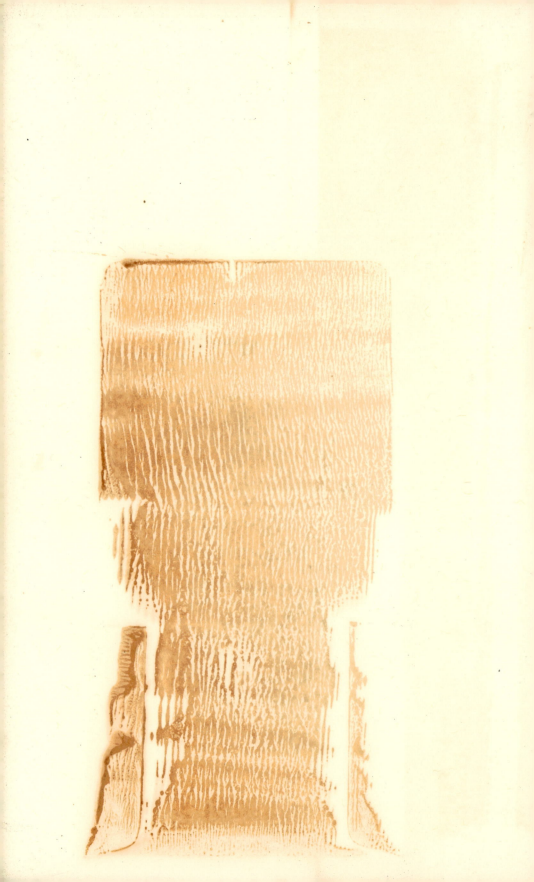